A SOCIO-ECONOMIC HISTORY OF GERMAN-CANADIANS

VIERTELJAHRSCHRIFT FÜR
SOZIAL- UND WIRTSCHAFTSGESCHICHTE

BEIHEFTE

HERAUSGEGEBEN VON
WERNER CONZE, HERMANN KELLENBENZ,
HANS POHL UND WOLFGANG ZORN

Nr. 75

FRANZ STEINER VERLAG WIESBADEN GMBH
1984

RUDOLF A. HELLING

A SOCIO-ECONOMIC HISTORY OF GERMAN-CANADIANS

THEY, TOO, FOUNDED CANADA

A RESEARCH REPORT BY
RUDOLF A. HELLING, JACK THIESSEN, FRITZ WIEDEN,
ELIZABETH AND KURT WANGENHEIM, KARL HEEB

EDITED BY
BERND HAMM

FRANZ STEINER VERLAG WIESBADEN GMBH
1984

CIP-Kurztitelaufnahme der Deutschen Bibliothek
A socio-economic history of German-Canadian:
they, too, founded Canada ; a research report / by Rudolf A. Helling . . . Ed. by Bernd Hamm. – Wiesbaden : Steiner, 1984.
   (Vierteljahrschrift für Sozial- und Wirtschaftsgeschichte : Beih. ; Nr. 75)
   ISBN 3-515-04014-5
NE: Helling, Rudolf A. [Mitverf.]; Hamm, Bernd [Hrsg.]; Vierteljahrschrift für Sozial- und Wirtschaftsgeschichte / Beihefte

Gedruckt mit Unterstützung des Förderungs- und Beihilfefonds Wissenschaft der VG WORT GmbH, Goethestraße 49, 8000 München 2

Alle Rechte vorbehalten
Ohne ausdrückliche Genehmigung des Verlages ist es auch nicht gestattet, das Werk oder einzelne Teile daraus nachzudrucken oder auf photomechanischem Wege (Photokopie, Mikrokopie usw.) zu vervielfältigen. © 1984 by Franz Steiner Verlag Wiesbaden GmbH. Printed in Germany

To Renée, Bernard, Anthea and Gianna

TABLE OF CONTENTS

Preface, by Bernd Hamm 9

Introduction 14

Chapter 1
   Germans in the Two Colonial Empires 16

Chapter 2
   From the Arrival of the United Empire Loyalists to
   Confederation 24

Chapter 3
   Mass Migration and New Settlements 32

Chapter 4
   The Impact of World War I 49

Chapter 5
   Post World War I Period 57

Chapter 6
   World War II and After 66

Chapter 7
   Education and the Preparation System 86

Chapter 8
   Institution and Social Structure 94

Chapter 9
   The World of Work 116

Chapter 10
   Political Experience 124

Chapter 11
   Recreation, Culture and Communication 132

Chapter 12
   Conclusion 149

Bibliography 152

Rudolf A. Helling
January 22, 1929 — September 10, 1982

PREFACE

Rudolf Helling, the senior author of this book, died of a heart attack Monday, September 10, 1982, in Trier (FRG). I invited him to spend his sabbatical year at Trier University to teach courses in our program on urban and regional planning and to work on joint research in ethnic minorities and German guestworker policies. Rudolf arrived with his wife Renee and daughter Gianna, on September 5, and the family moved into an appartment in the same downtown building where I lived. They made themselves at home, became acquainted with the city, Gianna went to the French highschool. We started talking about planned work. One evening I invited some of my collegues, collaborators, and students to meet him. We looked at the slides I had brought back from a trip to Canada in summer, Rudolf commented on them with admirably detailed knowledge: a stimulating, harmonious start to the winter term. Two days later I left for a conference in Heidelberg. When I came back to the hotel late at night, I found a small note in my letter box: Rudolf Helling is dead. I was shocked.

I met Rudolf for the first time in fall 1978, when he attended a Canadian-German conference on Urban Gestalt Research in Trier. We liked each other spontaneously. When I did some work at the University of Michigan, Ann Arbor, the following summer, he came to pick me up for a week-end. We roamed around Detroit, a city with which he was familiar since the time of his studies at Wayne State. He knew the city like the back of his hand. We discussed the crisis of urban societies, and Detroit was the perfect place to do so, with all the remainders of the 1967 riots, and Renaissance Center looking like the last tooth in the mouth of an old dying man. We strolled through the black and ethnic neighborhoods: this was his field, his commitment. From his house on the Windsor side of Detroit River, we overlooked the skyline of the city. On Canada Day, we visited the multicultural festival at Windsor's Teutonia Club. I did not know yet that this lively, colourful and peaceful event belonged in part to his achievements.

One year later, in winter 1980/81, Rudolf came to see me in Trier after participating in the Canada Days in Mannheim. I spontaneously asked him to present two guest lectures, one at the sociology department, and one in the department of geography. As he refused being picked up at the railway station, I met him at the campus entrance, a tall man in a fur coat with only a small bag. On the way to my office, he asked for a clear specification of the subjects he was expected to talk about, and for some information about the audiences. He did both lectures adlip, precisely meeting the knowledge of his audience, a lecturer whose fascination came from his detailed information and well-structured conceptions.

In summer 1982 I had an opportunity to go back to Canada, due to a fellowship I received from the Canadian government. Rudolf helped me to prepare the trip, calling contact persons, arranged for accomodation, took care for everything. He came to meet me at Detroit airport after an intensive study tour. We went to his cottage on Lake Erie where he invited me to spend some days reading and writing. We dropped right into a welcome party with all the neighbors and friends. He was cheerful and entertaining, and we had a wonderful evening. On one of the last days of my stay, I went to see him at his Windsor home. He had an emergency call from the German Club which gave me a chance to learn some more about his everyday work. A German immigrant couple had arrived in Windsor, after an odyssey throughout the U.S. and Canada, without money, without permission to stay and work, without their children they had to leave behind in Louisiana. Rudolf listened to their live story, and he was prepared to advise on any problem, fatigueless, commited, natural.

This is not the place to talk about the many details that made him a fatherly friend and highly esteemed scholar to me. These few remarks, however, are important in the preface of his last book. He never adhered to the publish-or-perish-principle of the common academic circus. His love was teaching on the one hand, and practical work on the other. His commitment was with his students, with ethnic minorities, with immigrants, with his family. He combined investing effort with serious commitment and a warmhearted character.

Let me roughly sketch some of the stations of his biography: Born on January 22, 1929 in Bochum (FRG), he attended Bochum highschool before beginning his studies in sociology, economics, and law at Bonn university. In 1952 he went to Wayne State University after having received a Fulbright Scholarship, where he received his B.A. in sociology. Back in Germany he continued his studies in Göttingen and received, in 1954, a State Award for scholarly work from the government of Lower Saxony. He left Göttingen to join the International Labor Office in Geneva as an intern and field officer in the Expanded Technical Assistance Program. In 1955 he returned to Wayne State to beginn his doctoral studies, receiving several awards and research grants, and subsequently his Ph. D. in 1962.

In 1956, Rudolf Helling began teaching at Assumption University, and became the first head of the Department of Sociology and Anthropology when Assumption became the University of Windsor in 1963. Several universities throughout Canada saw him as a visiting professor. He also served as a research associate to the Institute of Labor and Industrial Relations at Wayne State (1966–67) and as a research director to the Ohio Socio-Economic Profile (1966–70).

His continuous commitment was with multiculturalism and ethno-cultural minorities, in research and teaching as well as in practical work and policy advising. In 1965 he produced, after a two-year study of the Black, Chinese and Italian populations, a controversial and revealing report on racial and ethnic attitudes in Windsor for the Ontario Human Rights Commission. In chairing the Citizenship Committee of the 1972 Heritage Ontario Congress, he had the opportunity to contribute to the initiation of the Ontario Advisory Council on Multiculturalism and Citizenship, a member of which he remained since its origin in 1973. Among his special concerns were the fate and problems of the Mennonite community, where he attempted to help the Mennonite immigrants from Mexico. He travelled to Mexico several times, spoke to officials of the Mexican Government, the Canadian and German Embassies about ways of solving their problems, did research on the laws and regulations that affected them, and represented some of them in appearances before the Immigration Appeal Board. In his untiring efforts on their behalf. he worked closely with the Ottawa Office of the Mennonite Central Committee.

He maintained close contacts with the German Embassy in Ottawa and with the Consulate General of the German Federal Republic in Toronto. Through his membership with the Canadian German Chamber of Industry and Commerce, he made an important contribution towards bringing Canada and Germany closer together. A Canadian of German background, he lectured intensively on Canadian multiculturalism in both countries. His last assingment to the Federal Republic of Germany was, in his own words, "to try to serve the cause of multiculturalism in a different way in another land".

While multiculturalism remained his principal commitment, he was also actively involved in Windsor community services. His 1965 address to the Greater Windsor Foundation was described as "one of the most penetrating and comprehensive studies given of the city". He clearly foresaw the economic difficulties Windsor and Essex County would have to meet in the future and urged community leaders to change their perception that Windsor could remain a successful city by resting on its past accomplishments. Conscious of the coming technological revolution, his advise was to establish research and development centres in the city and to diversify its economy.

In 1977, his work in the field of multiculturalism was recognized with the Queen's Silver Jubilee Medal.

In late 1979, Rudolf had two heart attacks and remained in hospital for several months. Due to his heavy work load in teaching, writing, advisory meetings, traveling to Mexico and lecturing in Germany, he obviously did not find the time to pursue the publication of this book with full energy. He brought the manuscript with him when he arrived in Trier in September 1982, together with some background material, and wanted to take care for its publication in Germany.

It is not an easy task to take charge of the publication of a book which is not one's own. Lack of personal expertise in the author's accomplishment forbids commenting on substantial issues or updating the manuscript. So I decided to ensure as much authenticity as possible and provide only for minor corrections, most of them typing errors. Contents and style of the book have remained unchanged, even if some uncertainties could have been avoided, or Germanisms eliminated.

Together with the manuscript, Helling brought a microfilm role with documents photographed in William L. Clement Library, University of Michigan. He might have intended to include some of them in the book. Careful inspection revealed that most of them consisted of lengthy letters in old German handwriting which by far most of the potential readers would have been unable to understand. As they did not contribute to, or clarify, issues mentioned in the text, serving only as illustrative examples, I decided to drop them.

Rudolf Helling was a bold and outspoken social critic who did not hold back his own opinion or assessment of facts, as the reader will see. Even if some of his valuations will not be shared by everyone, it cannot be within the editor's responsibility, nor task, to mitigate, or accentuate, the opinions expressed. The book, although treating the history of Germans in Canada in general, also deals with the life history of its senior author.

Rudolf Helling's memory will be kept alive by the Rudolf A. Helling Bursary for the Study of Ethnic Groups in Canada established in his honour at the University of Windsor. The Multicultural Council of Windsor and Essex County dedicated to him a bronze plaque which is permanently displayed in the Windsor Multicultural Centre. This book may, apart from its value with respect to German-Canadians and multiculturalism, contribute to the memory of a man whose fighting spirit, scholarly expertise, tireless commitment to the problems of the poor and the weak, and warm-hearted character will not be forgotten.

The publication of this book was made possible by a generous grant from Verwertungsgesellschaft Wort; Franz Steiner Verlag and its director, Vincent Sieveking, agreed to produce the book and were helpful to solve many technical problems; Petra Thinnes dedicated some time for checking the bibliography and footnotes; and Lieselotte Anhäuser provided secretarial assistance. Their contributions are gratefully acknowledged.

Trier, December 4, 1983   Bernd Hamm

THE WRITINGS OF RUDOLF A. HELLING

Rudolf A. Helling: *Human Relations in a German Coal Mine.* Herten (FRG) 1954.
–: *Elliot Lake, Beginning,* Windsor 1960.
–: *A Comparison of the Acculturation of Immigrants in Toronto, Ontario, and Detroit, Michigan,* Detroit 1961 (doctoral dissertation).
Rudolf A. Helling and Nancy Zettlemoyer: *Immigrant Needs and their Fulfillment in Windsor,* Windsor 1961.
Rudolf A. Helling: *The Limits of Cultural Pluralism,* Geneva Park, Toronto 1961.
Rudolf A. Helling and Paul Lassaline: *Suburban Parish,* Windsor 1962.
Rudolf A. Helling: *The Social Background for Vocational Rehabilitation,* Detroit 1963.
–: *A Place Under the Crown,* Toronto 1964.
–: "Maltese Immigrants to Canada", *Malta Review,* April 1964, 7–11.
Edward Boyce and Rudolf A. Helling: *A Demographic Survey of Essex County,* Windsor 1965.
W. J. Gillen, Rudolf A. Helling and G. R. Horne: *A Survey of Labour Market Conditions, Windsor, Ontario 1964,* Ottawa 1965.
Rudolf A. Helling: *The Multi-Ethnic Society,* London 1965.
–: *The Position of Negroes, Chinese and Italians in the Social Structure of Windsor, Ontario,* Toronto 1965.
–: "La conception de l'élite et de la démocratie au Canada Anglais", *Cité Libre,* April-March 1966.
–: *Poverty Programs in Canada,* Evian 1966.

Rudolf A. Helling and J. Ransome: *Ohio, Socio-Economic Profile, Socio-Economic History of Ohio*, Columbus 1967.
Rudolf A. Helling and J. Rinehart: *Ohio, Socio-Economic Profile, Labor Force in Ohio*, Columbus 1968.
Rudolf A. Helling: *A Demographic Survey of London and Middlesex County, Ontario*, London 1968.
–: *Technological Changes in Canada*, Oberhausen (FRG) 1969.
–: *The Tree of Culture and the Marginal Man*, York University 1969.
Rudolf A. Helling, W. W. Isajiw, and S. S. Faber: *Unemployment in an Inner Core City Area*, Detroit 1969.
Edward Monahan, Jean Louis Allard, Clement Cormier, Rudolf A. Helling, E. C. Le Bel, Lucien Michaud, Joseph E. Roach, Edmund J. Roche and Phyllis G. Ross: *A Commitment to Higher Education in Canada*, Ottawa 1970.
Rudolf A. Helling: "Some Definite Opinions on Information and Advocacy", *Canadian Welfare*, vol. 47, July-August 1971, No. 4.
–: *Community Information Centres in Ontario*, Toronto 1971.
–: "Ein Bericht über die kulturellen Veränderungen in Kanada", *Zeitschrift für Kulturaustausch*, 1974.
–: "Religious Communities and Multiculturalism", *Proceedings of the Canadian Council of Christians and Jews*, 1976.
–: *The Role of the Churches in a Multicultural Society*, Toronto 1977.
–: *Controlled Acculturation Versus Institutional Survival: An Old Colony Mennonite Dilemma*, Cincinnati 1978.
–: *From Assimilation to Multiculturalism, the Challenges and the Limits*, Windsor 1978.
–: *The Tomatoes of Wrath-Migratory Farm Workers in Southwestern Ontario*, Windsor 1979.
–: *Dutch Immigration to the Tri County Area of Ontario*, Windsor 1979.
–: *Detroit-Windsor Perception by Ethnic Groups*, Trier 1979.
–: *Deutsche Einwanderer in Toronto und Kanada*, Windsor 1979.
Rudolf A. Helling, G. Romsa and B. Helling: *Multi-National Corporations, Foreign Ownership and the Impact on Industrial Communities, Regions and Countries*, Dayton 1980.
Rudolf A. Helling: *Illegal Immigration to Canada*, Toronto 1980.
–: *The Legal Status of Mennonite Colonies and of Mennonite Residents in Mexico*, Ottawa 1980.
–: *Old Colony Mennonites and Citizenship*, Windsor 1981.
–: *From United Empire Loyalists to Old Colony Returnees – the History of German Canadians in Essex County, Ontario*, Windsor 1982.
–: *Germans in Canada*, Edmonton 1982 (The Canadian Encyclopedia).
–: *Die Deutschen in Kanada*, Mannheim 1981.
–: *Johann G. Seume, Halifax, Nova Scotia 1782*, Windsor 1982.
Rudolf A. Helling (ed.): *Johann Gottfried Seume in Halifax. Lebenserinnerungen, Briefe, Gedichte*. Windsor 1982.

INTRODUCTION

Canadians of German background constitute the third-largest ethno-cultural group in this country, surpassed numerically only by those of British or French background. German Canadians, along with those of British and French background, formed the core of the early European settlements and contributed to the development of the land and its institutions. Their participation in French-Canadian and British-Canadian societies, however, has received scant attention, being overshadowed by the search of the other groups for their own identities. Historians have concentrated on the problems of accommodation between the British and French, as well as the survival of the nation against the giant in the south. Sociologists have concerned themselves either with quaint minorities living alternate lifestyles, or with problems of unequal treatment of minorities in Canada.

Little research has been undertaken on the life and experiences of the early soldiers, artisans, farmers and fishermen. Yet their past is still present with us in records and biographies, in artifacts or cultural traits, the origins of which have fallen into oblivion. More is known about European history and quite often the knowledge gained from the study of the European past is transferred to Canadian experience without question. German Canadians have been judged not by their contributions to this land, but by events in Europe. They have been, and sometimes still are, treated as scapegoats.

This monograph is an attempt to evaluate data judiciously and to combine known material with new findings and concepts. It assesses the contributions of German Canadians to the growth of this nation and the development of unique Canadian institutions. Much has been written about the retention of the European heritage in Canada in contrast to the development of new forms in the United States. Most of this deals with folklore rather than with the life experiences of people from many lands. This book is an attempt to follow one strand of many which make up Canada.

In recent years there has been a growing concern about Canadian identity. This identity represents an emerging consciousness of uniqueness and a growing sense of belonging. One aspect of the identity is the emphasis on evolution and compromise rather than violent confrontation. There are patterns of continuity; the past casts its shadow onto the present. Minority groups in Canada discover that in order to remain as identifiable entities, they have to search for their roots in the land and demonstrate their contribution to the growth of the nation.

For those who are not of British or French background, the concept of "the two founding races" – les deux peuples – implies inequality for all who do not fit into these categories. Native peoples see the concept as a manifestation of racism, an assumption of superiority based upon power; third group Canadians consider the statement offensive. German Canadians, because of their early arrival, numbers and achievements, could claim special status; to do so, however, would be adding dignity to a political slogan. Canadian society has moved towards a system of stratification which denies special claims for ascribed status positions and stresses the formal equality of all Canadians. Adding new special status relationships would defeat this goal. This study does not ask for special status for an ethno-cultural group; it describes the participation of a linguistic group in the building of this country.

From the earliest days of European settlement along the Atlantic Seaboard, German-speaking soldiers and settlers have contributed to this land. As soldiers, they defended the French cause at Louisburg and in Quebec, and the British cause as soldiers, settlers and citizens. They have participated throughout Canadian history from the earliest days of the colonial period, the settlement of the West and the growth of the industrial and post-industrial society. In the past, they operated on personal bonds, the feudal system, rather than in the framework of the nation-state; at present, they seek opportunities and peace in a turbulent world. In the dying days of the feudal system, they pledged personal allegiance to their sovereign, who in turn protected their freedom of conscience. In the days of the declining British Empire, they were outsiders who had to reaffirm their loyalty in a fervent manner. In the present period of the renaissance of nationalism, they are both committed to Canada and uneasy about further developments. The division of the world along ideological lines has created complications which affect the various minorities in Canada.

Among the German-speaking in Canada have been immigrants or settlers, exiles and sojourners. Immigrants have come for various reasons; some were pushed out of their homeland, others were attracted to Canada by the opportunities of a young nation. Once settled, they consider Canada their land. While they might wish to visit their homeland again, Canada is their country of orientation and commitment. Exiles consider their stay in Canada temporary, and fight as best they can for the various goals and objectives of their commitment. Sojourners reside temporarily abroad for economic or educational reasons, and consider themselves a part of their nation of origin and/or identification.

This study deals primarily with those who consider themselves as Canadians of German origin or background and their position within the country. Canada is richer as a nation if it incorporates into its culture the contributions of all those who have settled the land, tilled the soil and built the cities and industrial enterprises, but still have retained and adapted their own identity within a new world. This new world culture is not a time capsule, frozen in the memory of the events at the time of arrival, but a mingling of diverse traits into unique patterns. The recognition and presentation of these, as well as their acceptance in the society-at-large, is one of the goals of multiculturalism. Whether this acceptance of diversity will be permanent is a question of time and the position taken by the dominant groups. No single culture has grown rich in isolation; none can do so except by constant exchange and interaction. This continuous process will be studied among German-speaking Canadians.

Chapter 1

GERMANS IN THE TWO COLONIAL EMPIRES

Canadians of German background are in an ambivalent situation. On the one hand, many are among the most acculturated, non-English, non-French residents of Canada, often distinguishable from other Canadians only by their names. On the other hand, a minority of German-speaking persons cling stubbornly to their lifestyle, their religion and their peculiar culture. German-speaking people seem to have little in common except their language, and yet there is a feeling of shared identity, based on language, heritage and tradition. They come from many lands and their experiences and their lives reflect the trials and tribulations of European history. Some came to create God's Kingdom on Earth in this new and wide land, some came because of their loyalty to their monarch, some were pressed into service overseas, but the majority came because of the opportunities of the new world. For some, Canada was the land of second choice. Quota restrictions and the lack of land in the United States directed the flow of migration to Canada. Whatever the motivations and circumstances have been, these settlers and their children are part of this land.

The majority of Canadians of German background do not trace their origins to the present Federal Republic of Germany. They have come from Eastern Europe, the former Austrian Empire, the settlements in the valley of the Danube, Alsace, Lorraine, Switzerland and even Africa, South America and Mexico. Some came from ethnically homogeneous regions, others had centuries of experience in living as linguistic minorities among groups of different ethno-cultural backgrounds. A few, even in the minorities, were the traditional socio-economic leaders in their old countries; most, however, came from backgrounds just above the poverty level. The infinite variety of backgrounds and experiences enriched Canada in many ways, but also transplanted problems, such as old world hostilities, not germane to this country.

Before the first Industrial Revolution, the search for farm land was the main factor in out-migration. Western Germany permitted the division of property among all the children, which drastically reduced the size of the farms and made them no longer viable. In the North and East, only the first-born son received the farm and the other children had to search for their own land. Land was always scarce and expensive in Central Europe. It was seldom possible to acquire land through personal initiative alone; out-migration was the alternative. In search of land, German settlements expanded into Eastern Europe, Russia and the Balkan countries. Centuries later, the descendants of the settlers were expelled from the land and looked to the New World for another beginning.

The New World had always attracted the imagination of Europeans. There were dreams of fabulous riches, of adventures and success. First came the adventurers in search of quick wealth and the deportees who were serving as indentured labourers. Soldiers came to this continent when the rivalries of the Great Powers for the possession of land were transferred to North America.

The first power to lay claim to the northern part of this continent was France. In search for the North-West passage to China, the newly discovered continent was claimed in the name of the King of France. France had not yet developed into a national state, feudalism was on the wane and the absolutism of the Sun King had reached its highest point.

The heritage of the Thirty Years' War, 1618-1648, was the devastation of many parts of Europe, undertaken in the name of one religious faction or another. To determine the faith of their subjects was the prerogative of the ruler. Religious dissenters hoped to escape persecution in their homeland and sought refuge abroad, first in Europe and later in North America. New France was to be Roman Catholic; protestantism was the dominant religion in British North America.

In the seventeenth century, New France developed slowly in Acadia and Quebec. By 1700, New France had about 14,000 European settlers. This small number was surpassed by the rapid growth of the British settlements in the South. Neither the settlers of New France nor those of the British colonies were ethnically homogeneous. Among the French settlers were Roman Catholics from all parts of Europe, especially Scots, Irish and Germans. In the British colonies, there existed a similar diversity, especially in Pennsylvania, New Jersey and New York.

The first German who appeared in the records of New France was Hans Bernard. In 1664, he bought two arpents of land close to Quebec City.[1] He was one of the persons of non-French background who came in small numbers before 1700, but increased considerably after France granted citizenship rights to all Roman Catholic Europeans residing in North America in 1717.[2]

This fact cannot be seen as an acceptance of cultural diversity; rather it was an outgrowth of concern with religion. The concepts of nationality were not of great significance before the nineteenth century.

Before 1700, there were about thirty or forty permanent settlers of German origin in New France. They, with Scots and Irishmen, were the first European ethnic minorities in Canada. There is documentary evidence of three of these settlers, Andreas Wolf of Danzig, nicknamed Loup de Polonaise, Leonard Crequy of Cologne, and Andreas Spenner of Mayence.[3] These three appeared in the public records when they married French Canadian girls between 1687 and 1690.

Whereas the number of civilians was low, a considerable number of German-speaking soldiers served in New France, in Port Royal, Quebec and Louisburg, in

---

1 H. W. Debor, *Die Deutschen in der Provinz Quebec, 1664-1964,* (Como, Quebec, 1964), p. 4.
2 Cornell, P., Hamelin, J., Quellet, F., Trudel, M., *Canada, Unity in Diversity,* (Toronto, 1967), p. 51.
3 Institut Drouin, *Dictionnaire National des Canadiens Francais, 1608-1760,* Partie Genealogique, Tome 1, p. 324.

the eighteenth century. For a short time in 1755, Jean Herman Baron de Dieskau of Saxony was chief of all French troops in the colonies. The elite groups among the soldiers were German-speaking Swiss in the service of the French Crown. However, soldiers were also recruited from the principalities along the Rhine. The soldiers were encouraged to settle in the new land after the expiration of their military obligations. The largest group was garrisoned in Louisburg; however, because of the conditions and the location of the fortress, no settlement came into being.

The number of civilian settlers increased in the eighteenth century. Germans came in large numbers and soon participated in the life of the colony. There were about two hundred German families living along the St. Lawrence. Two settlers rose to prominence, Charles Joseph DeFeltz, a surgeon in Montreal, and Jean Lucas Schmid, a peominent seigneur in St. Michael de Yamaska and captain of the local militia.[4] These early settlers became completely immersed in the French-Canadian society, leaving few traces of their non-French heritage behind; only genealogical research could trace their family backgrounds.

With the conquest of New France, the interaction between Germans and French-Canadians continued. There were numerous marriages between disbanded soldiers and local women. Entirely new settlements were created in the Eastern Townships, especially in the Missiquoi Bay. Former soldiers and skilled craftsmen also settled in Montreal and Quebec City. After the original pioneer settlers, Quebec ceased to be a province of immigration with the exception of land acquisitions along the Ottawa River in Ottawa and Pontiac Counties. In the nineteenth century, Germans in Montreal were primarily in transit or sojourners who lived there for a limited time. In 1871, in Quebec, there were 8,136 persons of German origin in a total population of 1,191,516 or 0.7 per cent of the population. In the twentieth century, German-speaking urban settlers came to the big cities of Quebec but constituted a small percentage of the overall population. At present, over 80 per cent of German-speaking persons in Quebec are living in Metropolitan Montreal.

THE MARITIMES

While migrants to the Maritime Provinces were more numerous, they had features in common with the early German migrants to Quebec. They came early and settled, but subsequent migration waves bypassed the region. The integration of the population into the general fabric of society was soon completed; only in pockets was ethnic identity retained. From the earliest days of European settlement in the Maritimes, Germans were participants. They sailed with Cornwallis in 1749, but the first organized group arrived in Halifax in September, 1750, with the ship "Ann."[5] The passengers were refugees who previously lived in England. Nova

---

4 *Ibid*, Tome 11.
5 Winthrop P. Bell, *The Foreign Protestants and the Settlement of Nova Scotia*, (Toronto, 1961), p. 9.

Scotia admitted only Protestants for permanent residence, but they could be of various nationalities. The early settlers were Protestants from the Palatinate region and from Klein-Heubach along the Main River. Together with the Palatinates came French-speaking Montbeliards. This region, south of the Alsace, was part of Germany, but occupied by France under King Louis XIV. They were all called "Dutch" because they came by way of the Low Countries and because the term became the collective name for all non-British migrants of the eighteenth century. In Halifax, they settled close to the Citadel, on Goettingen and Brunswick Streets.[6] A small church on Brunswick Street, Old St. George's, close to the present McDonald Bridge, was their place of worship. The church still displays German characteristics, among them the traditional iron rooster weathervane on the tiny steeple.[7]

On May 10, 1753, the Colonial Council resolved that a settlement be established south of Halifax, under the name of "Lunenburg."[8] Prior to that time, Acadians had lived in that area, but they were expelled, shortly before the general expulsion from the Annapolis Valley. The settlers at Lunenburg were to receive fifty acres of land each, provided with accommodation and arms and supplied with materials and implements for housekeeping.

Over 1,453 persons who had come on the ships *Ann, Pearl, Gale, Sally, Betty, Murdock, Swan* and others proceeded from Halifax to Rous's Brook to develop the Township of Lunenburg. They cleared the land and established their own social order with three justices of the peace as the first government. Land was allotted in town lots, garden lots and three-hundred-acre farm lots. On the town lots, houses were to be built without delay.[9] Many of these houses are still standing, displaying a unique mixture of Old World traits and North American ingenuity. The school, entirely erected by local craftsmen, was the most prominent building.

The settlers, who had been farmers and craftsmen before coming to Lunenburg, adapted themselves to a new life by the sea. They became fishermen and boatbuilders, specializing in the Lunenburg schooner which slowly evolved as an ideal sailing vessel. During the American Revolution, they were attacked by a force of 100 privateers on July 1, 1782. Only the payment of a ransom of £1,000 prevented their settlement from being burnt to the ground.[10] Two hundred men from the Seitz Regiment, a German Regiment garrisoned in Halifax, came to the rescue, but too late.

Throughout the nineteenth century, the German language prevailed in Lunenburg County, within the interior of the county and in the town of New Germany. In the twentieth century, German characteristics have become less pronounced.

---

6 Thomas H. Raddall, *Halifax, Warden of the North*, (Toronto, 1948), p. 40.
7 G. I. Cooper, "The Germans in Nova Scotia, the Bi-Centenary of the Halifax Community", in *American German Review*, (Philadelphia, Pa., Feb. 1950), p. 24.
8 Mather Byles DesBrisay, *History of the County of Lunenburg*, (Toronto, 1895). Facsimile edition printed by Mika Studio, Belleville, Ont. 1972.
9 *Ibid*, p. 23, 28.
10 Bernhard Uhlendorf, *Revolution in America*, (New Brunswick, N. J., 1957), p. 519.

There are still 192 persons whose mother tongue is German (1975). Some of them do not know that they speak German and think that their language is a Dutch dialect. Whereas linguistic survival is minimal, cultural traits have been maintained to a greater degree. One indication of this is the easy change from Anglican to Lutheran Church membership. Most young men are confirmed in the Anglican faith during their teens; young women seldom get confirmed until marriage. If the prospective husband is Lutheran, the wife is expected to become Lutheran herself and usually does; when the fiance is Anglican, the prospective wife is expected to join the Anglican community.[11] This pattern follows historical traditions in Europe, but is not as frequent in North America. Other cultural traits, such as food items and handicrafts, are especially evident on Tamcook Island, where they have been preserved in isolation from the Nova Scotia mainland.

Between 1760 and 1770, slightly fewer than 1,000 German settlers from Pennsylvania and from Europe established themselves in Annapolis County in Nova Scotia. Prominent businessmen in Pennsylvania had received land grants in Nova Scotia on condition that they bring settlers into the province. Among these was General Anthony Wayne, who brought 20 Germans to the north shore off the Bay of Fundy in 1765. John Hughes acted as the agent for Anthony Wayne of Philadelphia, and the agreement was signed by nine Germans, among these Heinrich Stief and Michael Lutz, in 1766. Later, the German families settled in Albert County, Coverdale Parish, Elgin Parish and Hillsborough Township.[12] The latter areas later became a part of New Brunswick and are situated in the Petticodiac River Valley.

Before the American Revolution, the main settlements of Germans in the thirteen colonies had been in Pennsylvania. The Penn family had extended the invitation to European dissenters and allowed them freely to pursue their unique ways. German family bibles, printed in Philadelphia, can be found among many of the early settlers in the Maritimes. The *Stief* (Steeves) Bible in the New Brunswick Archives is an example. When settlers moved from Pennsylvania, they brought their own folkways and transmitted them to other settlers in the new areas. Thus, *Spaetzle* became the *poutain rapé* of the Acadians residing in the vicinity.

The first period of German settlement ended with the American Revolution. Up to that time, there was little conflict between the Germans' identity and their feeling of loyalty to the British monarch. Some were grateful for having received protection against religious persecution in their homelands and for being able to come to America. Others simply came in search of new opportunities. Germans who had settled in Quebec were also reconciled with their new status as British subjects.

The American Revolution created a crisis for the German settlers and a renewed involvement of German soldiers. To many of the settlers, breaking their oath of allegiance to the King was inconceivable, and thus they remained loyal to the

---

11 Information supplied by Dean Cooper of the Anglican Cathedral in Fredericton, New Brunswick, on March 29, 1976.
12 C. Alexander Pincombe, *The History of Moncton Township*, (Fredericton, 1969), p. 57.

British Crown. Others actively joined the American cause and took part in the war. The majority retained a cautious neutrality which had serious consequences after the end of the conflict.

German soldiers played an important part in the American Revolution. When fighting for the British cause, they were called mercenaries; if they fought on the American side, they were dubbed patriots. Numerous reports were written about the Hessians; few of them depicted the situation accurately. In the eighteenth century, soldiers in a standing army were recruited by dubious means by any state or monarch; volunteers were rare. Universal military service was practised in the nineteenth and twentieth centuries, but not before that time.

The Brunswick regiments were called to service by their Duke, the King of Great Britain. Other principalities had treaties with either Hanover-Brunswick or Great Britain. Among these were Hessen-Kassel, (ruled by a brother-in-law of King George III), Anhalt, Ansbach-Bayreuth, Hanau and Waldeck.[13] All troops were under the command of their own officers and reported to their own war departments. The records of the Hessian Army, preserved and available at the William L. Clements Library of American History, University of Michigan,[14] differ considerably from the commonly held opinions on the experience of the German troops in the American Revolution. Most armies were not under British command; they operated as allies in independent units. One important cause of misunderstanding was the inability of officers and men to speak English. The soldiers spoke German and the officers spoke German and French. Lack of communication and propaganda created monsters out of conscripts. The French contingent which fought on the side of the Americans also contained German troops, primarily from Zweibruecken,[15] who were considered as heroes.

Canada was defended by Brunswick troops under the command of Baron von Riedesel. He stayed for seven years in North America, as soldier, prisoner, and soldier again. Documents in the William L. Clements Library, as well as the vivid reports of his wife, gave interesting glimpses into army life as lived by the commanders. The Riedesel Reports speak about the battles and tribulations, as well as

13 Martha B. Clark, *The Hessians*, in Papers and Addresses of the Lancaster County Historical Society, Vol. IV, (Lancaster, Pa., 1900), p. 119–137.
Friedrich W. Sintenis, *Sintenis' Chronik der Stadt Zerbst, 1758–1817*, narrated by Reinholt Specht, Zerbster Jahrbuch, Jg. XV, Zerbst, 1930.
Stephan Popp, *Popp's Journal 1777–1783*, translated by Joseph G. Rosengarten, in Pennsylvania Magazine of History and Biography, Vol. 24 (Philadelphia, Pa., 1902), p. 25–41.
Carl Heiner, "Von Hanau nach Quebec" in *Volk und Scholle*, Heimatblaetter fuer beide Hessen, Nassau and Frankfurt a. M. Jahrgang IX (Darmstadt, 1931), p. 292–295.
L. Curtze, *Geschichte und Beschreibung des Fuerstenthums* Waldeck, (Arolsen, Speyersche Buchhandlung, 1850), XIII, (2), p. 6645.
14 There were two periods between 1776–82 during which German troops were active in Canada; first, in Quebec from November 6, 1776 to July 8, 1777 (see letter of Brunswick Army), and subsequently in garrison duties in Nova Scotia. (see letters of Loos, Schallern and Waldenburg to von Jungkenn).
15 A. B. Faust, *The German Element in the United States* (New York, 1927), Vol. 1, p. 344–9.

the social life under winterquarter conditions.[16] The Baroness introduced to Canada the custom of having a Christmas tree, at Sorel, Quebec, in 1781.

Other reports gave an insight into the life of the common soldier. Johann Gottfried Seume,[17] a student of theology at the University of Leipzig, decided to leave for Paris but was impressed at Ziegenhain and brought to Halifax for garrison duties. Life in the transport vessels was most disagreeable; the soldiers were pressed, packed and pickled like herring. Food consisted of peas and pork and peas, except later when they fished for cod. After twenty-two weeks at sea, the ships arrived at the shores of Acadia and reached the Bay of Halifax. Life in Halifax was unpleasant. The camp was on a rolling shore; there was little food and life was generally boring. Seume was kept busy in several functions of garrison duty. During his stay in Halifax he wrote, on October 24, 1782, the first German-Language poems written in Canada.

In his autobiography, Seume describes his experiences in the army, his observations of the natives and life in Halifax. At first, life in the army was difficult, but later he had sufficient time to pursue other interests. His observations about the Hurons — as he called them, were very positive and contrasted with European barbarity. Seume was an egalitarian who deplored the artificial restrictions placed on people by European conventions. Life in Halifax in 1782 appeared similar to subsequent war periods. Limited accommodations and high prices were already a part of life.

After the American Revolution, some of the disbanded soldiers chose to remain in North America. They were granted land in the Annapolis Valley of Nova Scotia and established the Waldeck Line and Hessian Line settlements. Several soldiers moved into New Brunswick and joined the German settlements in Albert County.

Prince Edward Island and Newfoundland were two provinces with hardly any German settlers: even now, fewer than 700 persons, or 0.6 percent of the population in Prince Edward Island are of German origin. Although the island of Newfoundland likewise had few inhabitants of German background, German missionaries played an important role in the settlements along the coast of Labrador. These missionaries belonged to the Moravian Brethren Community which was under the leadership of Count Zinzendorf. In North America, they worked with the Delaware Indians in Pennsylvania, Ohio, and Ontario and with the Inuit population of the coast of Labrador. Here, the main centres were Nain and Cape Mugford. A relatively small group, they were unable to maintain their activities indefinitely and became a part of the Grenfell Missions.[19] The Moravians were very fond of music,

---

16 Frederike Charlotte Louise von Mussow, Freifrau von Riedesel, *Briefe der Generalin von Riedesel auf dieser Reise und Waehrend ihres sechsjaehrigen Aufenthalts in America in den Jahren 1776 bis 1783 nach Deutschland Geschrieben* (Berlin, 1800), translated by William Stone, Joel Munsell, 1867.
17 Johann Gottfried Seume, *Mein Leben* (Berlin, no date) p. 61–78.
18 William L. Clement Library, University of Michigan.
19 Sir Wilfred Grenfell, *The Romance of Labrador* (New York, 1934), p. 158–9.

especially brass bands. Wherever Moravians worked, active musical groups were formed. As a consequence, the Inuits along the Labrador Coast had some of the best classical music groups in the country. Music appreciation was one of the permanent traits which were taken from the activities of the early Moravian missionaries.

Throughout the nineteenth century, few persons of German background settled in the Maritime Provinces. Many landed in Halifax, but only in transit to other parts of Canada. German settlements in the Maritimes remained static. Apart from Nova Scotia, where slightly over six percent of the population are of German background, less than one percent of the population of the other provinces are of German origin.[20]

---

20 J. J. Cooper, "The Germans in Nova Scotia", in *The American German Review* (Philadelphia, 1950), p. 22–24.

Chapter 2

FROM THE ARRIVAL OF THE UNITED EMPIRE LOYALISTS TO CONFEDERATION

With the withdrawal of British troops from the former Thirteen Colonies, the internal division of the population became more pronounced. The victorious Americans showed little magnanimity towards the Loyalists and harboured suspicions towards those who remained neutral throughout the war. As a consequence, most Loyalists were forced to leave the country or did so in anticipation of reprisals. Notwithstanding the Peace Treaty of Paris in 1783, the property of the Loyalists was confiscated and their personal lives were threatened.

The first groups in the exodus to the remaining British colonies were the members of the militia regiments and their families. Johnson's First Battalion, King's Royal Regiment, received land in the Bay of Quinte Region[1] and along the St. Lawrence River; Butler's Rangers settled in the Niagara Peninsula,[2] and other former soldiers chose Peel County and Fort York (Toronto). Another group founded settlements in southwestern Ontario.[3] From the Atlantic seaboard, soldiers and their families were evacuated to Nova Scotia. In 1783 alone, close to 20,000 settlers came by sea. In Nova Scotia, it was found that the refugees could not adequately be accommodated in the province and consequently New Brunswick was created to resettle the refugees.

German soldiers were a significant percentage in the militia groups, especially those from New York, New Jersey and Pennsylvania. Many German names appeared on the list of those who received land in compensation for their services. German soldier settlements were along the St. Lawrence River, in southern Essex County and in Albert County, New Brunswick.

After the militia came civilians who preferred to live under the British crown. Some were adventurers who were attracted by the newly available land. Among these was William von Moll de Berczy (1748–1813),[4] a German master of many trades and arts. He contributed to the original designs for the City of Toronto, was active in promoting a German settlement near Markham, and worked as a portrait painter. A Renaissance man, he was ill suited to the tedious job of community leader. Forever full of ideas, he found it hard to fulfill his dreams and promises in a

---

1 William F. E. Morley, *Prisoner Life in the Bay of Quinte* (Belleville, 1972).
2 For a list of the early German settlers, see G. Elmore Reaman, *The Trail of the Black Walnut* (Toronto, 1957), Appendix A, p. 216. Also, Jean N. McIlwraith, *Sir Frederick Haldimand* (Toronto, 1910), p. 256.
3 Ernest J. Lajeunesse, CSB, *The Windsor Border Region* (Toronto, 1960).
4 John Andre, William Berczy, *Infant Toronto as Simcoe's* Folly (Toronto, 1971).

raw and difficult land. Imbued with charm and skill, he lived in perennial financial straits, which ultimately contributed to his departure from Upper Canada.

More steadfast than the adventurers were the religious dissenters, primarily residents of Pennsylvania. Since they did not bear arms for the United States, they were accused of disloyalty and harassed. Many chose to move to Upper Canada. The first group established itself around Jordan, in the Niagara Peninsula in 1786. Later came the main stream between 1799 and 1812.[5] In 1803, the German Company[6] was founded which purchased land in the Grand River Valley, especially Waterloo County. This county became the centre of German settlements and the focal point of religious and secular activities.

In 1807, the present Woolwich Township, about 45,195 acres adjacent to the 60,000 acres bought previously, was purchased by the German Land Company. This township remained for over 60 years the area with the highest concentration of German settlers in Upper Canada, more than ninety per cent of the population being German. Until 1827, most Germans were Anabaptists and Fundamentalist Protestants. Most Anabaptists were Mennonites.

These people left Pennsylvania with their Conestoga wagons, the prototype of the prairie schooner, following the Susquehanna Trail which crossed the Allegheny Mountains. The trail crossed the Genesee River, either at Lewiston or Black Rock, and finally reached the Niagara River. This stream was traversed with flatboats. Huge forests had to be penetrated and movement was slow, seldom more than four or five miles per day. The entire journey, which now takes less than a day by automobile, took between 107 to 120 days.[7]

The migration of Anabaptists continued until about 1830, when the separation between Swiss Mennonites and Amish became visible.[8] For 130 years, there was hardly any Amish migration to Canada until new colonies were established in Elgin County, Ontario.

The first German Catholic settlers, mainly from Alsace and Baden, came between 1827 and 1830. St. Mary's Church and St. Jerome's College (Berlin, Ontario) became their spiritual homes in the new region.

In 1785, the western part of Quebec (Upper Canada) was divided into four judicial districts, named after German regions, Lunenburg, Mecklenburg, Nassau and Hesse. These districts were legal entities until 1791, when Upper Canada was formally established as a province. Of the districts, the most western was the District of Hesse, administered from Detroit. At the time of the American Revolution, there was a small settlement along the Detroit River which had been under British jurisdiction since the Peace Treaty of Paris in 1763. The bulk of the population was French-speaking. Officially, the land beyond the Great Lakes and the Detroit River was ceded by Britain to the United States of America. However, the British contin-

---

5 G. Elmore Reaman, *ibid.*, p. 44.
6 W. V. Uttley, *A History of Kitchener, Ontario* (Kitchener, 1937), p. 9.
7 *Ibid.* p. 8.
8 Orland Gingerich, *The Amish of Canada* (Waterloo, 1972), p. 161–167.

ued in possession of the district until 1796, when the Jay Treaties settled some of the outstanding differences between the two countries.

In 1796, the inhabitants had to choose between American and British citizenship. Those who opted for the latter, moved into what are now Essex, Kent and Lambton counties. During this time, about twenty German families received land grants in southern Essex county.[9] Early Kent County saw the work of German missionaries of the Moravian Brethren Church, similar to the work along the Labrador coast. The Moravians had converted the Delaware Nation to Christianity and to a peaceful way of life. When American settlers moved westward across the Allegheny Mountains, they did not differentiate between warlike and peaceful natives and burned two settlements, Sandusky, Ohio, and Gnadenhuetten, and killed the inhabitants who could not escape. Finally, under the leadership of David Zeisberger, they settled in Fairfield on the Thames in 1792. Zeisberger stayed in Fairfield between 1792 and 1798, during which time a townsite and a colony were established.

Zeisberger's diaries[10] describe the trials and tribulations of establishing a peaceful settlement in times of war and insecurity. The subsequent fate of Fairfield seemed to bear out Zeisberger's concerns and worries, for it was completely destroyed in 1813 during the War of 1812. Close to the settlement was the battleground on which Tecumseh, the famous warrior chief, lost his life. The Delaware Nation re-established itself on the south bank of the river, and Moraviantown, the new settlement, came into existence.

The War of 1812 signifies the end of the pioneer period in Upper Canada. By that time, soldiers, United Empire Loyalists and neutrals had gained their first foothold in the new land. German settlers lived south of Amherstburg, in the Grand River Valley, the vicinity of Newark (Niagara-on-the-Lake), York County, the Bay of Quinte and along the St. Lawrence River.

After a period of consolidation and limited success in attracting British settlers under Peter Robinson, new impetus was given to colonization with the establishment of the Canada Land Company. A royal charter was granted on August 19, 1829, and the company received approximately one million acres of land, to be opened for development. Most of the available land was in Southwestern Ontario, between Waterloo and Essex Counties. In 1829, the Huron Tract, close to the present townsite of Goderich, was opened. A trail connecting Goderich with western country roads was built to facilitate the opening of the region.

The opening of the Huron Tract did not proceed as fast as hoped for. English-speaking settlers were slow in coming and attempts were made to attract German and French colonists. The French, who came from France rather than Quebec, established St. Joseph on Lake Huron; the Germans lived in Hay Township. Most of the Germans were Anabaptists and Lutherans who became prosperous farmers. In 1846, the village of Zurich was built. It was named after the hometown of Conrad Grebel, the founder of the Anabaptist Movement in Switzerland. German charac-

9 G. Elmore Reaman, *ibid.,* p. 216.
10 Eugene F. Bliss, *Diary of David Zeisberger* (Cincinnati, 1885).

teristics are still evident, from the clock on the steeple of the Lutheran Church to linguistic retention of German traits and German-style food.[11]

However, some settlers did not like the land granting procedures of the Canada Land Company and preferred to homestead on Crown land instead. The Bruce Peninsula remained Crown property and was opened for settlement in the 1850s.[12] German settlers came in search of land, either from Waterloo County or directly from Europe. They separated along religious lines; Protestants lived in the Townships of Brant and Carrick, Mennonites in Saugeen, and Roman Catholics in Hepworth, Mildmay and Formosa. The Bruce County settlements retained their German identity until World War I, when pressures were applied to assimilate the settlers. Most residents of German background raised before World War I were fluent in the language. The subsequent generation neither speaks German nor identifies with the German-Canadian community. The German population of Grey County was in the southwestern part — Neustadt and Hanover, Bentinck and Keppel Townships, where they formed the majority of the population. Other German settlers came in small groups to Wellington and Perth Counties.

By the middle of the nineteenth century, German settlers were living throughout Ontario, with concentrations in the above-named regions. Most farmers were living in rural areas. Their houses looked slightly different from those of farmers of other backgrounds. Mennonite farms had traditional designs on their barns, such as symbols of good luck and prosperity. Other German-speaking farmers placed more emphasis on the construction of the barn than on the quality of housing. There were unique patterns of enclosure and trees were planted profusely around the houses and barns. These patterns contrasted strongly with French-Canadian farms which were devoid of trees around the houses, a reminder of the time when trees and bushes could conceal hostile natives and room for defense was needed. Theirs was a hostile country; the German settlers came during peaceful periods and knew little about the problems of the past.

Berlin (now Kitchener) was the centre of the German-speaking population of Ontario. Here they found the goods and services for the rural hinterland, and tradesmen and craftsmen settled. Small industries emerged in furniture-making, leather goods and tanning, milling and brewing. There was a great deal of diversification; no single company dominated the town.

Religion, rather than nationality, provided the bonds among the settlers, their social institutions and their educational institutions. This was quite evident among the Waterloo County Mennonites and Amish. During the nineteenth century, the differences between the two groups became more pronounced. They were based on life-styles and church discipline rather than upon theological interpretations.[13] Group control was exercised to obtain conformity with the desired patterns; transgressors were exhorted, shunned or permanently excommunicated. Lutherans,

---

11 James Scott, *The Settlement of Huron County* (Toronto, 1966), p. 170–175, 295–297.
12 Norman Robertson, *The History of the County of Bruce* (Toronto, 1906), p. 337–393.
13 Orland Gingerich, *ibid.*, p. 21.

the other large Protestant group, stressed the unity of language and religion which reinforced the patterns of ethnic identity. Lutherans, however, did not exercise the level of control over their members that the Anabaptist group did. They depended primarily on education to maintain group identity. Roman Catholics experienced the greatest difficulties in maintaining their ethnic identity. When they first arrived, they brought their own priests, who established churches and schools. Soon the schools were under great pressure to conform to the patterns of English-speaking separate schools. Only if a religious congregation was in control of an educational institution was language maintenance emphasized. In general, the Irish-oriented Roman Catholic Episcopate had little room for third groups; the English-French dualism was the major preoccupation of the day. Awareness of cultural difficulties was a late discovery among the Roman Catholic local clergy. Newcomers were expected to adapt, rather than be recognized for their unique contributions. In general, large religious organizations cared little about language maintenance. The small groups, however, thought religion and ethnicity to be inseparable.

At the time of Confederation, the main areas of settlement in the Maritimes, Quebec and Ontario had been established. Land for agriculture was still available, albeit mostly in the inaccessible parts of the country. The Canadian Shield, the rock formation which made the penetration of Northern Quebec and Ontario difficult, was sparsely populated and hardly opened for lumbering, fishing, and trapping. The Maritimes, Quebec, and southern Ontario had already reached the limits of agricultural settlement under the conditions of that time. Young farmers found land more difficult to obtain.

The value of land depended upon the accessibility of transportation. This was first by waterways, and after the middle of the nineteenth century by railroad. New markets and opportunities opened up. The small towns, hitherto in isolation, provided the services for the hinterland and allowed for expansion of primary production and distribution. Railroad communities prospered; those without access stagnated or disappeared altogether.[14]

The Maritime Provinces depended on water transportation. The Lunenburg settlement prospered and flourished because of the unique combination between agriculture, fisheries and accessibilities to the markets of the seaboards. German settlements in the Bay of Fundy already experienced the economic deterioration which became so evident in the twentieth century. The change from water transportation to railroads put the Maritimes at a disadvantage and they remain disadvantaged today.

Two major waterways were established in Upper Canada, the Rideau and the Trent Canal systems. Ottawa owed its existence to the Rideau Canal; so did Smith Falls. Originally built for military purposes, the Canal opened up the interior of eastern Ontario for lumbering and agriculture. The Trent Canal, more oriented to

---

14 J. M. S. Careless, *Union of the Canadas: The Growth of Canadian Institutions, 1841–1857* (Toronto, 1967).

commercial purposes, developed numerous towns and villages and laid the basis for small industries around Peterborough.

Whereas canals were the main avenues for opening the American West, the railroad fulfilled this function in Ontario and the Western provinces. Within a relatively short period, Ontario was criss-crossed by railroads. The bush trail and the Conestoga wagons were the symbols of the pioneer farmer who cleared his land by slash and burn methods and who had limited access to the market economy. The railroads ended this phase of development and initiated a new phase of agricultural and industrial growth.

The early pioneers had to be as self-sufficient as possible. Little money was available, and all the food was grown on the farms; hunting and fishing supplemented the staple diets. Each small hamlet had a grist mill which operated on a share-cropper basis. Many of the early millers were of German background.[15] They were the first to use the rolling mill which was substituted for the grist mill because of greater efficiency.

In the cycle of cutting down the virgin forest, pioneer farming and systematic agriculture, German settlers were seldom involved in the first two stages. More often than not, the German farmers bought the crudely prepared land from the homesteaders, who frequently stayed in the bush until the land patents were granted and then moved on.

German farmers were less mobile and remained in the region where they settled. The farms were developed under a system of shared labour with different roles assigned to men, women and children. The children started with the herding of small animals, such as geese, and progressed to more adult tasks. There was great emphasis on the participation in work by all members of the family. This work ethic was especially evident among the Ontario Mennonites and Amish. There was little faith in the value of education beyond basic knowledge, and accomplishments were measured in farming skills rather than school grades. The children were directed to the ways and means of farming with a keen sense of marketing. There was great emphasis on frugality, hard work and thrift. Capital accumulation was valued as providing young sons with the possibility of establishing a farm and daughters with suitable dowries.

In closed communities, there was a co-operative lifestyle. The group depended primarily on its own resources and manpower. Whenever a member built a house or a barn, all others participated in the work. This was reciprocated on occasions. The community also acted as the main agency of social control and discipline. There were codes of accepted behaviour which only the young people could transgress occasionally. Social responsibility was taken for granted, including the care of the elderly by the members of the immediate family. Several generations either lived together in one household or in close proximity to one another.

Social responsibility was, however, restricted to conforming members of the

---

15 Mabel B. Dunham, "Mills and Millers in Western Ontario" in *Western Ontario History Nuggets No. 9* (London, 1946).

family, the extended family and the members of the congregation. Only in times of dire emergencies did it extend to co-religionists and hardly ever to outsiders. The farming communities were inward-looking and participated little in civic and public affairs.

In urban areas, the patterns of frugality were maintained. From an early age, all members of the family were expected to be gainfully employed. The family pooled the resources and kept expenses to the minimum. Although in the nineteenth century, women of English or Scottish background seldom worked outside the home, Germans did not have these restrictions. Young women worked as domestics or in the emerging small factories which were little more than cottage industries. There was no social stigma among German women for having worked as domestics or in factories. The button and textile industries especially attracted women workers who worked long hours for small wages. Since outside employment was seen as temporary, in preparation for marriage, there was great emphasis on the amount of savings or dowry which a young bride could bring into marriage. Young men were assessed for their ability as breadwinners and providers. However, in each case, the extended family was expected to help. Especially among Mennonites, ostentatious display of wealth was frowned upon. Jewelry was scarce and the European custom of having jewelry as a kind of last resort insurance was not practised.

During the nineteenth century, a half-way type of German Canadian culture emerged. German, in the archaic form, remained the principal language of primary-group communication and worship. On the other hand, business activities and public affairs were conducted in English. Germans preferred people of other backgrounds as business partners; they liked to conduct business at arm's length rather than in a quasi-primary group setting.

One of the most important changes was the emerging separation of church and state. Many German language churches had depended upon the state to enforce religious conformity. In the new land, this was not possible and the congregations themselves were responsible for orthodoxy and discipline. Informal sanctions replaced the government. Religious schisms were common because of different interpretations and lifestyles. German Protestants created many new religious interpretations.[16] At the level of social interaction, voluntary associations performed many of the functions which in Europe were handled by public institutions. Many voluntary groups were separated along denominational lines, especially among Lutherans and Roman Catholics.

Denominational cohesion became a significant factor in ethnic group survival. This survival was not based on nationalism, because most immigrants had hardly any feeling of being a single identifiable group. Regional and denominational differences created a variety of patterns with little German self-awareness.

Most Canadians of German linguistic background, as British subjects under a German dynasty, had no split loyalties and little concern about the future. The events in Europe which led to the formation of the German Empire in 1870—1

---

16 G. Elmore Reaman, *op. cit.*, p. 179.

were of little interest to the Ontario residents. This was in contrast to policies pursued by Germans in the United States who were passionately involved in the affairs of the homeland. One of the reasons for the absence of involvement was the relative scarcity of refugees from the abortive 1848 German Revolution, especially the middle class intellectuals, who in the United States became an important rallying focus of German life and activities. Canada, a young country with little for a professional class, was bypassed by most refugees, and those who came stayed only for a short time before moving to the American Mid-West.

Some changes in attitudes towards the homeland occurred after 1871. As in Germany, the war with France fanned the flames of nationalism, so the events in Europe were used as rallying points in Canada.[17] In times of success, there was little awareness that minorities should develop their own institutional identity in Canada without relying for prestige upon events in their homelands. Only the Anabaptists, who abhorred all military activities and ostentatious display of national sentiments, remained aloof. All others felt that the unification of Germany and the economic prosperity elevated the status of Germans in Canada and acted accordingly. The Alsatians, who were becoming German subjects instead of French citizens, considered this matter with apprehension, because of the conflict between linguistic and national sentiments. Similar reservations existed among German-speaking Canadians of Swiss and Austrian origin. Since the number of these minorities within minorities was small at that time, the reservations were muted.

Before the advent of modern means of communication, German-language newspapers served as transmitters of news. Another means of communication, postal service, was slow to grow. In 1837, Berlin, Ontario, inaugurated partial postal service. With the coming of the railroads, the service was expanded into a daily delivery system. In the nineteenth century, reports of travellers were eagerly awaited and circuit-riding ministers were welcome for the news they carried with them, as well as for their preaching. The isolation of the early settlements created a hunger for news and information which could seldom be satisfied. News was often late in reaching the hinterland.

---

17 M. V. Uttley, *op. cit.*, p. 187.

Chapter 3

MASS MIGRATION AND NEW SETTLEMENTS

At the time of Confederation, the majority of Germans in Canada, somewhat over 200,000, lived in Ontario. Outside that province, there were a few isolated pockets of German settlers. In Quebec, they lived mainly in Montreal, where they numbered about 1,440 in 1881, and in Pontiac County along the Ottawa River. The German presence in Montreal was continuous, but never large. A German Mutual Aid Society had existed since the 1850s.[1] However, the Germans of Montreal were frequently sojourners who remained in the city for a short time before continuing their migration to points west.

The Maritimes had about 47,000 Germans, 20,000 of whom lived in Lunenburg County, Nova Scotia. In the nineteenth century, a mixed pattern of Anglo-Nova Scotian and German traits had evolved. Although English had become the usual language of interaction, German was still spoken. There were many Germanisms in the expressions, especially in the use of German proverbs in English translation.[2] The decrease in isolation, due to regular transportation patterns and lack of continuous immigration, militated against language maintenance. Other German settlements, such as those in New Brunswick, disappeared through intermarriage and the substitution for German of English and to a lesser degree, French. The elites of German background, such as the Tuppers and Steeves, were aware of their heritage and proud of their tradition.[3] Nonetheless, their connections with German-Canadian institutions were tenuous.

Towards the last part of the nineteenth century, German settlements in Ontario changed from self-sufficient farming to the market economy and to small-scale industry. With improved economic standing, there was increased awareness of public affairs, especially in southwestern Ontario. Two events, both in Berlin, Ontario, symbolized the change, the *Saengerfest of 1879*,[4] and the *Kirmes of 1894*.[5]

1 *Statuten der Deutschen Gesellschaft zu Montreal in Canada* (The Statutes of the German Community of Montreal in Canada) (Preston, C. W., 1859) and list of subsequent members.
2 Helen Creighton, "The Folklore of Lunenburg County, Nova Scotia," *National Museum of Canada, Bulletin No. 117* (1950), p. 78.
3 The Steeves Family Bible had been donated to the New Brunswick Public Archives. Unfortunately, the first pages are missing; however, it seems to be a Sauer, Philadelphia, Pa., print.
4 Mabel Dunham, *Grand River* (Toronto: 1945), p. 127.
5 Mabel Dunham, *ibid.*, p. 128 ff.

The *Saengerfest* reflected primarily the expression of an immigrant culture with ties to the Old World. Patterned after singing competitions in Germany, it was a mixture of patriotism and conviviality. The patriotism was divided between the Old World and the New. While homage was given to Germany, Canadian and American choirs, from as far away as Chicago, Illinois, participated. Attendance was estimated between 12,000 and 20,000. This event demonstrated also the growing strength of the German-Canadian community.

German craftsmen established themselves in wood processing and furniture production, rubber goods, tanning, breweries, textiles and button-making. With industrial development, new lifestyles emerged. Yet most remembered the pre-industrial society of a romantic Germany, a society of the world of the Brothers Grimm, not one of industrial life and urban development. This nostalgia reflected itself in the Kirmes of 1894. The event was the recreation of the folk-festivals of historic Germany. The Town of Berlin was decorated as a small village, streets were made to resemble old country market squares. Old dresses heightened the nostalgia for the "Good Old Tymes" with regional costumes and family heirlooms on display. An abundance of food and drink was provided in booths and tents. The highlight of the event was the Harvesters' Homecoming Procession, in which the Queen of the Harvest was honoured in a parade.

The Kirmes attracted a great deal of attention throughout Ontario and was attended by the Lieutenant Governor and the German Consul General. Whereas the Saengerfest could be seen more as a desire for recognition, the Kirmes affirmed the standing of German-Canadians in public life. Only a group which felt economically and socially secure could indulge in a nostalgic recreation of the past.

Although centered in Berlin, Ontario, German manufacturers established themselves in Preston, Hespeler, Elmira, Hanover, Chesley, Walkerton, and Southampton. The most prominent German-Canadian business families were the Boehmers, Breithaupts, Heintzmans, Kaufmans and Krugs.

Towards the turn of the century, participation of German-Canadians in political life encountered few difficulties. There was representation at the municipal, provincial and federal levels. Best known in municipal politics were Victor Lang in Grey County and Sir Adam Beck in London, Ontario. The latter was the first mayor of London and later became one of the developers of a province-wide hydro-electrical power grid system. Others were mentioned in a famous speech about the Germans in 1908.[6]

Two German-Canadians served in the Provincial Legislative Assembly, Dr. Lackman and Mr. C. M. Bowman. The federal ridings of Waterloo County, and Grey and Bruce Peninsula were also held by persons of German background. Participation in government services and cultural events was also active.

Until the opening of the Canadian West brought many German-Canadians to the new territories, integration into the economic, political and social life was pro-

---

6 *House of the Commons Debate, April 14, 1908*, Mr. H. Miller (South Grey), Ottawa, 1908, p. 6826–6833.

gressing rapidly. Most German-Canadians were at least as prosperous as the average Canadian family.[7] While politically less influential than persons of Anglo-Saxon background, they did not suffer informal or formal exclusion from political processes either. There were few problems of social acceptance; German-Canadians had formed their own institutional network. In the nineteenth century, it was possible for a convert from Judaism, educated in Germany, to become Anglican Bishop of Huron with his See in London, Ontario, and founder of the University of Western Ontario. The Right Reverend Isaac Hellmuth[8] frequently referred to his German connections and educational accomplishments. Being of German background was a matter for pride. This attitude was to change with the outbreak of World War I.

THE PRAIRIE PROVINCES*

The Prairie Provinces form a distinct unit; they share a common climate, geographical pattern, history of settlement and economy. Separated from the eastern part of the country by the wide, barren and sparsely populated Canadian Shield, they have developed a unique identity; boundaries between the provinces are manmade superimpositions. The western boundaries are the Rocky Mountains which once formed a difficult barrier to British Columbia. The climate is severe: there are short, hot summers and long, cold winters. Harvesting in the fall is a race against time, as the grain has to be brought in before the onset of winter. In many areas, fall seeding is impossible and spring seeding is the alternative. This again creates race against time; only a few weeks are available for the intensive work of preparing the ground and seeding. A wet spring can prevent this work and make it difficult for the fall harvest. Apart from the dry lands of southern Alberta and Saskatchewan which unless irrigation is applied is suitable only for ranching, the Prairies have just enough precipitation to allow a good yield of summer grain. Fruit is not grown on a commercial scale, vegetables can be grown on irrigated land, but wild berries are pentiful. The Prairies are rich in mineral resources, coal, natural gas and oil, and potash. However, the primary industries are the result of discoveries in the last thirty-five years; the early settlers came in search of land.

In May, 1670, the Hudson's Bay Company was granted territorial rights over the watershed of the Bay. All rivers flowing into Hudson Bay from the headwaters to the mouth and the territories between the rivers were to be under the control of the Company.[9] This monopoly was challenged, first by New France and later by

---

7 This has been described by Bruce Creighton, Luella Sanders *High Bright Buggy Wheels* (Toronto: 1951), a theme which was also apparent in the H. Miller speech in the House of Commons, *ibid.*, p. 6826–6833.
8 A. H. Crowfoot, *This Dream, Life of Isaac Hellmuth* (Toronto: 1963).
9 W. L. Morton, *Manitoba, A History* (Toronto: 1957), p. 11.

* R. A. Helling, University of Windsor with the co-operation of Jack Thiessen, University of Winnipeg.

the competing North-West Company. However, the union between the latter and the Hudson's Bay Company again established the domination of the Hudson's Bay Company from the Lakehead to the Pacific Ocean. Although there were trading posts throughout the Prairies, attempts at settlement were primarily made in the Red River Valley. Many of the settlers were fur traders and Metis, the offspring of white men and native women.

In 1812, Lord Selkirk tried to colonize the Red River Valley and induced Scottish Highlanders to homestead near Fort Garry. The settlement was a failure. A similar fate occurred to German-speaking soldiers who were settled there in 1817.[10] They occupied land opposite Fort Douglas, on a small stream called German Creek. However, the DeMeuron and Von Wattenwil settlers were not prepared for the viscissitudes of living in isolation with annual spring flood conditions. In 1821 only sixty-five residents remained. In that same year, another group of Swiss settlers were given land close to the DeMeuron soldiers. They, too, left soon for St. Paul, Minnesota, and St. Louis, Missouri. Soldiers and craftsmen were not suitable for the rigorous farming conditions of the Prairies, the constant struggle for food and the long periods of isolation from the outside world.[11]

Among the settlers of 1821 were the Rindisbacher family. Peter Rindisbacher (1806–1834) came to the Selkirk Settlement as a boy. Later, he obtained a position as clerk with the Hudson's Bay Company and soon discovered his talents as a water-colour artist. His vivid descriptions of the frontier and native life around the Hudson's Bay forts left an everlasting impression. As the first practising artist west of the Great Lakes, he left numerous genre pictures of life in the wilderness. Governor Bulzer was so impressed that he organized a buffalo hunt to allow Rindisbacher to depict the hunt in accurate drawings and paintings which have become the Canadian antecedents of George Catlin and other artists of the American West. The flood of 1826 forced the Rindisbacher family to leave for St. Louis, where Peter died in 1834.

The first half of the nineteenth century was not yet the time for large scale settlement of the Canadian West. Some tough Scotsmen and French-Canadians were able to survive as subsistence farmers, equally dependent upon grain and the hunting of wild animals. With luck, they grew enough grain to supply the trading stations; in adverse times, they depended upon the land for meagre support. In 1835, 658 Europeans lived in the Prairies, and by 1849, there were 1,052 heads of families. Of these, only two were Swiss, a good indication of the abandonment of the Red River Settlement by that group. After 1856, the growth rate accelerated somewhat. In 1856 the inhabitants totalled 5,042 and by 1870, they totalled 12,228.

In the nineteenth century, a steady stream of settlers moved into the American

---

10 Friedrich von Grafenried, "Sechs Jahre in Kanada," *Tenth Yearly Report of the Geographical Society* (Bern, Switzerland: 1890).
11 George Bryce, *The Romantic Settlement of Lord Selkirk's Colonists* (Toronto: 1909), Chapter XII.

Prairies. They learned how to farm the treeless land and to survive under extreme weather conditions. At the end of the American War between the States, most homestead land was pre-empted, yet more farmers in search of land moved to the west. Canadians had justified fears that the United States would annex the British colonies and the Hudson's Bay Territory. Some of it, the Oregon Territory and the Red River Valley south of Pembina, was already claimed or threatened. If American settlers inhabited the British colonies, sooner or later they could invoke the principle of manifest destiny which had been successfully used against Spain and Mexico. The territorial rights of the Hudson's Bay Company had lapsed in 1859 and Britain was willing to cede the land gradually to Canada. Shortly after Confederation was established, British Columbia joined the Dominion in 1871, the same year the province of Manitoba was created in the Prairies. One of the conditions of British Columbia joining was the establishment of a transcontinental railroad.

Such a railroad was only possible if the large land masses were subdivided and opened for settlement. Construction on the Canadian Pacific Railroad began and the township system of land division was established by the Federal Order in Council of April 25, 1871.[12] The Dominion Land Act of 1872[13] created the homestead in the size of a quarter section, 160 acres, and the conditions under which the land could be acquired by settlers.

The basic conditions were a filing fee of $10.00, the building of a house and the cultivation of at least 40 acres within three years.

At first, the impact of this organization remained small. Canadian farmers were used to pioneer in woodland areas, not on the open Prairie. They followed the river valleys and had small settlements in and around Winnipeg, St. Boniface, Portage La Prairie and Edmonton.

It became desirable to look for immigrants who were familiar with homesteading on a treeless prairie, but preferably not American. William Hespeler, a native of Baden who had migrated to Canada in 1850, became an official immigration agent in Alsace-Lorrain, and travelled to the Mennonite colonies in the southern Ukraine. In August 1872, Hespeler contacted the Mennonites and discussed the possibilities of homesteading in the Canadian West.[14] The Russian authorities were concerned about Hespeler's activities and did not grant him a permit as emigration agent. However, he succeeded in arranging for a delegation of Mennonites to come to Canada and inspect for themselves. In 1873, there were three Mennonite delegations from Russia and Prussia; among the delegates were also two Hutterites.[15] The representatives of the Bergthal and Kleine Gemeinde, the former near Berdyansk, close to the

---

12 *A Memorandum on the Subject of Public Lands in the Province of Manitoba,* April 25, 1871, Canada Gazette, Vol. IV, January – June, 1871.
13 *An Act Respecting the Public Lands of the Dominion,* Statutes of Canada, 1872, Chapter 23 (Ottawa: 1872).
14 Frank H. Epp, *Mennonites in Canada, 1786–1920* (Toronto: 1974), p. 187.
15 *Ibid.,* p. 189.

Sea of Azov, and the latter on the Dnieper River, close to Borozenko, seemed to favour Canada after a visit to Manitoba. On July 23, 1873, the delegation received the statements by the Canadian government, which outlined the conditions of settlement, freedom from military service and the right to educate their children. The latter condition was not within the federal jurisdiction and was withdrawn without the Mennonites being advised of the change.[16] The first seventy families came from Borozenko in June 1874 to Manitoba, followed by one thousand families from Bergthal and Chortiza. Altogether, about 6,931 persons arrived between 1874—1880.[17] The settlement took place in two regions, the East Reserve, east of Niverville and west of Steinbach, and the West Reserve, east of Morden and west of Rosenfeld with the United States boundary as the southern delineation.

Within twenty-five years of their coming, most Mennonites prospered beyond their greatest dreams. However, their original plan, to live in a new land in their own communities with a minimum of outside interference, had not been realized. There were several groups, the Old Order Mennonites, who made the minimum adjustment to the new society; others were influenced by the various branches of the American Mennonite churches, others became members of the evangelistic churches or became secularized to a much greater degree than originally envisioned.

The Mennonites, especially in the West Reserve, proved that Prairie land was fertile and could sustain permanent agricultural settlements in areas which had hitherto been considered to be frozen wastelands. They paved the ways for other settlers who came in groups before World War I. The Mennonites also proved exemplary in the payments of their debts. By 1892, they had paid back to the Canadian government the transportation money loaned to them, except for a rebate of $24,000 in consideration of the poorer migrants.[18]

Within the first twenty-five years, the reserve system which allowed block settlement was changed into the township system; the West Reserve was divided into two municipalities and the East Reserve coincided with the Township of Hanover. At first, the two governmental systems existed side by side, but in 1898, the reserves were abolished and the township system prevailed.

In the 1890s, a new wave of Mennonites came from Europe and settled in the Rosthern Area, located on the South Saskatchewan River between Saskatoon and Prince Albert. Old Colony Mennonites, from the West Reserve, obtained four townships in the Hague Osler Area between Saskatoon and Rosthern. Mennonite groups from Ontario and the United States settled in Alberta between 1893 (Carstairs) and 1915 (Duchess).[19] Another reserve of Old Colony settlers was established in 1904 near Swift Current along the CPR line.[20]

Initially, the Mennonites were welcomed as pioneer settlers. Their social organi-

---

16 *Ibid.*, p. 192—193.
17 *Ibid.*, p. 200.
18 *Ibid.*, p. 226.
19 *Ibid.*, p. 310, Table 2.
20 *Ibid.*, p. 317, Table 3.

zation did not yet clash with the civil government. However, there were seeds of discontent which became significant areas of disagreement later, the main problems being participation in secular government, the school question and the exemption from military services.

While Mennonites were not the only German-speaking pioneer settlers, they formed in the early days the largest single block. Without their experience, the migration policies and patterns would have taken different directions.

After 1870, Winnipeg became the major transportation centre for the West and the colonization of the Prairie Provinces. At first, river boats provided the connection with the American railroad system, but after 1878 a railroad connected Winnipeg with St. Paul, Minnesota, and in 1882 the Canadian Pacific Railroad traversed the Canadian shield for the first time.

Winnipeg became of great significance to the German settlers. Among the early inhabitants was Christian Schultz, a native of Amherstburg, Ontario, and a leading opponent to Louis Riel. The ancestors of Christian Schultz came from Schleswig-Holstein. After the Riel Rebellion, Sir Christian became prominent in the affairs of Manitoba and served as Lieutenant Governor of Manitoba from 1888–1895. As early as 1871, a German Society was founded by J. Sanderman, G. Rath and E. Kuhlton.[21] For the next ten years, the number of Germans in Winnipeg remained small; in 1881, there were fewer than two hundred. With the coming of the railroad, the situation changed dramatically. In 1891, about ten percent of Winnipeg's population was German-speaking. The most prominent German-speaking resident was Wilhelm Hespeler, whom on January 16, 1882, the Emperor Wilhelm I appointed German Consul in Winnipeg.[22] Since that time, Winnipeg had a German consular representative, first as honorary consul, later as a career representative, and since April 1976 as an honorary consul. Later, Hespeler became active in the political life of the province. In 1899, he was elected to the Manitoba Legislature and in 1900 and 1904 became the Speaker of the House. This was the first time that a naturalized European had obtained this position.

In 1901, Winnipeg had a population of 42,340, of which 2,283 were Germans, 1,147 Austro-Hungarians and 35 Swiss. This increased in 1911 to about 8,000 Germans, 6,620 Austro-Hungarians and 112 Swiss.[23] Over 10,000 German-speaking residents consisted as a sizable minority among the 128,157 inhabitants. In contrast to the farmers in the rural hinterland, the urban residents were primarily skilled craftsmen. German-speaking settlers formed the lower middle class, but except for Hespeler and Schultz, they were not part of the economic and social elite which

---

21 Gotthard L. Maron, *Facts About the Germans in Canada* (Winnipeg: 1920), p. 33.
   However, the Deutsche Vereinigung von Winnipeg, 1892, 121 Charles Street, claims to be the oldest German Association in Western Canada.
22 Werner Entz, "Wilhelm Hespeler, Britischer Parlamentarier aus Baden," *Mitteilungen* (Stuttgart: 1957), 7 Jahrgang, Nummer 3, p. 171–173.
23 It should be noted that among the Austro-Hungarians, there were substantial numbers of Poles and Ukrainians.

was primarily composed of descendants of the early Scottish settlers and migrants from Ontario.

With the extension of the railroads westward, other German settlements were established in Manitoba. Most of the German-speaking settlers in the Prairies did not come from regions within the German Empire. They were primarily from Austria-Hungary, the Balkan Countries and the Russian Empire. *Volksdeutsche* (ethnic Germans) exceeded *Reichsdeutsche* (German Nationals) numerically, especially in the rural areas.[24] The internal tensions between the two groups remained noticeable up to the present time.

The reserve system of group settlement was one of the important patterns in the Canadian West. The railroad companies, sometimes the government, arranged with leaders of a particular group the settlement of entire townships. The promoters, in turn, assembled the potential migrants, shepherded them, with the assistance of the railroad companies, to Canada and via immigrant trains to the West. As a rule, the groups were organized along denominational or ethnic lines, or both. Even today, these patterns can still be recognized in the communities of the Canadian West. By 1890, German-speaking Lutherans had established themselves close to the Mennonites in Steinbach, Rosefield, Emerson, Gretna and Morden. In Northern Manitoba, they settled at Grahamdale, Moosehorn, Camper and near Glenella. East of Winnipeg, there were reserves at Beausejour, Whitemouth and Brokenhead. Other communities were Friedensfeld, Staubach and Waldersee. German Catholics arrived later but were few in comparison to the other denominations.

The pre-World War I migration of Germans to Manitoba amounted to about 35,000 persons or 7.5 percent of the total population. They were exceeded by Ukrainians, who formed the second largest group after those of Anglo-Saxon origin. This rank order lasted: in 1971, Ukrainians were 16 percent of the population and Germans 12 percent.

Before World War I, immigrants made little adjustment to life in Manitoba. Most German-speaking settlers had their own schools and their own social institutions and were only marginally affected by the social life in the larger community. As pioneer settlers, they were concerned about survival, rather than integration.

The Manitoba School crisis affected not only English-French relations in Canada, but also the German-speaking communities of Manitoba, especially the Mennonites.[25] Many Old Colony Mennonites considered the legislation a breach of faith by the Federal Government. It was of little concern that the Federal Government had promised concessions which were ultra vires because they were in the domain of the provinces. Old Colony Mennonites considered this action as the beginning of the erosion of the covenant, and World War I confirmed their suspicion. Other

---

24 The Imperial German Government issued regulations discouraging emigration; although they were rescinded in 1898, they specifically excluded Manitoba and the Northwest Territories of Canada.
Norman MacDonald, *Canada's Immigration Policy: 1840–1903* (Toronto: 1957), p. 219.
25 Frank H. Epp, *ibid.*, p. 340.

groups tried to effect compromises, primarily in the fusion of religious instruction and instruction in the mother tongue, stressing the unity between religion and ethnicity.

With the extension of the railroads into the Western Prairies and the foothills of the Rocky Mountains, settlers followed the railroads and began homesteading. Prior to this time, Saskatchewan was part of Rupert's Land, under the domination of the Hudson's Bay Company. Indian tribes followed the trail of the buffalo according to season. An occasional European traveller and trader followed the rivers and the trails. One of these travellers was Maximilian, Prince of Wied, a small principality along the Rhine, who spent a considerable time in the region. His observations about the geography and the animal world, as well as about the native tribes with whom he came into contact, were among the earliest reports on the Canadian West written in the German language. He travelled through Western North America between 1832–1834. From his base on the Missouri River, he followed the migratory cycle of the natives, observed their social structure and customs and described the fauna and flora of the land.[26] His excursions were well described and were translated into several languages. Other travellers, either before or after Prince Wied, had German members in their expeditions, among these Governor Simpson of the Hudson's Bay Company. These travels, however, did not lead to permanent European settlements.[27] Only the railroads made those possible. With the building of the transcontinental railroad, Southern Saskatchewan became available for settlement. Other lines opened up the northern part of the province, first by a combination of water and rail transportation, and later by connecting railroad networks.

Saskatchewan was one of the first regions in Canada where neither British nor French settlers formed a majority. Although British settlers were the largest single group, those of other origins than British and French together formed the majority of the population. The non-British residents lived in the countryside, whereas settlers of British background settled in the towns and cities.

Saskatchewan is the province with the largest percentage of persons of German origin. Over twenty-five percent of the population is of German background. Most of these settlers who were *Volksdeutsche,* had come before World War I. Former citizens of the German Empire were in the beginning discouraged from moving into the Prairies, which in the latter part of the nineteenth century were considered unfit for European settlement.

The first German migrants to Saskatchewan came from the United States. They were followed by German-speaking Austro-Hungarians and settlers from Russia.[28] These early pioneers came after 1880. In 1885, the Edenwald settlement, the first German reserve, was founded twenty-five miles northeast of Regina.[29]

26 Maximilian, Prinz zu Wied, *Reise durch Nord America* (Coblenz: 1839/41).
27 Governor Simpson speaks of permanent settlers in the Forts of the Hudson's Bay Company. Sir George Simpson, *Overland Journey Round the Ward,* 1841–42 (Philadelphia: 1847).
28 Carl Peterson (ed), *Handwoerterbuch des Grenz- und Auslandsdeutschtums* (Breslau: 1938–40), Vol. 3, p. 270–71.
29 Herbert Wilhelm Debor, *The Cultural Contributions of the German Ethnic Group to*

Most German settlements followed denominational lines, like those established a few years earlier in Manitoba. German Lutherans and other Protestants settled between 1885 and 1890 in Nendorf, Markineh, Davin, Southey, Kronan, Brightholm, Leask, Esk, Lanigan, Melville, Yorkton, Leader, Edenwald, Ebenezer, Rhein, Langenau, Gorlik, Stornoway and Hartfield. The first known Catholic colony was Josephstal (1886), followed by Katharinental (1891) and Odessa,[30] Kendal, Mariahilf, Landsheet, and Maryland before 1900. A very large colony, St. Peter's, was settled in 1902 by German Roman Catholics under the leadership of Benedictine Monks from Collegeville, Minnesota. It consisted of thirty-six townships (later increased to fifty), in Northern Saskatchewan, around Humboldt and Muenster.[31] In 1905, a second German Catholic group settlement, St. Joseph's Colony,[32] was formed with seventy-seven townships in the Tramping Lake area. Shortly before, in 1904, smaller colonies were founded in Landau, Bergfeld, Holdfast, Spring Valley, Quinton, Raymore, and Kronberg, close to Leader, next to the Protestant settlement which was formerly called Prussia and Bellimun. Catholics moved in between 1910–1912.

Mennonites came to Saskatchewan in 1891, when they established the Rosthern settlement.[33] There were twenty-six settlements before 1920, ranging from Aberdeen to Woodrow.[34]

The growth in the number of German settlers in Saskatchewan was dramatic. In 1901, there were fewer than 5,000, but in 1911, German-speaking residents numbered over 100,000. The majority still came from outside the German borders and from the United States. Before World War I, Saskatchewan which became a province only in 1905, was in the pioneer stage. Three centres became important for the German-speaking population: Saskatoon for the German Lutherans, Rosthern for Mennonites and St. Peter for German Roman Catholics.

The Lutherans were mainly members of the Missouri Synod, a group with a long tradition of German language maintenance. In 1913, they established a seminary for the education of the clergy, which was later affiliated with the University of Saskatchewan. Because of the close relationship between the Lutheran Church and the government in the countries of origin, the development of a unique Canadian identity became a difficult process which had not yet been completed. While Lutheran settlements gained a reputation for exemplary economically development and a high degree of social cohesion, their cultural development was minimal. One possible reason might have been the dependence upon American church structures rather than upon an independent religious organization.

Canada, Report to the Royal Commission on Bilingualism and Biculturalism (Ottawa: 1966), p. 17 ff.
30 *Sessional Papers,* 1887, No. 12, p. 75.
31 Very Rev. Peter Windschiegle, OSB, *Fifty Golden Years* (Muenster: 1953).
32 C. A. Dawson, "The German Catholics," in *Group Settlement,* Part IV (Toronto: 1936), p. 275–352.
33 Frank H. Epp, *op. cit.,* p. 311.
34 Frank H. Epp, *ibid.,* p. 317, Table 3.

German Baptists who had settled in Russia during the nineteenth century left the country because of the Russification policies at the latter part of the century. In 1887, they founded Ebenezer, a settlement which was expanded in 1914 with the addition of Rhein and Stornoway. Other Protestant settlements were Lemberg (1890), Neudorf (1896), Hill Farm (1900), Lipton (1907), Gull Lake (1907), and the Morse Area (1909–1912).

Rosthern became the centre of Mennonite life. Medical services were soon available and educational facilities were established. A secondary school was formed. The graduates of this school became primarily teachers and these in turn formed the nucleus of leaders of the German-speaking community.

The position of German-language instruction was ambiguous. In the early days of settlement, the schools were under religious auspices. There were no obstacles to education in the mother tongue. When a system of public education was established, schools came under the supervision of the territorial government. The School Act of 1901 provided in clause 136[35] that the School Board in any district – subject to the regulations of the Department of Education – could employ one or more competent persons to give instructions in a language other than English to all pupils whose parents or guardians signified a willingness for their children to receive instruction. German-language schools availed themselves of this opportunity. When Saskatchewan became a province, pressures were initiated to increase the English content of instruction. After 1910 there were pressures for the abolition of third-language instruction; these pressures intensified during World War I, and culminated in the complete ban on German in 1918.[36]

As already mentioned, German Catholics had two major settlement areas, St. Peter's and St. Joseph's colonies. St. Peter's colony was traversed by several railroad lines; from east to west by the CNR mainline from Winnipeg to Edmonton, built in 1904, from south to north by the CPR from Humboldt to Melfort (1921) and since 1930 by the CNR from Young to Prince Albert. The colony was situated on fertile, gentle rolling parkland and produced excellent wheat, even during the drought of the 1930s. The founding of this colony was due to the lack of available land in the United States and to the tradition of the Benedictine Monks who had served in similar roles in Germany throughout the Middle Ages. Reverend Bruno Doerfler O. S. B., and three men from the newly formed German Land Company led by Gerhard Ens of Rosthern, selected the Hodoo Plains as the site of the colony. Land was purchased from the North Saskatchewan Land Company, about 108,000 acres at $4.50 per acre with a down payment of 50¢. Six hundred families came in the first year, primarily from the American Mid-West. Many of these were second-generation Americans, whose parents had arrived from Germany between 1860 and 1880. They brought their cattle, machines and household effects along. First came the males to homestead; their families followed a year later. This nucleus was joined

---

35 An Ordinance Respecting Schools, Ordinances of the Northwest Territories, Chapter 29, 1901, clause 136. Saskatchewan School Act 1901, clause 136 (Regina: 1903).
36 Norman Ward and Duff Spafford, *Politics in Saskatchewan* (Toronto: 1968), p. 139.

by Germans from Southern Russia and from Westphalia. Most were deeply committed Roman Catholics who organized themselves into a complete institutional network. Churches, schools and parishes were established at Leofeld, Muenster, Anaheim and Dead Moose Lake. In 1911, Muenster became a fully autonomous Abbey with ecclesiastical jurisdiction, the only *Abbey Nullius** in English-speaking Canada. In the same year, a convent and hospital were established at Humboldt. Humboldt rather than Muenster flourished and also became the centre of the colony. Due to location problems, the Abbey experienced difficulties and in 1970 had to give up the college which was established in 1926, and the school. At present, Muenster is a shadow of its former self, and the dream of establishing a German Catholic focal centre and giving German culture in the Prairies a home has slowly vanished. While prospering economically, the colony had lost its identity. One of the reasons for the lack of success might have been that the struggle between the Irish-dominated English-speaking Roman Catholic clergy and the French-Canadian clergy left little room for other groups to maintain their identity.

St. Joseph's, the second German Catholic colony, was geographically larger than St. Peter's colony but did not reach the significance of the latter. In August 1904, about one thousand families settled in the Quill Plains, in Townships 37—39, Ranges 18—25.[37] Most families came from the United States and from Russia. The spiritual leadership was provided by the Oblate Fathers and Bishop Pascal of Prince Albert. In 1911, about 5,300 Germans lived in the colony. Due to severe weather conditions and economic problems, the colony did not prosper. Few families retained their German heritage, the majority acculturating rapidly.[38]

Other colonies were established in the semi-arid areas in the south west of the province, mostly by Germans from Russia. However, these settlements slowly disappeared with changes in agricultural methods from subsistence farming to large-scale commercial enterprises.

By World War I, most of the colonies were in existence. The majority of the farmers were subsistence farmers engaged in mixed farming and animal husbandry. The migration policies of the pre-war period were designed to attract foreign immigrants to the land and British and Canadians into the towns and cities. Since the economic, political and cultural activities were controlled by the urban elites, "third group" Canadians had little impact upon public life. Some who came from the United States wanted to retain their American citizenship. Many members of religious minorities participated in public life only through intermediaries. Originally, the division of the population in Saskatchewan was English, French and foreign. With the decrease of the French impact, which became evident when Irish bishops took over the Sees hitherto occupied by French-Canadian bishops, the dualism was between British and foreigners. They were separated by a deep rift

---

37 F. Lange, *Sessional Papers*, 1906, No. 25, 11, p. 114.
38 P. Schweers, *Maria Immaculata* (Marburg: 1907—08), p. 312—15, 344—49, 380—85.

* an independent ecclesiastical organization which is not under the jurisdiction of the local bishop.

indicated by socio-economic standing and personal lifestyles. There was little accommodation except on an ad-hoc political alliance basis. Saskatchewan had patterns of religious and ethnic segregation, which decisively influenced opportunities as well as limiting mobility.

Alberta, one of the youngest settlement areas in Canada, also had a large influx of German-speaking settlers. John Steinbruck, the first German travelling through Alberta, had joined the Mackenzie expedition.[39] They left Fort Chipewyan on Wednesday, June 3, 1789 and followed the river system leading into the river which later became the Mackenzie River. They followed the Peace River, the Slave River and the Great Slave River.

Throughout the nineteenth century, the land was traversed and the foothills explored in search of a pass through the Rocky Mountains and ultimately to the West Coast. Permanent settlements were not established by these travellers. The International Boundary Commission was the first group which worked in the West, measuring the 49th parallel and establishing reference points. The Northwest Mounted Police moved simultaneously westward in 1873–74 but would not have succeeded without the help of the British-American mixed commission. Shortly thereafter, the Canadian Pacific Railroad reached Alberta. With the advent of the railroad, settlement began on a large scale. Ten miles from the railroad lines was considered to be the limit of permanent settlement. In 1882, the first German settlers homesteaded in Pincher Creek,[40] thirty miles west of Fort McLeod, the garrison of the North-West Mounted Police. These early arrivals were followed by 630 migrants in 1889 who came to the vicinity of Medicine Hat and the south Saskatchewan River at Dunmore, Josephsburg and Seven Persons.[41]

As in Saskatchewan, the settlers in Alberta were divided along denominational lines. The first arrivals were Lutherans from Russia and the United States.[42] The newcomers were ill prepared for farming in the semi-arid region of Southern Alberta and lacked the skill which Charles O. Card and his fellow Mormons possessed and practised a decade later. Some of the colonists re-settled in Northern Alberta after 1889, the Lutherans around Hoffnungsau and Rosenthal, later called Stoney Plain,[43] and members of the Reformed Church to Josephsburg in the Fort Saskatchewan area.[44]

With the opening of the Calgary and Edmonton Railway in 1892, new lands became available. Besides establishing colonies in Josephsburg, there were homesteads in Duffield, Beaver Hill (1892), Rabbit Hills (1892), Spruce Grove and Glory Hills (1892), Leduc, Golden Spike, Egg Lake (1894), Beaver Lake (1894), Victoria

---

39 John Blue, *Alberta, Past and Present,* Vol. 1 (Chicago: 1924), p. 26.
40 Herbert Wilhelm Debor, *ibid.,* p. 18.
41 Howard Palmer, *Land of the Second Chance, A History of Ethnic Groups in Southern Alberta* (Lethbridge: 1972), p. 183 ff.
42 Howard Palmer, *op. cit.,* p. 183.
43 James B. Hedges, *Building the Canadian West* (New York: 1939), p. 92.
44 James G. MacGregor, *A History of Alberta* (Edmonton: 1972), p. 166.

(1894), Wetaskiwin and Barshaw.⁴⁵ German Baptists from Russia lived primarily at Rabbit Hills and Leduc.

Canadian immigration officers made serious efforts to recruit German settlers from the United States with quite successful results. For example, in 1893, after a campaign in Chicago it was reported that "some twenty heads of families left in June and took up homesteads on the lines of the Calgary and Edmonton Railroad. They took with them sums of money averaging about $500 per family. Some of these have since sent for their families and all have been self-supporting." It was also reported that "seven of the best farmers went west, to spy out the country, with the result that they entered for seventeen homesteads, and a whole settlement of about sixty families will move west in the early spring of 1894. These people are principally Pennsylvania Germans and their descendants, and are progressive and prosperous and are not excelled by any class of settlers."⁴⁶ The immigration of these settlers resulted in a block settlement of Germans in the Edmonton-Wetawiskiwin-Camrose triangle.

The Moravian Brethren established a colony for refugees from the Ukraine in Bruderheim in 1894. They were joined by other Protestants who homesteaded there as well as in the vicinity of Edmonton. After 1896, the newly opened areas between Edmonton, Fort Saskatchewan and Leduc were occupied by Germans. East and west of Red Deer were also new settlements; those east of Red Deer were in Stetller and Castor.⁴⁷

Most German settlers in Alberta were Protestants. Although many colonies were established, they lacked the cohesiveness of the Saskatchewan settlements. On the other hand, they placed a stronger emphasis on the unity between language and religious maintenance.

The settlers came in large numbers between 1901 and 1914. In 1901, there were 10,676 Germans in Alberta and Assiniboia West. In 1911, out of a total population of 393,320, there were 36,862 Germans. In addition to the German ethnic population, there were 26,424 Austro-Hungarians and 1,200 Swiss. There were Poles, Ukrainians, Roumanians, and Hungarians among the Austrians, but with the addition of the Russian Germans, it is estimated that about 50,000 were of German ethnic origin.

Not all Germans were farmers; although Sir Clifford Sifton wanted "none but agriculturalists, we do not recognize the labourers," nevertheless labourers did come.⁴⁸ Germans preferred Lethbridge, Medicine Hat, Edmonton and Calgary. Employment in the coal mines of Lethbridge and Medicine Hat was also one of the ways for a new immigrant to support himself in the winter.

The history of German-Canadians in British Columbia began in the Vancouver

---

45 Howard Palmer, *ibid.*, p. 183.
46 *Sessional Papers of 1894*, Vol. 13, 111, p. 150, 159.
47 Howard Palmer, *ibid.*, enumerates the founding of the various colonies.
48 Sir Clifford Sifton, "The Immigrants Canada Wants," in Howard Palmer, *Immigration and and Rise of M. lticulturalism* (Toronto: 1975), p. 34–38.

Island Colony about 1850. Dr. John Sebastian Helmcken,[49] the physician of the colony, was born in London, England, of Hanover parentage. Fluently bilingual, he played an important role in the growth and development of the Vancouver colony and the province of British Columbia. He owed much of his influence in the early days to his being the son-in-law of Governor Douglas. Later, he earned influence by his achievements. At first, he opposed Confederation with Canada, but later he helped negotiate the entry of British Columbia into the Dominion of Canada.

In the 1850s, the entire white population of Vancouver Island was 3,024, most of whom lived in and near Victoria.[50] In addition, about 5,000 natives were trading at the Hudson's Bay Post. This tranquil co-existence changed dramatically with the discovery of gold in the Fraser River Valley. Several thousand adventurers drifted into the colony, among these Germans who had missed their luck in the American gold rush. One immigrant, Frank Laumeister, was active in transportation, road building and mining. He tried to introduce camels as pack animals in the interior of the province with hilarious results.[51] The natives were terrified and the whites could not stand the smell of the animals. The experiment was soon abandoned.

In 1863, a second gold rush started with the discovery of the Bakerville Gold Mines in the Cariboo Mountains. Due to those gold rushes, the population of British Columbia increased considerably and by 1870, the total white population of the province was 10,586. About 4,000 lived around Victoria, 1,360 in New Westminster, 1,067 in the Yale district and 1,637 in the Cariboos. In 1881, the total population was slightly under 50,000. Of this total, 15,417 lived in New Westminster, at the mouth of the Fraser River, 7,550 in the Cariboos, 9,200 in the Yale Goldfields, 7,301 around Victoria and close to 10,000 in Northern Vancouver Island and West Coast communities. Among these persons, there were 160 Germans and Swiss in New Westminster, 94 in the Cariboos, 115 in Yale, 138 in Victoria and 138 in Northern Vancouver Island.

The population of British Columbia in 1891 grew to 98,173. Germans were concentrated in New Westminster and Victoria and to a lesser degree Northern Vancouver Island. By 1901, the population had almost doubled to 178,657. Most people lived in the Yale-Cariboo area followed by the Burrard District (City of Vancouver), Northern Vancouver Island, New Westminster and Victoria. About 1,100 Germans lived in the Burrard District, 3,000 in the Yale-Cariboo, 840 in New Westminster, about 750 in Victoria and 700 on Northern Vancouver Island. In 1911, the population was 392,480. Of these, 11,880 were Germans, 7,015 Austro-Hungarians and 796 Swiss. They lived in Vancouver, the Kootenays and the Yale-Cariboo District. The number of Germans in pre-World War I British Columbia was

---

49 British Columbia Historical Association, *Victoria, B. C., 1843–1943* (Victoria: 1943), p. 10.
50 *Censuses of Canada,* 1665–1871, Vol. IV (Ottawa: 1876), p. Lii.
51 Bruce Ramsay, *A History of the German Canadians in British Columbia* (Winnipeg: 1958), p. 8.

low, when compared with the Prairie Provinces, but higher than in the Atlantic Provinces.

The early adventurers and gold miners did not leave a permanent mark on British Columbia. That role was given to more stable residents who worked as craftsmen, businessmen and farmers and started to develop a viable economy. Numerous Germans were active as farmers in the vicinity of Victoria, the Fraser Valley and later, the Okanagan Valley. They established woodworking and lumbering facilities. Some brewmasters built the Victoria Brewery and others were well known as businessmen. In the 1860s, Germans in Victoria formed the Germania Sing Verein[52] which soon reached its peak of popularity and continued to last for many years, until World War I. Other entrepreneurs were active as cigar makers[53] and as operators of the British Columbia Express Company. The German settlement in Victoria continued to prosper until 1912, the year of the great financial debacle, when real estate prices plummeted from their former heights.

The largest city in the West started relatively late, beginning with a saw mill in 1862, the laying out of the town-site of Granville in 1870 and the petition for incorporation as the City of Vancouver in 1886. After the arrival of the Canadian Pacific Railroad in 1887, Vancouver became the most important shipping terminal and largest city in the province. German-born residents played an important part in the growth of the city. Early business men included the Oppenheimers and the Grauers.[54]

In 1892, German businessmen established a chapter of the Sons of Hermann Lodge, the first in Canada. This lodge was deeply involved in the social life of the community and organized a great many activities. A German-language newspaper, the *Westliche Kanadische Post* (West Canadian Post) was printed in 1906 and dealt with community information in the entire province. A second paper, the Vancouver German Press, was started in 1911 by Dr. Karl Weiss.

In the first decade of the century, Gustav Constantin Alvo von Alvensleben was one of the most colourful residents of the city. After resigning as an officer in the German army, he arrived in Vancouver in June, 1904. During the real estate boom of 1905, he became an active speculator. He was reputed to have invested about seven million dollars, money given to him by German investors from the Empire.[55] Soon becoming the centre of German activities, he organized the *Deutsche Klub* as an organization of the German business elite.

The Depression of 1912 curbed the boom in real estate, and World War I signalled the end for the time being. Von Alvensleben was absent at the beginning of the War, and never returned to Canada. His numerous companies collapsed or were confiscated as enemy property. Some of the leading political figures of that time availed themselves of the confiscated property at bargain rates, a process which was, to a lesser degree, repeated in World War II.

52 Bruce Ramsay, *ibid.*, p. 42–43.
53 Harry Gregson, *A History of Victoria, 1842–1970* (Victoria: 1970), p. 33.
54 Bruce Ramsay, *ibid.*, p. 47.
55 Alan Morley, *From Milltown to Metropolis* (Vancouver: 1961), p. 128.

In general, German migration to Canada occurred in several stages from the colonial period until World War I. At first, there were the settlements of disbanded soldiers and individual adventurers. Then came the United Empire Loyalists who began the settlement of Upper Canada and opened up new areas in the Maritimes. Soon, these were followed by the Pennsylvania Germans, who moved along the Trail of the Black Walnut into the Grand River Basin of Ontario. Several decades later came the colonists who tamed the forests of the Bruce Peninsula and Grey County and other wooded regions.

Ethnic Germans came to the Prairies and broke the ground for the wheat fields of the subsequent eras. Germans in British Columbia developed similar patterns. There were the colonists on Vancouver Island, the adventurers in the gold fields and later the farmers in the Fraser Deltas and the Okanagan Valley. There were the artisans and businessmen in the towns and cities. They were indeed one of the founding peoples of Canada, albeit an ignored people, caught in the greater French-English dualism. During all this time, they were brought here against their will as soldiers, welcomed as settlers and preferred because of their thrift, hard work and industry.

Chapter 4

THE IMPACT OF WORLD WAR I

World War I was the turning point in the history of German-Canadians and signified the end of the first phase of colonization. Until 1914, there were few problems of dual identity. The older generations of migrants had gradually adjusted to the new land and the new migrants were still in the process of securing an economic base. As immigrants, Germans from Germany were preferred migrants,[1] although the German Empire had some reservations about having its subjects settle in Western Canada. Germans from Austria-Hungary who had settled in the West, with their German-speaking friends from Russia, also experienced only minor difficulties. Germans from the United States were ardently welcomed and received whatever government help was available.[2] All this changed with the outbreak of the European War in August 1914.

At first, the attitude of the Canadian government towards immigrants who were not British subjects was conciliatory. Canada at that time had four categories of residents: 1) British subjects either born in the United Kingdom or its dependencies, 2) British subjects naturalized under the Imperial Naturalization Acts which conferred full citizenship privileges upon the grantee, not only in Canada, but in other dominions as well, 3) British subjects naturalized in Canada with citizenship rights limited to Canada and 4) resident aliens. The conciliatory attitudes were expressed in the Canada Gazette of August 15, 1914:

> In accordance with the Proclamation, restrictive measures will be taken only in cases where officers, soldiers or reservists of the German Empire or of the Austro-Hungarian Monarchy attempt to leave Canada or where subjects of such nationalities engage or attempt to engage in espionage or acts of a hostile nature or to give information to, or otherwise assist the King's enemies. Even where persons are arrested or detained on the grounds indicated, they may be released on signing an understanding to abstain from acts injurious to the Dominion or the Empire.[3]

In 1912, about forty families of German officers had settled in Hussar, Alberta. In 1914, a group of sixty reserve officers tried to return to Germany via New York. They were subsequently captured by the British navy and interned for the duration of the war.[4] In 1914, Bishop N. Budka first asked Ukrainians to join the homeland

---

1 James S. Woodsworth, *Strangers within our Gates or Coming Canadians* (Toronto: 1909), p. 100.
2 H. Troper, "American Immigration to Canada, 1869–1914" in Howard Palmer, *Immigration and the Rise of Multiculturalism* (Toronto: 1975), p. 41–42.
3 Proclamation of August 15, 1914, respecting immigrants of German or Austro-Hungarian Nationality, *Orders-in-Council, op. cit.* p. LXL, LXVI.
4 Howard Palmer, *Land of the Second Chance, op. cit.*, p. 187.

in the war against Serbia, but subsequently reversed his stand and instead stressed loyalty to Canada.[5]

The hostilities against German-Canadians slowly built up. In 1914–15, there was emphasis on the loyalty of nearly half a million citizens of Canada who were of German origin.[6] Nevertheless, private individuals and groups of people menaced the well-being of persons of German background or ancestry. German-born professors at the University of Toronto were threatened with dismissal. Sir Adam Beck was attacked because of his German parentage and H. J. Glaubitz of the London, Ontario, Public Utilities Commission was forced to resign.[7] The largest number of dismissals occurred against Austrians who bore the brunt of the persecution of Western Canada.

Anti-German sentiments were especially virulent in British Columbia. The province was in the midst of a severe recession, the population was predominantly male and consisted of recent arrivals who were easily agitated. Riots against immigrants, especially from Asia, had occurred before 1914. In the summer of 1914, *The Komagatu Maru*, a Japanese ship, attempted to land 374 East Indians who were British subjects. Due to riot conditions, these people were prevented from disembarking. At the time, it was rumoured that the ship had been chartered by German interest groups for the explicit purpose of sowing dissention.[8] Within a short time after the beginning of hostilities, an attempt was made to remove all enemy aliens from the Pacific coast to the interior. Quite a few persons were pressed to leave Vancouver for the United States, as authorized by the Order-in-Council of April 24, 1915.[9] Furthermore, immigration to British Columbia was prohibited from October 1, 1915 to March 31, 1916. As a consequence, about eight thousand enemy aliens left for the United States.

On June 12, 1914, Canada enacted a law respecting British Nationality, Naturalization and Aliens[10] which granted British subjects status worldwide, rather than only in Canada as the old naturalization law did. As a transitory measure, the older legislation remained in effect until January 1917, primarily so that homesteaders could qualify after three years' residence instead of the five under the British law.

In English-speaking Canada, judges refused to naturalize enemy aliens. Judge G. H. Thompson, a county court judge in British Columbia, refused to naturalize individuals on the grounds that "no enemy alien has the right to apply to the civil

---

5 *Canadian Annual Review*, 1914, p. 275–278.
6 Statement of Prime Minister Borden, quoted from Joseph Amedee Boudreau, *The Enemy Alien Problem in Canada, 1914–1921*, doctoral dissertation, University of California, Los Angeles, Modern History, 1965, p. 30–31.
7 Desmond Morton, *The Canadian General, Sir William Otter* (Toronto: 1974), p. 327.
8 Agnes Rothery, *The Ports of British Columbia* (New York: 1943), p. 327.
9 Order-in-Council authorizing the emigration of alien enemies at Vancouver to the United States, April 24, 1915, P. C. 858 (Ottawa: 1916), p. 610.
10 *An Act Respecting British Nationality, Naturalization and Aliens*, 12 June 1914, Cp. 3, reprinted in the Report of the Secretary of State for Canada for the Year ending March 31, 1915, p. 202.

courts during the war."[11] Judge Meredith also refused naturalization of enemy aliens in the Spring Assizes of Waterloo on February 16, 17, 1915.[12] On the other hand, Judge Archambault in Montreal permitted the naturalization in the Fall of 1914. In general, naturalization during the war was severely restricted. An Order-in-Council of September 13, 1917 authorized the naturalization of "alien enemies who have resided for many years in Canada, on its being shown that they are clearly in sympathy with the United Kingdom and its allies in the present war, and that they have not pro-German or other alien enemy affiliations or connections."[13] The effect of this Order-in-Council was minimal; the number of naturalized enemy aliens did not increase.

The War Times Election Act of 1917[14] dealt with two major issues, conscription and the disenfranchisement of those who claimed exemption from military service or were suspect in their loyalty to Canada or the cause of Britain. In French Canada, conscription was the major issue. English-Canadians even proposed, as did the Toronto *Mail and Empire*,[15] "that French-Canadian opponents of conscription and 'seditionmongers' be disenfranchised." The Act itself disenfranchised all Mennonites (exempted from military service by the Order-in-Council of August 13, 1873), all "Doukabors" (exempted from military service by Order-in-Council, December 6, 1898), every naturalized British subject who was born in an enemy country and naturalized subsequent to March 31, 1902, and those whose "mother tongue" was a language of an enemy country and who had been naturalized subsequent to March 31, 1902. Under the strict interpretation of the Act, even former Swiss citizens were disenfranchised. While Armenians were exempted from enemy registration in 1914,[16] they were refused naturalization in 1915[17] and disenfranchised in 1917. The Act applied to those whose mother tongue was German, Hungarian, Yiddish, Ukrainian, Czech, Slovak, Slovenian, Croatian, Bulgarian, Macedonian, Turkish, Albanian, Arabic and Greek.

It was ironic that the War Times Election Act came into force after the Imperial Election Act of 1914, which confirmed the same rights, privileges and obligations upon naturalized British subjects as natural born. The War Times Election Act initiated a period of differential treatment of Canadians which lasted until 1977.[18] Naturalized citizens remained under the threat of disenfranchisement and involuntary loss of citizenship. In May 1919, for example, the government passed a bill that provided for the deportation of aliens, British subjects born outside of Canada

---

11 Joseph A. Boudreau, *op. cit.*, p. 29.
12 Sessional Paper No. 29, *Report of the Secretary of State for Canada*, for the year ending March 31, 1915, p. 215–225.
13 P. C. 2552, September 13, 1917.
14 War Time Election Act, September 20, 1917, 7–8, Ch. 39.
15 Quoted from Joseph A. Boudreau, *op. cit.*, p. 109.
16 Joseph A. Boudreau, *ibid.*, p. 33.
17 In the decision by Judge Meredith, Waterloo, Ontario, 16, 17 February 1915, Sessional Paper No. 29, *op. cit.*
18 An Act Respecting Citizenship, C–20, 1976.

and naturalized citizens.[19] The Citizen Acts of 1927 and 1946 also allowed the involuntary loss of Canadian citizenship.[20]

In return for disenfranchisement, there was also freedom from conscription. While this aspect was pleasing to such groups as otherwise non-exempt Mennonites, it added ammunition to the accusations of slackerism raised against persons of Central European background.

The hostilities against German-Canadians increased considerably after the torpedoing of the steamer Lusitania. A number of Canadian passengers were killed, especially fourteen from Victoria, B. C. The role of the Lusitania in the British War effort had never been fully explained,[21] but the propaganda value of the Lusitania became great and had far-reaching consequences. In Victoria, hundreds of men raided the Kaiserhof, a German-owned hotel and club, and destroyed it.[22] Simon Leiser's Wholesale Grocery in Victoria was raided. Mob agitation was so intense that Sir Frank Barnard, the Lieutenant Governor, whose wife was a Canadian of German descent, was threatened.

In Alberta, Arthur Trainor, reacting to the sinking of the Lusitania, was charged with sedition because he said: "Ha, ha, ha, so they got her at last." First convicted, he was freed by the Alberta Supreme Court.[23] In contrast, two Albertans, Oscar Felton, an American-born Canadian, was convicted for saying, "I would like to see the Germans come across the channel and wipe England off the map," and George Cohen, a furniture dealer "stated to have been a German officer," was convicted for making disparaging remarks about Canadian soldiers at the Battle of Langemarck.[24] A German club was destroyed in Calgary[25] and a club in Montreal. The National Club of Toronto resolved to dismiss from membership anyone of German or Austrian extraction "not thoroughly loyal to Britain."[26]

Berlin, Ontario, became the symbolic focal point of anti-German sentiments. Local businessmen were afraid that goods labelled "made in Berlin" would not be acceptable. On September 1, 1916, the town was renamed Kitchener. In Toronto, the playing of German classical music was deplored and even signs for German beer brewed in Ontario were prohibited.[27] It was somewhat ironic that the Governor General, the Duke of Connaught, continued to call himself, among other titles, the Duke of Saxony and Prince of Saxe-Coburg and Gotha.

Acts of disloyalty among enemy aliens residing in Canada consisted of assisting

---

19 Desmond Morton, *op. cit.*, p. 335.
20 For example, see Rapport du Secretaire d'Etat du Canada pour l'Année Financiare close le 31 Mars 1947, La Commission de Revocation, p. 78, 79.
21 Colin Simpson, *The Lusitania,* (Boston: 1972).
22 Harry Gregson, *op. cit.*, p. 198–99.
23 Joseph A. Boudreau, *ibid.*, p. 44.
24 Joseph A. Boudreau, *ibid.*, p. 43.
25 W. B. Fraser, *Calgary,* (Calgary: 1967), p. 94.
26 Desmond Morton, *ibid.*, p. 341.
27 Werner A. Bausenhart, "The Ontario German Language Press and its Suppression by Order-in-Council in 1918," *Canadian Ethnic Studies,* (Calgary: 1972), Vol. IV, No. 1–2, p. 37.

enemy reservists to escape over the American border. In 1915, Paul Nazew was acquitted of treason for helping a reservist escape. In the same year, Emil Nerlich was first convicted but then had his conviction overturned.[28] Plans for sabotage in Canada were developed by German-Canadians, among these an attempt to dynamite a bridge leading into Canada from Vanceboro, Maine to St. Croix, New Brunswick.[29] None of the acts of sabotage came to fruition, although at some time it was assumed that the Canadian House of Parliament was ignited by German saboteurs on February 3, 1916.[30]

In the course of the war, 8,579 male prisoners were interned. In addition, 81 women and 156 children accompanied their husbands and fathers.[31] Of these, slightly over three thousand were enemy reservists. In addition, the British government had an internment station in Amherst, Nova Scotia. Most of the interned were not Germans but Austrian citizens, about six thousand of whom were released in 1916. About two thousand were Germans and there were continuous disagreements between the Registrar of Alien Enemies, Major General Sir W. D. Otter, and the German interns. The internment camp at Kapuskasing, Ontario, was the focal point of controversies. In 1915, the German government sent a *Note Verbale* via the American Ambassador in Berlin. A detailed Order-in-Council dealt with the objection,[32] which also stated that there are only about one hundred German civilians interned in Canada, a figure which was not consistent with Sir William Otter's subsequent report.

Most internments were on the basis of local complaints primarily depending on gossip rather than facts. The most ardent German nationalists had escaped across the border to the United States in hope of reaching Germany. As a consequence, Canada did not have a nucleus of potential internal enemies.

Many internees were collected at random or when they became unemployed, a device used frequently in British Columbia.[33] Internees were also the prey of unscrupulous patriots. At Toronto, several thousand dollars worth of cash and valuables confiscated from prisoners vanished. A militia colonel in Sault Ste. Marie used the threat of internment to extort a bank book and then a mortgage from a young Austrian, desperate because his wife was expecting a baby. As a final insult, the man was ordered to shave his mustache to make him look less like a German and threatened with death if he made trouble.[34]

The internment camps, especially in the Rocky Mountains, were poorly equipped and the inmates subjected to indignities and abuse.[35] Morrissey and Vernon

---

28 Joseph A. Boudreau, *ibid.*, p. 42, 43.
29 Joseph A. Boudreau, *ibid.*, p. 14.
30 Desmond Morton, *ibid.*, p. 341.
31 Desmond Morton, *ibid.*, p. 362.
32 Order-in-Council respecting the objection of the German Government to the compulsory labour of interned Germans, P. C. 2039, August 28, 1915, War Document, p. 717–721.
33 Desmond Morton, *op. cit.*, p. 338.
34 Desmond Morton, *ibid.*, p. 335.
35 Desmond Morton, *ibid.*, p. 339.

were the focal points of ill-treatment. At Vernon, the commandant finally fled to the United States rather than face an investigation.[36]

Sir William Otter attempted to provide for an orderly system; however, political interferences and popular pressures, which at one time demanded the deportation of 85,000 enemy aliens, countervailed. In the course of internments, over one hundred prisoners died: a few were shot by guards and the others succumbed to illnesses aggravated by the poor conditions and locations of the camps. Between 1919 and February 1920, over 1,800 internees were repatriated to Germany via the Netherlands.[37]

The most sweeping powers under the War Measures Act were given to country or district court judges on February 14, 1919. They could intern upon summary complaint by a municipal authority or by "any person whose complaint may in the opinion of the judge be accepted as reasonable evidencing a feeling of public apprehension entertained in the community."[38] As a postwar measure, these powers were ideally designed for witch-hunting purposes. Prior to this time, on January 26, 1919, a crowd of Winnipeg ex-soldiers wrecked with impunity, among other places, a brewery owned by a naturalized German.[39] The above powers were used against aliens involved in some way in the Winnipeg General Strike in 1919 when close to one hundred aliens were deported from Winnipeg to Europe.[40]

Beside curtailment of individual freedom, internment and public hostilities, the German-speaking Canadians experienced limitations in the use of their language by the press and in education. Under the War Time Measures Act and Order-in-Council No. 94 of November 6, 1914, newspapers prejudicial to the war efforts were prohibited from importation and from the use of the Canadian mails. This immediately affected newspapers from Europe. In the course of time, German language newspapers printed in the United States were prohibited entry. An Order-in-Council of August 14, 1916 summarized the prohibited newspapers. They were 15 German language, 4 Irish, 1 Syrian, 1 Yiddish, 2 Hungarian, 1 Croatian and 1 Ukrainian newspapers.[41] German-language newspapers were heavily censored but initially not prohibited. The Alberta Herold[42] was the first to suffer. After several attempts by the Conservative opposition in the provincial legislature to suppress the paper and to prosecute the editors for treason and sedition, the paper ceased publication voluntarily in July 1915. Most papers continued publication, but their contents were carefully censored. Between 1915 and 1918, these papers were frequently

---

36 Desmond Morton, *ibid.*, p. 344.
37 Desmond Morton, *ibid.*, p. 362.
38 Order-in-Council of February 14, 1919, P. C. 332.
39 Desmond Morton, *ibid.*, p. 354.
40 In 1919, about 98 Europeans were deported from Winnipeg, Manitoba. *Sessional Papers* No. 18, 1920, 1921.
41 *Post Office Notice,* (Ottawa: 1916), August 14, 1916, War Documents, No. 961, p. 2169–71.
42 James C. McGregor, *A History of Alberta* (Edmonton: 1972), p. 231.

attacked by English-speaking newspapers; contents were deliberately misinterpreted to show pro-Central Power biases. Finally, in September 1918, all publications in the languages of any country or people at war with Great Britain were prohibited.[43] This action spelled the end of the first-generation immigrant press.

Conditions in Western Canada and Ontario differed somewhat as described by two diverging articles on the matter.[44] Germans in Saskatchewan had founded in March 1914, the *Deutsch-Kanadischer Provinzialverband von Saskatchewan* under the leadership of Conrad Eymann.[45] The association wanted to protect German-Canadian interests and had a meeting in September, 1914. Their resolution dealt with "stirring up hatred and race feelings" and asked for a greater recognition of the German contributions in the province. It was a most inopportune time to have such an organization. Although they once succeeded in presenting their views before Prime Minister Borden in 1915, their activities were curtailed in 1916 and came to an end.

World War I was a time of fierce identification with everything British and the elevation of English as the only national language. In the nineteenth century, sentiments of this kind were expressed by Lord Durham in his report to Queen Victoria.[46] The problem flared up again in the Manitoba School Crisis and became contentious in Ontario, Saskatchewan and Alberta. In Ontario, the pressures were primarily directed against French-language schools. A strange alliance between Bishop Fallon of London, Ontario, and Protestant leaders resulted in the abolition of bilingual schools. German language schools in Ontario were private, church-affiliated institutions with little but local significance and were easily suppressed. In February 1916, the Anti-German League in Toronto dedicated itself to eliminating German products, immigrants and influences from Canada. The first goal was driving naturalized Canadians of German background out of the public service. German had virtually disappeared as a subject of study from schools and universities. In Manitoba, unilingual English instruction was made mandatory on August 21, 1916.[47] Among those affected were the Old Colony Mennonites who considered this Act a breach of previous solemn commitments. In Alberta, unilingual instruction was proclaimed on March 30, 1915 and in Saskatchewan on December 18, 1918.

The behaviour against enemy aliens in World War I can be best explained in terms of scape-goating. War-time propaganda was developed to a high degree and used for political purposes, yet the actual enemy was several thousand miles away. Other outlets for aggression had to be found and immigrants became the victims by

---

43 Werner Bausenhart, *op. cit.*, p. 35.
44 The Suppression of German Language Press in September 1918, in Werner Bausenhart, *op. cit.*
45 Joseph A. Boudreau, *op. cit.*, p. 39.
46 Lord Durham's Report on the *Affairs of British North America* (Oxford: 1912), Vol. 11, p. 70-72.
47 Werner Bausenhart, *ibid*, p. 43.

proxy. Again, the poor and helpless, especially the Austrians, were most severely affected. Having recently migrated, they depended upon their labours to sustain themselves. Germans from Germany were usually more educated and skillful in dealing with the conditions at hand. General Otter considered them as more dangerous because of their social standing.[48] The German Government, through their protective powers, who looked after the interests of internees, first the United States, later Switzerland, could offer some counterpressures to the greatest excesses which occurred in the internment camps.

The end of the war did not spell an end to the restrictions and anti-alien propaganda. For some time, the re-integration of former soldiers into civilian life created further hostilities against those who did not serve in the war or were thought to have profiteered.

German-Canadians remained suspect. Publications in German were only resumed in 1920. Migration from Europe was still prohibited, and migration from the United States suspect. Mennonites suffered greatly in the post-war period; for some time, their immigration was also prohibited by an Order-in-Council.[49]

World War I signalled the end of large-scale migration from Europe. Until the war, financial considerations were the prime movers of people. In the post-war period there were entirely different patterns of migration, often in reaction to the closing of the American borders. For those prohibited from entering the United States, Canada became the "Land of Second Chance."

---

48 Desmond Morton, *ibid.*, p. 333.
49 Frank H. Epp, *op. cit.*, p. 405 ff.

Chapter 5

POST WORLD WAR I PERIOD

The post-war period signalled the end of large-scale agricultural migration to North America. The United States, whose frontier was closed a generation earlier, curtailed mass migration during the war and at the end of hostilities moved to a quota system of immigration, based on national origin and country of birth. Persons born in Germany had a quota of 25,814 immigrants per year.[1] All other countries, with the exception of Great Britain (65,361 persons) had significantly lower quotas although the statutory minimum was one hundred. Most countries exhausted their quotas rapidly; they had more people wishing to emigrate than allotments. Between 1920 and 1968, Canadians were outside the quota system; migration of Canadian-born persons to the United States was relatively easy. Between 1920 and 1968, over one million Canadians moved to the United States. Since then, migration has been sharply curtailed. On the contrary, the numbers of returning Canadians exceeds the out-migrants.

Canada was one of the principal beneficiaries of the changes in American immigration policies. People who dreamt about moving to America selected Canada instead. This country did not introduce, except in a limited way, a formal quota system. Admissions were geared to attitudes and economic conditions, orders-in-council, and regulations directed the flow of immigrants.

After a period of re-integration of the veterans, it was the desire of the Canadian government to attract primarily farmers to this country, who would work on the land and settle. Native Canadians were increasingly reluctant to live on the farms. Before 1920 and 1930, rural areas grew only slowly, the surplus population moving into the cities and to the United States. Were it not for immigration, the exodus from the farms would have been accelerated. The post-war period was also one of rapid industrial growth. Most of the industrial workers at that time were native Canadians; the employment of immigrants was primarily in agricultural and service occupations. Canadian unions at that time were craft unions which rigidly controlled admission to their occupations. It was difficult for immigrants to qualify.

The migration of persons of German background started slowly. Between 1919 and 1922, a few settlers of German origin came to Canada from the United States. Among these were the Hutterites who had received an Order-in-Council in 1899, granting exemption from military service. Afterwards, however, they settled in the United States and were severely persecuted during World War I.[2] This persecution

---

1 Rufus D. Smith, "Immigration and Government" in Francis J. Brown and Joseph S. Roucek, *One America* (New York: 1947), p. 515–523.
2 Frank H. Epp, *op. cit.*, p. 397.

in turn motivated the Hutterites to go to Canada again and colonies were established in Manitoba and Alberta.

Migration of Mennonites and persons of German background was again permitted in 1923. In that year, 1,258 Germans, 1,368 Austrians, and 235 Swiss came to Canada. In 1924, over 3,000 migrants arrived in this country who claimed German background. From 1925 to 1930, immigration was accelerated. While in 1925 German-speaking migrants were still under 7,000, from 1926 to 1930 immigration was over 10,600 a year, reaching a peak of 14,500 in 1928. Most immigrants did not come from the German Republic but from the former Austro-Hungarian Empire, Poland and Russia.

Canada after World War I differentiated between preferred and non-preferred immigrants. The former were citizens of the Old Commonwealth, France, Belgium, Holland, Switzerland, Sweden, Norway, Denmark and the United States. After 1927, German citizens were also placed in the preferred category. These immigrants were admitted if they had sufficient means not to become a public burden, or proof of employment. Citizens of all other countries were only to be admitted if they were farmers, farm workers or their immediate relatives. Women were admissible if they were willing to work as household help.

During the post-war period, the Canadian Pacific Railroad and the Canadian National Railway[3] were entrusted with bringing immigrants to Canada, primarily to the West. The railroads provided transportation and accommodation to prospective settlers, sold them land and later moved the agricultural products. The railways also worked with denominational groups in assisting migrants in their settlements. The German Roman Catholics and Lutherans had committees in Winnipeg, Manitoba, and the Mennonites in Rosthern, Saskatchewan.[4]

In most cases, the checkerboard settlement practices of ethnically and religious homogenous townships continued throughout the 1920s. One justification for this pattern was the concept of the Canadian mosaic. Loosely used at first, the concept became idealized by John Murray Gibbon.[5] According to it, the ethnic groups coming to Canada were encouraged to settle as blocks, maintain their own cultural identity, but somehow integrate and interact with members of other groups to form a harmonious society. The churches, especially the Roman Catholic Church, supported this concept enthusiastically because group settlements served as control mechanisms and provided for the maintenance of religious practices. The Roman Catholic Church not only used this approach towards immigrants, but also preferred it for internal migrants, such as French-Canadians settling in the West.

During the 1920s, the policies of the Canadian government were directed towards the immigrant farmer. Immigrants were expected either to homestead on newly opened land, such as the Peace River Region, or to take over the farms which

---

3 Carl Peterson, *Handwoerterbuch des Grenz- und Auslandsdeutschtums*, 3. Band (Breslau: 1938), p. 261.
4 Frank H. Epp, *Mennonite Exodus* (Altona: 1962), Part 111.
5 John Murray Gibbon, *Canadian Mosaic, The Making of a Northern Nation* (London: 1938).

were abandoned by the original settlers who moved to the cities or the United States in large numbers. Not all immigrants remained on the farms. In most cases, they worked as farmers for three to five years, but then followed the general exodus to the towns and cities. However, in contrast to native Canadians, they were seldom able to obtain admission to the United States. Some hoped that they would eventually be admitted and located themselves in the border regions, such as Essex County, Ontario, the Niagara Peninsula and the lower mainland of British Columbia.

After World War I, the Old Colony Mennonites decided that Canada had broken the Covenant of 1874 and the government could not be trusted. From 1919 onwards, they searched for other areas where they could live without governmental interference and pursue their own lifestyles. After numerous inquiries in Latin America, they were able to obtain a colony in the State of Chihuahua near the municipality of San Antonio, later Cuauhtemoc. Starting in 1923, about 6,000 members of the Reinland-Mennonite Church sold their land and moved to the new colony, which was located on the east slopes of the Sierra Madre.[6] At that time, the conditions in Mexico were favourable to group settlements. The Old Colony Mennonites were permitted to settle under the provisions for communal farming ventures which were enacted in the first phase of the Mexican Revolution. The same provisions, however, subsequently created difficulties, with repercussions into the 1970s. Since the ownership of the land was held by the leaders, albeit in trust, this arrangement violated the laws concerning *latifundia* which restricted the acreage which a person might possess. The colony as well as daughter colonies have expanded to over 30,000 persons and re-created the problems of landless peasants.[7]

Old Order Mennonites seldom became Mexican citizens by naturalization, but retained their Canadian citizenship. Problems arose a generation later about the status of the Mexican-born children. While Canadian laws grant citizenship to children born in wedlock to Canadian fathers but not mothers — a situation to be remedied with the Citizenship Act of 1977 — the procedural regulations were cumbersome and difficult for peasants with limited mobility and education. As a consequence, the Canadian government made the return to Canada most difficult for the children of emigrants.

There is little hope for the permanent integration of the majority of Old Order Mennonites into Mexican life. Ultimately, the Old Order people will again have to migrate. However, the fate of these expatriated Canadians does not arouse great concern among the authorities. At present, they are people with rudimentary education, limited resources and few linguistic skills, either in German, Spanish or English.

Mennonites in Russia found their lives considerably changed after the Revolution. For several years, they were in the regions affected by the Civil War; later they found themselves a persecuted minority. A great number decided to emigrate.

---

6 Walter Schmiedehaus, *Eine Feste Burg ist unser Gott* (Cuautemoc: 1948).
7 Harry Leonard Sawatzky, *They Sought a Country, Mennonite Colonization in Mexico* (Berkeley: 1971), p. 197.

Canada again became the country of preference and all those who could be admitted intended to migrate to this land. On June 2, 1922, the Order-in-Council restricting the immigration of Mennonites was rescinded.[8]

From 1923 to 1930, about 10,000 Mennonites entered Canada. These were classified as *Russlaender* in contrast to the *Kanadier* who had come after 1874. In general, the *Russlaender* were more educated than the *Kanadier*, who were the more conservative group among Mennonites. Within two generations, the members of the group established themselves and have become an integral part of Canadian life.

German cultural activities resumed slowly after the proscriptions and pressures of World War I. In 1920, newspapers were again permitted to be printed in the German language. The revival of the press was short-lived, from a peak of about 40,000 copies to a total of 21,000 copies within a decade.

German social and fraternal groups also restarted their activities. Winnipeg was the principal city of third-language groups who were active in Manitoba and other Prairie provinces. The Manitoba Free Press recognized early the significance of other than British groups and started a program in compliment to residents of foreign origin. The flag of each country was flown during national holidays of ethno-cultural groups. Slowly this procedure became one of the accepted rituals of Canadian intergroup relations.[9] Whether the ceremony contributed to recognition and harmony among 'other Canadians' has been open to debate. Quite frequently, the flag-raising ceremonies created strife and discord.

Another change which occurred in the post-war period was the shift from religious to national identity. During the war, the Canadian government judged the groups according to ethnic and linguistic criteria, rather than religion or cultural expressions. As a consequence, groups which formerly would not have interacted with each other because of religious divisions found themselves in alliance and co-operation. Also, before the war, regional differences were seen as significant differentiation factors among migrants. In Canada, they were treated alike whether they came from an advanced region or a backward one.

The War had also affected schools which offered instruction in languages other than English. The termination of language instruction which occurred during the war continued in publicly supported schools. Private schools were permitted after 1922 to use other languages of instruction than English, provided they otherwise followed the officially approved curriculum. Most of these were church schools, such as Hutterite, Mennonite and Lutheran (Missouri Synod) institutions. Children who attended church-supported schools with German as an integral part of the curriculum maintained the use of the language longer than children who attended public schools or Roman Catholic Separate schools. While both systems in the 1920s wholeheartedly accepted the "melting pot" approach, the Roman Catholic

---

8 Frank H. Epp, *Mennonite Exodus, ibid.,* p. 105.
9 Letter of E. H. Macklin, President and General Manager, Manitoba Free Press Company, Winnipeg, November 28, 1922, to the Consul General, Germany, Montreal, P. Q.

Separate School system became the most vociferous proponents of the melting-pot ideology.

The second decade also saw the development of evening and Saturday schools[10] where children who attended public or separate schools were instructed in German. From the beginning, Saturday schools were designed to reach as many children as possible. While Saturday schools did not create students who were fluent in both languages, they allowed the maintenance of the German cultural heritage. Saturday schools continue to the present, interrupted temporarily by World War I, but not prohibited as in World War II.

The formation of the German-Canadian National Association[11] in 1927 intended to provide for the group's interests on a broad scale. Among minority groups in Canada, there has always been the concern that the group's interests were neglected in cultural and political arenas. The founding of national associations was an attempt to overcome internal divisions as well as to develop pressure groups. More often than not, these national organizations succeeded in unifying newcomers. They were less likely to succeed in influencing the political decision-making process.

In order to promote unity among German-Canadians, annual meetings, called *Deutsche Tage*[12] (German Days) were introduced in 1928 in the major cities of each province, primarily in Western Canada. The Days were marked by exhibitions, cultural performances, meetings and public addresses by political and association leaders. The events were designed to elicit a feeling of in-group identity and to overcome the divisions within the German community. German Days were held in Edmonton, Winnipeg, Vancouver, Kitchener and Regina. The Edmonton, Winnipeg and Kitchener Days were considered successful, the Vancouver and Regina Days less so. The number of Germans in Vancouver was small and broad support was missing.

The lack of success of the Regina meeting was less comprehensible; Germans formed the largest minority group in the province and were almost one-quarter of the entire population. The Days were held on August 9 and 10, 1930. Great care was taken not to offend public opinion which had turned strongly anti-European. No German flag was flown and the provincial representative at the ceremonies, the Minister of Health, Monroe, stressed the necessity of becoming better citizens by assimilating into Canadian ways. However, the provincial government of the time had come into power on a wave of anti-German and anti-immigration sentiment. At the time, the KuKlux Klan[13] was active in Saskatchewan. The citizens

---

10 Letter of the German Consulate, Winnipeg, to the German Foreign Office, 15th April, 1929, p. 1.

11 Letter of the German Consulate, Winnipeg to the Foreign Office, Winnipeg, Germany, of 15th April, 1929. See also the analysis of Werner Entz, "Der Einfluss der deutschsprachigen Presse Westkanadas auf die Organisationsbestrebungen des dortigen Deutschtums 1889–1939" in Historical Society of Mecklenburg, Upper Canada, *Deutschkanadisches Jahrbuch*, Vol. 11, 1975, p. 119–136.

12 Letter of the German Consulate, Winnipeg, to the Foreign Office, Germany, 16th August, 1930, also Werner Entz, *op. cit.*, p. 125, 126.

13 Norman Ward and Duff Spafford, *Politics in Saskatchewan* (Don Mills: 1968), p. 108–109.

were frightened by the image of an "Alien Flood." It was also stressed that the large number of children foreigners had would inundate and dilute the Canadian way of life. The Dominion was asked to establish a solid wall against those who could not be assimilated. The Anglican Bishop of Prince Albert, the Rt. Rev. George Exton Lloyd,[14] wanted Saskatchewan to be British only and regarded other Europeans as "dirty, ignorant, garlic-smelling (and) unpreferred." The pressures of the time made politicians of German background defensive about their origin. For example, the Provincial Minister of Health in the Liberal Saskatchewan Government which was defeated in 1928, Dr. Ulrich, stressed in his biography of that year[15] that his father, an Alsatian immigrant, fought on the French side in the Franco-German War of 1870–71.

After March 21, 1931, immigration came to a standstill. The only admissible immigrants were white British and American citizens who had proof of sufficient means to maintain themselves and to seek work without becoming a public burden. Wives and children under eighteen years of Canadian residents, if their maintenance was guaranteed, were still allowed into the country. Farmers who had sufficient cash to purchase land for a minimum of $1,000.00 were also admitted.

The effects of the changing policies soon became evident. Whereas in 1930 the total migration to Canada was 104,806, it fell to 27,530 in 1931. Of these migrants, 797 were Germans and 37 Swiss. Between 1932 and 1936, immigration decreased further, reaching the lowest point in 1935 with 11,277 immigrants, of whom 230 were German and 38 Swiss. During this time, net immigration to Canada was negative. Some immigrants returned to their countries of origin voluntarily; others were persuaded to leave or even deported for becoming public charges.

The Great Depression from 1930–1940 affected newcomers significantly more than the rest of the population. There were strong pressures not to hire immigrants for the few jobs which were available. The immigrants who came during the 1926–27 wave had not yet established their economic base. Farmers suffered under the poor crop conditions which lasted for four to five years and created extreme hardship conditions in Western Canada. Many lost their farms in the dust-bowls of the 1930s; only the Northern Saskatchewan farmers were slightly better off. Some immigrants had arrived in Canada without their families, planning to establish themselves and bring the family over later. Many families remained separated throughout this time, the war period and the post-war events. Some families were never reunited.

The Depression with the resultant hostility towards immigrants was, to some extent, responsible for mutual aid and co-operation among immigrants. During the 1930s, numerous clubs were founded, such as the Alpen Club in Vancouver,[16] Club

---

14 Norman Ward and Duff Spafford, *op. cit.*, p. 116. Watson Kirkconnel, "Western Immigration" reprinted as Nativism under Attack, in Howard Palmer, *Immigration and the Rise of Multiculturalism* (Toronto: 1975), p. 56–58.
15 Greene's *Who's Who of Canada*, 1928/29, p. 195.
16 Bruce Ramsay, *A History of the German-Canadians in British Columbia* (Vancouver: 1958), p. 51.

Teutonia in Windsor, Ontario,[17] mainly for social purposes but also for mutual aid. In Vancouver, a German Mutual Aid Society, *Wirtschaftsbewegung,* was founded in 1938. The members promised to buy each other's goods and offer discounts.

In Germany, the National Socialist Party had gained power in 1933. There was renewed interest by the German government in working with Germans abroad and overseas, not out of concern for Germans, but in pursuance of ideological goals. The early refugees warned against the dangers of the regime, but mainly in vain. Subsequent refugees, prior to World War II, found Canada not receptive to outsiders with the exception of two groups, Sudeten Germans and Internees. Starting in 1934,[18] the German Consulate in Winnipeg became active in the reorganization of German associations along Nazi Party directives. Groups which were formerly mainly interested in social and fraternal activities were infiltrated and reoriented towards the goals of a National Socialist Germany. Throughout Canada, a German League of Canada, Inc. (Deutscher Bund, Kanada Inc.), was established.[19] The Bund followed the general format of Nazi organizations abroad, as in the United States and Latin America. Those who joined had to declare that they were of German background, had neither Jewish or Negro ancestors and submitted themselves to the directives of the leaders. The Bund claimed to be an association of all German Aryans who supported the ideals of the New Germany. The members promised to promote the political creed of the New Germany amongst Germans, as well as Canadians, in order to promote mutual respect. The members of the Bund promised to obey the laws of Canada as honourable and respectable residents. They also promised not to interfere in the internal policies of Canada. They promised to be proud of their names, their background, and aspirations and to maintain their heritage. Finally, they were admonished never to forget their homeland.

These goals, as such, were innocuous and primarily directed towards the Canadian public. Further plans were the establishment of a system of indigenous leadership. Bernhard Bott, the president of the Central Committee of German-Canadians, Regina, had early discouraged the placing of German leaders abroad. He suggested instead that suitable leadership candidates be sent to Germany on scholarships for education and indoctrination. This was done; several candidates were sent to Germany, received an education and returned. Few of these became convinced National Socialists. On the other hand, the system also prevented the infiltration of potential enemy agents. The Canadians who went to Germany were known and could be placed under surveillance in case of hostilities.

Bott was primarily regarded as an idealistic and overly-enthusiastic journalist. As an ardent apologist for the Third Reich, he dismissed any criticism of Germany

---

17 *Geschichte des Teutonia Vereins* (Windsor: 1965).
18 Confidential Memorandum of Bernhard Bott, the Editor of the Regina Courier of August 25, 1934 to the German Foreign Office, Division VI A; also Werner Entz, *op. cit.,* p. 132–34.
19 German League of Canada Inc. (Deutscher Bund Kanada), 32 King Street South, Waterloo, Ontario, Application Form and Guidelines.

and German-Canadians as a Jewish-Communist plot. He tried to initiate a boycott of Jewish goods in Canada, but the Canadian Jewish Congress, in turn, recommended in 1938 that Jewish employers dismiss their employees of German background.

With Dr. Heinrich Seelheim, the German Consul in Winnipeg until 1937, Bernhard Bott tried to mobilize the German ethnic group into open demonstrations of loyalty to Nazi Germany and a demand for German cultural autonomy in Canada. There were about fifty branches of the Bund and a few cells of the National Socialist party and the German Labour Front. The principal function was the dissemination of propaganda. In 1934, Bott, dissatisfied with the existing German Language Newspapers, *Der Courier* and *Der Nordwestern,* proposed to the German Foreign Office a newspaper favourably inclined to the "New Germany."[20] This paper came into being in 1935 with the financial support of the German Consulate.[21] *Die Deutsche Zeitung für Canada,* printed in Winnipeg, became the principal instrument of German propaganda. Well written, the paper disseminated the Nazi point of view. It also contained an English-language section, which, according to the suggestions of the editor, was to be handed to English-speaking friends of the readers. The last edition was printed on August 30, 1939. Upon the outbreak of the war, Bott was arrested and placed in an internment camp. Later he was released and continued to live in Winnipeg until his death. The paper had a circulation of about 6,000 copies. Based on this figure, the number of Nazi sympathizers in Canada was not very large, since the number of Nazi-oriented groups received the newspaper. Werner Entz[22] estimated that about one per cent of the Germans in Canada supported Nazi ideologies.

Before World War II, even Mennonites were well disposed towards Hitler. Having been rescued, primarily by German intervention, from Russia, they were favourably disposed towards the folk-unity ideas. In later times, they recognized the duplicity of the approach and refused to go along any further. For a short period, *Der Bote* and *Die Rundschau* published anti-Semitic articles in the 1930s but later discontinued the practice.

Most German-Canadians looked at the National Socialists with mixed feelings; there were supporters and strong enemies. The German language newspapers, after initial support, generally took exception to the developments in pre-World War II Germany.[23] The strongest opposition came from the German Communists, a small but active group in Canada. Their own newspaper, *Deutsche Arbeiterzeitung*[24] was published for a few years but folded up because of lack of support.

20 Confidential Memorandum, *ibid.,* p. 4.
21 Werner Entz, "120 Jahre Deutschkanadische Presse" in Institut fur Auslandsbeziehungen, *Mitteilungen,* Juli-September 1957, 7. Jahrgang, No. 3, p. 181.
22 Werner Entz, Jahrbuch 1975, *op. cit.,* p. 134. Another study was conducted by John Offenbeck, *The Nazi Movement and German-Canadians, 1933–1939,* unpublished thesis (London: 1970), University of Western Ontario.
23 Confidential Memorandum: *ibid.,* p. 5, 6.
24 Ostdeutscher Kulturrat, *op. cit.,* p. 11.

Canada did not accept large numbers of refugees prior to World War II. Suffering from the prolonged depression, the country was unwilling to accept impecunious refugees. Between 1933 and 1936, slightly more than three hundred persons from Germany were admitted annually. In 1937 and 1938, Canada admitted about six hundred persons in each year, in 1939, the number was increased to 1,100 admissions. Most of these were Sudeten Germans, about whom a separate report will be made. The pre-War period saw a few arrivals of Jewish refugees; these came primarily during the War as reported by Kurt and Elizabeth Wangenheim. In 1940, Otto Strasser, once Hitler's collaborator who broke with him on ideological grounds in 1930, and had fought him ever since, arrived in Canada. For most of the time, Strasser lived in the Annapolis Valley until he returned to Germany. A highly controversial person, silenced throughout the War, his role in Canada was never fully explained. Other pre-War refugees were a group of Augustinian Roman Catholic monks who opposed Hitler and were forced to flee the country. They settled in Monastery, Nova Scotia, close to Antigonish.

Chapter 6

WORLD WAR II AND AFTER

THE SUDETEN GERMAN SOCIALISTS IN CANADA*

Sudeten German newcomers to Canada never appear as a separate entry in Canadian Statistics, but are included in the data for "Germans," "Austrians," "Czechoslovaks," or under still other headings, depending on the time and the circumstances of their arrival. But in any history of German-Canadians, a certain group of Sudeten Germans merit special consideration: the Sudeten German Social Democrats who settled in Canada in 1939. Their title to a separate and special treatment rests partly on the unique quality of their epic and tragic experiences, partly on the fact that they were the only politically homogenous group of German-speaking immigrants in Canada in the twentieth century, and, most importantly, on their remarkable maintenance of a specific political, social and cultural cohesion which continues to set them apart from other Canadians and other German-Canadians, as an autonomous cultural group and a socially identifiable segment in the Canadian mosaic a generation after their first arrival in Canada. Moreover, these socialists have practically pre-empted the Sudeten German concept in Canada; to speak of Canadian Sudeten Germans usually means to speak of pre-war refugees.

The ancestral homes of these Sudeten Germans lay in the heavily industrialized German-language areas of Bohemia and Moravia, which were parts of the Austrian Empire until they were handed over to Czechoslovakia in 1918. For the next two decades, the people of Sudetenland, where social democracy had sprung up even before it was organized in Germany,[1] and whence much of the early strength of socialism in Austria had come, found themselves reluctant citizens of a new Czechoslovak Republic ruled by strongly nationalistic and conservative biases. The history of the *Deutsche Sozialdemokratische Arbeiter-Partei in der Tschechoslowakischen Republic* (German Social Democratic Workers' Party in the Czechoslovak Republic), abbreviated DSAP, from its founding in 1919 to its voluntary dissolution in 1939 is an unhappy one, full of frustrations, bad luck, and eventually betrayal by its allies. Few political parties have ever been as shamelessly abused as the DSAP was by a state it had supported loyally.[2] But in September of 1938, the

---

1 Sudeten Jahrbuch (1973), p. 52. September 30, 1863, at Asch in western Bohemia, was the date and place of the first social democratic club. The first organizer is identified as Johann Martin. Social Democracy in Germany was not organized until 1869, by August Bebel.
2 The story of Sudeten German social democracy has been the subject of a number of recent publications, such as, Martin K. Backstein, *Wenzel Jaksch und die sudetendeutsche Sozial-*

* Fritz Wieden, University of Windsor.

Government of Czechoslovakia, under its President, Dr. Benes, was clearly ready to yield the Sudetenland to Hitler's Germany and it was almost as eager to rid itself of all Sudeten Germans, including those who had steadfastly opposed Hitler and had defended the Czechoslovak Republic.[3] It was clear that the DSAP would now quickly change from a political party into a band of refugees. The leader of the DSAP, Wenzel Jaksch, called a meeting of the DSAP Executive Committee to take place in Prague on 30 September 1938. Willi Wanka, the leader of the DSAP Youth Organizations and youngest member of the Executive, had just returned from a World Youth Congress at Vassar College in Poughkeepsie, N. Y., and had just brought the news that the Sudetenland would be ceded to Germany; he had been told as much as he had passed through London on his way to the United States. At that moment, Canada was first mentioned as a future home for Sudeten German Socialists: Jaksch took the floor and declared that if there should be no more room in Europe for freedom-loving Sudeten German Social Democrats, who refused to bow to Nazism, then perhaps there might be room for them on the plains and in the forests of Canada.[4]

Wanka, who was an eyewitness of the scene and who knew Jaksch as well as anybody, has doubted that the DSAP Chief had any concrete ideas on a Canadian immigration plan; in fact, he thought that Jaksch acted on intuition.[5] But that intuition proved better than it first might have seemed; Jaksch lost little time in following it up and flew, accompanied by Wanka, to London the very next day in order to put an emigration scheme into motion.

Jaksch and Wanka had contacts in England, especially with some trade unionists and with some officials of the British Labour Party. They intended to use these contacts to enlist help for a scheme consisting of three phases: 1) to find the means of transporting a maximum number of refugees, including socialists, Jews, German and Austrian anti-Nazis, and other foes of Hitler, from Czechoslovakia to temporary havens in Northern and Western Europe; 2) to look for a country which would accept a large number of Sudeten Germans as immigrants; and 3) to move as many immigrants as possible to that country.[6]

---

demokratie (München, 1974); Karl Bosl, *Das Jahr 1945 in der Tschechoslowakei*, (München, 1971); Wenzel Jaksch, *Europas Weg nach Potsdam*, 2nd ed. rev. (Köln, 1970); Collegium Carolinum, *Beiträge zum deutsch-tschechischen Verhältnis in 19. und 20. Jahrhundert* (Bd. 19, München, 1967). See also the bibliographies in each of these volumes which list a large number of periodical articles.

For documentation, see Ernst Nittler, ed., *Dokumente zur Sudetendeutschen Frage 1916–1967* (München, 1967).

3 Bachstein, pp. 161–163 and 180–81; Jaksch, p. 346. About 20,000 Sudeten German opponents of Hitler were expelled from Czechoslovakia by Czech gendarmes and sent into the German-occupied areas.

4 Reported as a paraphrase quotation by Karl Kern in *Sudeten Jahrbuch* (1961), p. 39; and confirmed by Willi Wanka in *Sudeten-Bote* (Juli/August, 1969), p. 13. See also Bachstein, p. 178.

5 Willi Wanka, *Sudeten-Bote* (Juli/August, 1969), p. 13.

6 For further details on the whole operation, see Bachstein, p. 177–185; Willi Wanka, "Be-

The first task, bringing endangered Sudeten Germans from Czechoslovakia to temporary safety, required a great deal of organizational skill and countless hours of overtime work at the DSAP headquarters in Prague. It also required constant lobbying in Britain, chiefly by Willi Wanka and his wife, Mizzi, who set up a base in two rooms on Taviton Street in London. Financing the first leg of the trip seemed to have been the responsibility of the DSAP treasurer, Siegfried Taub, who remained in Prague until March 1939.

The second task, namely, finding a country which would accept most, if not all, of the Sudeten German emigrants, proved to be difficult. Britain would at first grant only 50 visas a day and most other countries were far from eager to accept destitute foreigners into their labour forces. But Britain generously provided some assistance money: the British government gave four million pounds to Czechoslovakia for the resettlement of refugees dislocated by the Munich Agreement, while private collections for the "Lord Mayor's Fund" and the *"News Chronicle* Fund" brought in another two hundred and twenty-five thousand pounds.[7] Prominent Britons, including Professor Robert Seton-Watson, the Mayor of London, and the editor of the *News Chronicle,* opened some doors to Jaksch and Wanka, who were able to see Malcolm Macdonald, the Minister for the Dominions, the day after their arrival in England.[8]

A number of countries were considered as permanent havens for the Sudeten German socialists: these included East Africa, Bolivia, Brazil, Norway, Denmark, Australia and New Zealand.[9] But interest in Sudeten German immigrants did not seem to be high: New Zealand, for instance, wanted only carpenters, electricians, and bricklayers with a good command of the English language.[10] Soon it became clear that only Canada would be likely to accept a large number of Sudeten Germans and offer a reasonable opportunity for resettlement.

Willi Wanka pursued the prospects for resettlement at London's Canada House with considerable energy. Though he found Vincent Massey, then the Canadian High Commissioner to Britain, rather aloof, he received hearty encouragement from Lester B. Pearson, Mr. Massey's deputy.[11] A negotiating team, consisting of Franz Rehwald, a trade unionist and DSAP economic expert, Father Emmanuel Reichenberger, a Catholic priest and longtime chairman of the Sudeten German *Volksbund deutscher Katholiken* (National Association of German Catholics), and an official of the Czechoslovak Ministry of Social Welfare, went to Canada to secure the terms

---

gegnungen und Episoden aus meiner Flüchtlingsarbeit". *Sudeten-Jahrbuch* (1969), p. 102–112, and "Wie die Kanada-Aktion finanziert wurde", *Sudeten-Bote* (Juni, 1968), and "Sicherung des Lebens", *Sudeten-Bote* (Juli/August, 1969), p. 13–16; Eugen de Witte, "Die sudetendeutsche Emigration 1938", Sudeten Jahrbuch (1952), p. 97–104.

7 Wanka, "Begegnungen", p. 105–106; Bachstein, *op. cit.,* p. 179–183.
8 Wanka, "Sicherung", p. 14.
9 Bachstein, *op. cit.,* p. 183. See also Emil Kutscha, "Sudeten Germans in Canada", *American-German Review,* XXIII (February/March, 1957), p. 30–31.
10 Wanka, *Sudeten-Bote,* (Juli/August, 1974), p. 8.
11 Information received from Willi Wanka in September, 1974.

of settlement. In early January of 1939, Rehwald cabled Wanka the terms under which the Canadian government was prepared to accept Sudeten immigrants: they had to be physically fit, suitable for land settlement, supported by a settlement grant of $1,500.00 per family, and all those who were inexperienced in farming would have to work for at least two years under supervision while clearing the land and erecting farm buildings.[12] Rehwald rushed back to Czechoslovakia to organize further transports to Britain, which now would open its doors to further refugees as there existed an opportunity to settle refugees already in Britain by emigrating to Canada. The first Canadian immigration missions arrived in Sudeten refugee camps in Britain and in Czechoslovakia in late January 1939.

The Canadian immigration terms, although the best anyone could obtain at that time, presented some problems. Whether or not the upper limit of 5,000 immigrants[13] would be reached depended to a great extent on the amount of money available. To use up the quota of 5,000 immigrants, much more money would have been needed than had been collected.[14] But then, a number of Sudeten German refugees in Czechoslovakia were caught by Hitler's occupation of Czechoslovakia on March 15, 1939, and never made it to the free world.[15] About 230 Sudeten Germans settled in Sweden, another 200 in Denmark, Norway and Finland.[16]

The first group of Sudeten settlers left Britain for Canada on the CPR line Montcalm on April 8, 1939 and by the end of the summer of 1939, all the Sudeten settlers had reached their Canadian destinations. In keeping with the terms outlined in January 1939 by the Canadian government, $1,500 was apportioned to each family and $900 for each single man or woman; $35,000 out of these apportionments were set aside for administrative purposes. Canada's two major railways were charged with the task of transporting and settling the refugees. The Colonization and Agricultural Department of the Canadian Railways took charge of 148 families and 34 single men, totalling 525 people; these would be settled on abandoned farms

---

12 The original cable is still in the possession of Mr. Wanka. See also *Sudeten-Bote* (Juli/August, 1974), *passim*.
13 See Karl Kern, *Wenzel Jaksch: Sucher und Künder,* 2 Vols. (München, 1967), 1, p. 262.
14 About £500,000, i.e., approximately $2,500,000 by the exchange rates then prevailing, had been set aside for the Sudeten settlement; see Bachstein, *op. cit.*, p. 179 ff. To bring 5,000 Sudeten Germans to Canada would have required almost twice the available sum, plus transportation costs from Europe to Canadian destinations. Transportation costs from Czechoslovakia to Britain and Sweden were largely borne by the DSAP; see Bachstein, *op. cit.*, p. 192–94.
15 To keep a quorum in the Party Executive in Prague, many of the leading DSAP functionaries had remained there. Some were allowed to emigrate by the Nazis; Party Chairman Jaksch fled to the British Legation in Prague, and escaped a few days later in disguise, reaching Britain via Poland. A train carrying more than 400 Sudeten German socialists was stopped by German Army officers near Moravska Ostrava, but allowed to cross the border when an accompanying Englishman told the officers that these people were all Jews. See also Kern, *op. cit.*, 1, p. 260–76.
16 See Rudolf Hubner, "Die Sudetendeutschen in Skandinavien", *Sudeten Jahrbuch* (1952), p. 81.

in the St. Walburg, Loon Lake, Brightsand and Goodsoil areas of Northern Saskatchewan. The Canada Colonization Association, a subsidiary of the Canadian Pacific Railway Company, assumed the responsibility for 152 families and 37 single men, numbering 518 souls. They were to be settled on uncleared land in the Tupper Creek (now Tomslake) region of Northeastern British Columbia.

The story of the actual settling of the Sudeten Germans contains numerous features found in other accounts of immigration: hope was followed by disappointment, and individual kindness by official apathy, and there was, of course, never enough money for badly needed supplies. But it must be remembered how the whole settlement was arranged: Franz Rehwald and Father Reichenberger were in a great hurry, and the Canadian authorities had no time to examine farming facilities in remote areas in midwinter. The settlement scheme proceeded with much improvisation because its terms were often vague. This vagueness and many language difficulties caused misunderstandings between the settlers and the railway companies. Worse still, few of the settlers had any experience in farming whatsoever. A distressed CNR agent reported that of his five hundred charges, only half a dozen knew how to milk a cow, only one man knew how to harness a horse, and the majority "of the women did not know how to make bread, and fewer could make butter."[17] Farm prices were depressed and farm yields were often reduced by inclement weather.[18] The common denominator of nearly every kind of difficulty lay, of course, in the fact that the resettlement scheme attempted to convert a group of skilled industrial workers from one of Europe's reputable manufacturing areas into homesteaders at the fringes of North American civilization. To use the resettlement monies in order to establish the Sudeten Germans in industrial jobs might have been a more efficient way, but would have invited the fury of hundreds of thousands of Canadian unemployed workers.

The outbreak of World War II soon opened new prospects for the Sudeten settlers: the construction of the Alaska Highway offered jobs paying one dollar per hour to the cash-starved settlers in the Tomslake area, and the shift of Canadian industry to war production opened up a number of new jobs in Eastern Canada. Without objections from either the railway settlement companies or the RCMP (which controlled the movement of all aliens during the war), about one-third of the settlers quit their farms and joined the industrial labour force in labourshort Ontario and Quebec.[19] None of these Sudeten Germans reported instances of anti-German bias, or disagreeable encounters with Canadians who had yielded to the blind passions of wartime propaganda. In what might be regarded as an astonishing

---

17 Ken Hand, "Remember the Sudeten Czechs?", *Canadian National Magazine* (9 February, 1952), p. 16. For similar observations, see also H. J. Siemens, "Report of the Sudeten Settlement, Tupper, B. C." unpublished Report of the Canadian Colonization Association, Edmonton, Alberta, October 20, 1955.
18 Willi Wanka reported to the writer that much of the 1941 crop was damaged or lost because of an August snowstorm in the Tomslake area. The settlers shared what was left.
19 See *Vorwärts Festschrift* (Toronto, October, 1971), *passim;* also Franz Rehwald, "Ein Urteil über die Kanada-Aktion", *Sudeten-Bote* (Juli/August, 1974), p. 22–24.

example of Canadian official tolerance, the Sudeten Germans of Hamilton, Ontario, founded their Sudeten Club on November 7, 1941, when most German-Canadian clubs had either ceased to exist or had been disbanded by Canadian authorities and while a victorious German *Wehrmacht* had reached the outskirts of Moscow.

The Canadian Sudeten Germans maintained close contact with their central organization-in-exile, *Treuegemeinschaft Sudetendeutscher Sozialdemokraten* (Loyal Union of Sudeten German Social Democrats),[20] which set up its headquarters in London and was chaired by the last DSAP chairman, Wenzel Jaksch. The fortunes of war and the tricks of politics proved unkind to the Sudeten Germans and it soon became clear to DSAP veterans in England, Canada, Sweden and elsewhere that they could not return to the Sudetenland.[21] The savage penal laws decreed by the Czechoslovak government against all Germans and Hungarians who were, or had been, citizens of that Republic,[22] prompted most Canadian Sudeten Germans to remember the doublecross of 1938 and to forget any attempts of retrieving their homeland; the expulsion of their countrymen by the Czechs in 1945 also led them to initiate an aid and immigration program which, amongst other charitable programs, would bring the surviving relatives and friends of Canadian Sudeten Germans to Canada. A delegation of Sudeten Germans visited the Minister of Immigration, urging the government to lift its ban on immigrants from Germany and Austria.[23] But the ban was not completely lifted until 1951. Willi Wanka spent eighteen months in the refugee camps of Germany, taking advantage of whatever exemption he could find in the rules barring German immigration and fighting a battle or two against military occupation bureaucrats on the side.[24] He was able to bring home

---

20 By 1945, Canadian Sudeten Germans had supported the *Treuegemeinschaft* in Britain with donations totalling $628.00; see *Vorwärts Festschrift* (October, 1971), p. 7.
21 It is impossible to give even a thumbnail sketch of the historical developments which left the Sudeten German socialists in 1945 political orphans. A good deal of research has recently been published on this subject: e. g. Ladislav Feierabend, *Prag-London Vice-Versa*, ed. Gotthold Rhode, (Bonn, 1971); Friedrich Prinz, *Wenzel Jaksch – Edvard Benes: Briefe und Dokumente aus dem Londoner Exil 1939–45;* and Bachstein, Jaksch and Nittler, quoted above.
22 See *Sbirka zákonu a nárizeni státu československého,* (Collection of Laws and Decrees of the Czechoslovak State), rocnil 1945 (yearly vol. 1945): # 5 of May 19, 1945 regarding the confiscation of property of Germans and Hungarians; # 6 of May 17, 1945 on the reduction of food rations for Germans; # 12 of June 21, 1945 regarding the confiscation of land owned by Germans, Hungarians, and other "traitors to, or enemies of the Republic"; # 16 of June 19, 1945 on the punishment of "traitors" and "criminals", which terms covered a large variety of German, Hungarian, Czech and Slovak organizations specified in the same law; # 18 of June 19, 1945 adding some ceremonial prescriptions to # 16; # 28 of June 20, 1945 providing for the take-over of property confiscated from Germans and Hungarians; # 33 of September 2, 1945 depriving all Germans and Hungarians of their Czechoslovak citizenship; # 71 of September 19, 1945 consigning all Germans and Hungarians to forced labour; and # 140 and # 141 of October 26 and November 6, 1945 closing all German universities and colleges.
23 Gottlieb Leibbrandt, *Canadian-German Society Festschrift 1947–1972* (Waterloo, 1972), p. 32; Vorwärts Festschrift (October, 1971), p. 7–8.
24 See Wanka, "Begegnungen", p. 108–112.

some close relatives of Canadian Sudeten Germans to Canada. As the political and economic conditions in Germany and Austria, which had received most of the more than two million Sudeten German expellees, improved, the desire to move from there to Canada naturally diminished. On the other hand, few of the Sudeten settlers in Canada returned to Germany or Austria after 1945.

Many of the original settlers still live on, or near, their first Canadian homesteads in British Columbia and Saskatchewan. Time has, of course, taken its toll. Many have passed away, and most have given up farming and moved to towns and cities because of their advanced age. Some of the settlers of 1939 have changed to non-farming careers: one is the manager of a medical centre, another is a postmaster and still another is the executive secretary of the Ontario Federation of Labour.

Canada's Sudeten German socialists have long become firmly integrated into Canadian life, though they retain their German language and preserve their political and cultural identity with consummate skill. In politics, they have generally lent support to the CCF, and later to the NDP, though it should be noted that the mode of supporting Canadian socialist aims has produced amongst them a deep ideological schism which has yet to heal completely. They are organized in two national societies, each with its own monthly paper: the *Zentralverband sudetendeutscher Organisationen in Kanada* (Central Union of Sudeten German Organizations in Canada) has its headquarters in Toronto, where it publishes the *Vorwärts,* and *The Westkanadische Arbeitsgemeinschaft der Sudetendeutschen* (Western Canadian Union of Sudeten Germans) is domiciled in Pouce Coupe, B. C., in the Middle of the original Tomslake settlement, where it publishes the *Sudeten-Bote.* These organizations now maintain good relations between each other.

Perhaps the most remarkable fact of the Sudeten German presence in Canada is the cultural productivity of which this relatively small group of immigrants can boast. Limits of space and time allow nothing more than mentioning creditable efforts at lyric poetry and an amazing output of painting. At the 1974 Sudeten German reunion in Loon Lake, Saskatchewan, no less than ten Sudeten Germans exhibited their paintings, and more their handicraft. It would not be easy to find a comparable group of Canadians who can match this score of cultural expression; but like so many other interesting Canadian stories, a thorough record of Canada's Sudeten Germans and their cultural achievements remains to be written at some future date.

THE GERMAN RELIGIOUS AND POLITICAL REFUGEES*

A relatively small proportion of the present German population in Canada arrived after fleeing from Germany or Austria to escape from National Socialist oppression. The majority of the religious refugees were Jews, although members of other faiths were also threatened at times. The other main category of refugees included those who were persecuted for their political convictions.

* Elizabeth and Kurt Wangenheim, Toronto

Individuals who had families or friends to act as sponsors immigrated quite "regularly" during the 1930s. Some made their way to Scandinavia and later, by diverse routes, to Canada. During the War, a few managed to cross to Moscow and from there by Trans-Siberian Railway to Vladivostok and (prior to December, 1941) to Vancouver, via Japan. One group of Jewish refugees was able to secure exit visas in 1941 and get safe passage across Vichy France, to Spain and Portugal, and in 1944 across the Atlantic. A small number survived the war years in concentration camps and came via displaced persons' camps in Canada around 1948–1950 (together with other Jews from Eastern Europe, who had also been in camps). Also, in recent years, a number of Jews of German origin have come from Israel, which had been their earlier refuge upon flight from the National Socialists.

At the beginning of the nineteenth century, Jews, living in Prussia and in other German principalities, became subjects of these countries with all the rights which had been granted to the other subjects. They emancipated themselves quickly and fitted well into the structure of the German society, predominately in the middle class as merchants, manufacturers, industrialists, bankers and professionals. They were important not only in the economic life, but also in academic and cultural affairs, as university professors, writers, artists, actors, theatre directors, composers, conductors, musicians, and publishers. In their various religious practices, whether as orthodox, liberal or reformed, they identified themselves primarily as Germans, becoming highly assimilated in their appearance, speech and behaviour. Any identification with Eastern European Jews was avoided. During the various pogroms in Eastern Europe before and after World War I, when Eastern Jewish refugees passed through Germany, the German Jews kept a strict social distance from these refugees, considering them to be culturally and socially different and alien to them, and a threat to their own position in Germany. When the National Socialists came to power in 1933, with their anti-semitic policy and master race ideas, they wiped out in a few years all that the German Jews had achieved over more than one hundred and twenty years.

Artists, writers, civil servants, and younger professional people, who were forbidden to work in their regular occupations, were immediately affected by the National Socialist takeover in 1933–34. Older independent professionals were able to continue practising until about 1936, after which they were restricted to a Jewish clientele.

Initially, Jewish businessmen and manufacturers were not restricted by legislation, though the owners of the larger enterprises were put under National Socialist Party pressure to sell or transfer ownership to "Aryans." Students were first refused entry to universities and later children were excluded from the regular elementary schools. By November 9, 1938 — the date of the *Kristallnacht* — a pogrom was organized by the National Socialist leaders all over Germany (including the annexed Austria) demolishing all remaining Jewish establishments, putting fire to synagogues, and taking many Jewish men of all ages into concentration camps, with any release dependent on emigration. Simultaneously, stringent economic laws were passed against Jews, expropriating all Jewish property, real and personal, against token compensation.

There had been a steady Jewish emigration from Germany since 1933 to various countries in Europe and overseas. Now the need for a much larger and accelerated emigration had risen. Since many countries were refusing entry visas, immigration became difficult or even impossible. Some persons crossed illegally into other countries, where they found shelter in special refugee camps. So-called children transports — for juveniles up to age sixteen — were arranged from Germany to England, where families had volunteered to accept such children in their households. In addition, the British government had consented as an emergency measure to the establishment of a transit refugee camp (called the Kitchener Camp) for men who had either been released from concentration camps on condition of emigration from Germany, or who were otherwise in immediate danger from the National Socialist authorities, while awaiting visas or transportation to other countries.

Persons who had either converted from Judaism to Christianity or were offspring of Jewish parents but baptized at birth experienced the same hardships as the German Jews. Protestants and Catholics also left National Socialist Germany for religious reasons and persecutions. There were many political refugees from Germany who had either been members or supporters of various political parties and their organizations, or who had expressed by many ways — speech, writings, art, teachings, convictions, philosophy — an attitude which the National Socialists considered hostile and dangerous to their own aims and *Weltanschauung*. A clear line cannot be drawn between the political and religious refugees, as some individuals fell in both categories.

The economic situation of the majority of the refugees was rather precarious. Language difficulties, lack of certain skills, problems of recognition of diplomas and degrees, restrictions regarding work permits for foreigners left only limited areas open for employment in many cases. However, this situation changed with the beginning of World War II and the subsequent manpower shortage.

Once hostilities began, the government had to cope with the questions of aliens and especially those from enemy countries. In Great Britain, tribunals were set up to deal with about seventy-six thousand persons of German or Austrian origin. Three categories were possible: category "A" enemy aliens to be interned right away; category "B" refugees from National Socialist oppression restricted to a certain area which they could leave only by prior reporting to the local police; category "C" refugees from National Socialist oppression free from any restrictions. Sixty-five thousand persons were classified "C"; about eight thousand were in the "B" category and about six thousand were in the "A" category.

In May 1940, after the German invasion of Belgium and the Netherlands, all aliens in the British coastal areas were interned under special war-time emergency regulations. Later, they were interned on the Isle of Man, and subsequently some were shipped either to Canada or Australia and held there in custody for the British government. At least three boats with a mixed load of German prisoners-of-war and civilian internees left for Canada. One of them, the "Arondora Star," was torpedoed and sunk in the Irish Sea with heavy losses of life. The other two, the "Ettric" and the "Sobieski," landed in Canada at Quebec City between July 10 and 15, 1940, and their passengers were sent to various internment camps. Several hundred passengers of the "Sobieski" were entrained at Quebec City on July 15, 1940, and brought to Trois Rivières.

The majority were political and religious refugees of all age groups and various social strata. The Canadian authorities, completely unfamiliar with and unaware of the deep hostility between German political and religious refugees and other German nationals, sent the group from the "Sobieski" to an already existing internment camp "T" at the Trois Rivières exhibition grounds, where German merchant navy men, mainly National Socialists, were kept. When the National Socialists saw the "Sobieski" group, they sang some of their most violent anti-semitic songs and uttered threats and curses. They also destroyed all the food and other preparations made for the new arrivals. In view of this completely unexpected situation, the Canadian authorities had to make new arrangements. They put the "Sobieski" group in the huge exhibition hall which lacked all the necessary facilities to house and feed so many people. This makeshift arrangement lasted for about four days until the National Socialists were transferred to another camp and the "Sobieski" group took over the regular internment camp. The stay in camp "T" lasted for about a month, long enough to set up a kind of organizational machinery but not to let the inmates become acquainted with each other.

> An incident demonstrates further the lack of knowledge of the German refugee problem by the Canadian authorities at that time. The intelligence officer announced that the Swiss Consul, as the representative of the protective power for Germany, would come and visit the camp and accept any complaints from the inmates. When the speakers for the refugees told him that they refused any contact or dealings with the National Socialist government or any representative acting on its behalf, the officer replied that the inmates must be traitors to Germany. The officer was unaware of the ideological dimensions of the War and thought only in national categories.

On August 12, 1940, all the inmates of the camp were transferred to a new camp, "B," located in the forests of New Brunswick. Work there was limited, for besides kitchen work, only wood-cutting was available for small parties and occasionally work at an experimental farm, for small groups only. Various cultural groups sprang up, dealing with theatre or music; choirs were formed, lectures were given by experts in various fields, services were held for the various denominations, and a coffeehouse was opened with its own small band. These activities provided the inmates with an opportunity to get acquainted with each other, and to find out about their various social backgrounds.

In October 1940, it was announced that the Gentiles were to be shipped to a different camp. Some of the Jewish inmates objected to this separation and asked the commanding officer to be permitted to join the Gentiles for reason of conviction, as they had always fought against any form of discrimination. The request was granted.

On October 17, 1940, this group was sent to a new camp "A," near Farnham,

Quebec. Some of the people who had arrived in Canada on the "Ettric" and who had been kept at the camp in the Citadel of Quebec City were also sent to this camp. The Jews and Gentiles among these were not separated, and approximately eight months later, on June 22, 1941, about one hundred and sixty inmates of camp "B" arrived also at camp "A' " so that one cannot speak of a general policy of separation on religious grounds.

The life in camp "A" became active in many ways. School classes were established for the younger boys, so that they could continue with their education. Teachers and professors among the inmates, assisted by some of the interned students from Oxford and Cambridge, taught the boys from books and other materials supplied by the Y.M.C.A., Jewish organizations, the Quakers and other groups. The students of the camp school passed their matriculation examinations with excellent results. Artists gave exhibitions of their work and actors and musicians contributed their talents in many ways. Later on, possibilities for work were created when a woodworking factory was opened to manufacture pre-fabricated huts and ammunition boxes. A tailor shop was also established and facilities were set up for making camouflage nets.

Contacts were slowly established with various religious organizations, Quaker, Y.M.C.A., the Roman Catholic Church, Jewish organizations, and the Canadian refugee organizations. Senator Catherine Wilson, the Canadian representative for the High Commissioner of Refugees of the League of Nations, visited the camp and helped to improve some of the conditions of the refugees inside the camps. She also explained to the Canadian authorities that the refugees were strongly anti-National Socialist and started to organize the machinery for release from the camps. Some of the interned refugees, especially scientists and other specialists, had already been returned to the United Kingdom, where they were released. Of the approximately 2,500 interned refugees in Canada, about 1,500 returned to the United Kingdom during 1940 to 1943.

The first release in Canada was granted in February 1941 to a juvenile whose widowed mother lived in Canada. Meanwhile, the various organizations trying to help the interned refugees found sponsors for interned students as a means for their release. The first students were released under this scheme in Canada at the beginning of October 1941, and a considerable number were subsequently released. By this time, a shortage of manpower, especially of skilled labour, developed in Canada, and the authorities became slowly aware that an untapped reservoir existed among the interned refugees. One project was the government-sponsored establishment of a machine shop at Lachine, Quebec (Machine Industries Ltd.), which was run and managed almost entirely by released refugees, who lived on the premises in camplike surroundings. They were all highly qualified people, such as professional engineers, toolmakers, other skilled craftsmen and accountants. They were paid the going rate of wages, but they were not completely free as they had been released for this specific employment.

The project started at the end of January 1942, after camp "A" inmates had been transferred about January 23, 1942, to camp "N" at Sherbrooke, Quebec, to join other refugees. The life in camp "N" became much more relaxed and demonstrated a better understanding of the refugee problem by the authorities. Nearly every month, groups returned to England for release. The British Home Office had sent to the Canadian authorities a list of those refugees who could be released and those who should be kept in custody for the duration. More and more releases in Canada were granted, some for work on farms, some to certain jobs in the cities. If a released inmate quit his job, he was returned to the camp by the R.C.M.P. but could be later released again for a different job. Prospective employers appeared at the camp to interview inmates, to find out whether they were suitable for certain jobs. Even the Canadian government interviewed a certain number of inmates, inquiring whether they would be qualified and willing to work in postal censorship. Due to the many returns to the United Kingdom and to the release in Canada, the occupancy of the camp was reduced to less than fifty percent.

On November 25, 1942, the remaining approximately three hundred persons were transferred to the last remaining refugee camp "I" on the Isle aux Noix, near Montreal, which contained about seventy persons who had either come to camp "I" directly from the "Sobieski" or were later transferred there from camp "B." Camp "I" inmates expected either immediate release in Canada or return to the United Kingdom for release. This was, in fact, what happened to those who had been declared eligible for release by the Home Office. About twenty-five to thirty persons joined the Canadian postal censorship in Ottawa; many others went to jobs or returned to the United Kingdom. The camp was dissolved in August 1943. Those few people who had been declared ineligible for release were returned to England.

A total of nine hundred and seventy-two interned refugees were released in Canada between 1940 and 1943. They stayed on in Canada, were subsequently given the landing permits required under the Canadian immigration laws and became naturalized commencing in 1946. They entered into various phases of Canadian life and were found in most of the Canadian provinces. Those who had passed their senior matriculation in camp, or who had been released as students under sponsorship, entered and graduated from Canadian universities. Others who already had European degrees, or who had not yet finished their studies, were given certain credits for the continuation for their studies in their respective professions. Those who had been businessmen or skilled labourers found opportunities to establish themselves or were able to get employment using their skills. Among academics, some became prominent in their various disciplines. There were also impressarios and well-known artists. Many worked for the C.B.C. as musicians, producers or consultants. There were painters and art gallery owners. One former refugee is the owner of a well-known art gallery, which became instrumental in supporting and exhibiting Canadian artists. Among a sample of one hundred and seven persons, the following occupations were found in a study in 1973:

OCCUPATIONAL STATUS OF FORMER REFUGEES IN CANADA

Professions, general	18
Medical Science	11
Natural Scientists	9
Artists	5
Musicians	10
Performers & Directors	5
Ministers of Religion	3
Managerial	11
Professors & Teachers	16
Craftsmen	10
TOTAL	98

Nine persons died between 1945–1973

In addition to this large number of male refugees who came via internment camps, there were others, both male and female, who arrived in Canada "more regularly," before, during and after World War II.

All these refugees faced certain difficulties in becoming structurally assimilated into Canadian society. Because of the significant cultural differences between German and Austrian (and German-speaking Czech) Jews and Jews from Eastern Europe, this group had little in common with the existing Jewish communities in Canadian cities. (The very early German Jewish migration to Canada had virtually disappeared into the core culture, as had the early Spanish-speaking Sephardim). While some of the "camp boys" did become at least marginally linked to the existing Jewish community through marriage to Canadian Jewish women, a considerable number of others married non-Jews and a few found mates among German-speaking Jewish women who arrived as legal immigrants during or after the War.

Some of the refugees were agnostic or converts to Christianity. However, those who retained a commitment to Judaism often had difficulty in fitting into existing synagogues, whether Orthodox, Conservative or Reform.

After the War, as more and more German-speaking Jews arrived from England, from displaced persons camps, from Israel and from other places of temporary settlement (such as South Africa and Shanghai), German Jewish communities grew up in Metropolitan areas, such as Toronto and Montreal. In Toronto, a Reform Synagogue *Habonim* was established, which resembled more closely the type of Reform Judaism developed in Germany, Austria and Czechoslovakia than the type of Reform Judaism which had evolved in North America from Eastern European Orthodoxy. This served as both a religious and a social focus for individuals and families who had previously had only one formal social organization.

The second generation of this group shows little sign of perpetuating a German Jewish community. Some of them take an active part in the social and religious life of the larger Jewish community, becoming members of various synagogues, joining Jewish men's and women's organizations and participating in the social activities of Jewish cliques. But they have as little commitment to the German language as the Canadian-born members of Eastern European Jewish families have to Yiddish; their cultural assimilation had diminished many of the cultural factors which divided their parents and enables them to identify as Canadian Jews. Others take little or no part in Jewish affairs, having most of their social contacts with non-Jews.

While many of the German Jewish refugees lost all their relatives and friends in the extermination camps, others have families and friends scattered almost literally over the world's globe. Many keep up social ties through letters and travel. However, the main link for all German Jews is a New York German-language weekly newspaper, the *Aufbau*. In addition to world news, a strong section on art, literature and drams, and news of the various New World Club activities in the United States, the *Aufbau* also provides news of the activities of German Jews throughout the world.

A large proportion of the German Jews now in Canada are of urban middle class origin and the older ones had often been well established in their fields before being forced to emigrate. While a small proportion were able to transfer funds to other countries, the majority came with little or no money. In addition, many had difficulty in re-establishing themselves in their own profession or another approximating its social position. Others were too old or psychologically disturbed by their experiences or both to do anything except menial work. Many of the refugees have been helped to attain a degree of financial security by restitution payments made by the West German government. These varied from small one-time payments to young people who had been deprived of their right to an education, payments for property, furniture and jewels which had been confiscated, lump-sum payments or pensions for loss of profession. Those who had been civil servants were reinstated with some degree of seniority and given the choice of returning or of "retiring" with titles and part pension. Some who had been manufacturers and other entrepreneurs were able to regain ownership and then sell their businesses.

Many of the German Jewish refugees in Canada have been ambivalent in their attitudes towards other German immigrants. Among the refugees in general, a large percentage felt and expressed an emotional revulsion against Germany and all those Germans who had at the very least tolerated the National Socialists' oppression of Jews and other minorities. Consequently, many wished to have no contact with the Germans who began to immigrate to Canada in large numbers around 1950. However, at the same time the cultural heritage of these Jews was German: they thought, spoke and wrote in German and, especially for the intellectuals, their positive image of themselves was linked to their experience as well-educated members of the earlier German intellectual and sometimes social elite.

In the early period of their life in Canada, many of them were cut off linguistically and psychologically from enjoyment of and participation in the artistic and cultural life in Canada. Consequently, some were attracted to German theatrical and other cultural groups established in the 1950s, primarily by new German immigrants. However, here and elsewhere, social contacts between the Jews and German immigrants were usually accompanied by a considerable hesitation on the part of the Jews. One expressed the attitude of many: "Every time I meet one of them, I wonder 'Where were you during the *Kristallnacht*? Where were you when they rounded up our parents and herded them away to the camps? Maybe you were one of the officers or soldiers in the camps.' Even though we know from personal experience that not all Germans were anti-semites and some did their best to help us, nevertheless, we want to be very sure of the background of any German we meet here before we have anything to do with him or her."

THE WAR PERIOD

The treatment of German-Canadians in World War II differed significantly from World War I. In the latter, a great deal of emotional propaganda was unleashed for patriotic purposes; in World War II, there was a feeling that a duty had to be done, rather than that a war by proxy had to be fought in Canada.

With the outbreak of hostilities, Canada in September 1939 required that all enemy aliens register and sign an undertaking to observe all laws of Canada and not to convey any information to anyone whomsoever. Those who refused to sign such an undertaking, or failed to live up to the conditions imposed, were to be interned as prisoners-of-war.[25] An Order-in-Council of September 3, 1939 had established the office of Registrar General of Enemy Aliens.[26] In that month, 16,355 enemy aliens were registered.[27] Shortly after the outbreak of the war, ninety-seven German citizens and two hundred and ten Canadian citizens of German background were interned.[28] The two hundred and ten Canadian citizens were considered to be active followers of Nazi ideologies or were functionaries in the Bund.

In 1940, Canada required the registration of all persons of German and Italian racial origin. This registration attempt proved futile and was strongly attacked by John Diefenbaker, among others. A new Order-in-Council, P. C. 3751, was issued which required the registration of all persons of German and Italian birth and all nationals of those countries dominated by Germany and Italy, unless these persons had acquired British nationality prior to September 1, 1922. Approximately 82,500 registered. Of these, 30,000 were Germans; there were also 21,500 Czechoslovakians and Austrians.[29] All persons registered were considered as parolees, unless they had Exemption Certificates which were given to those whose loyalty to Canada was unquestionable. This registration affected more Italians than Germans, since the majority of Germans were not natives of Germany but former citizens of countries not affected by the registration provisions. Until World War II, about one-eighth of all residents of German background were born within the boundaries of the German Reich.

Between April 1, 1940 and March 1941, 375 Germans and Canadians with

---

25 Government of Canada, Order-in-Council, September 2, 1939, Canada Gazette.
26 Government of Canada, Order-in-Council, September 3, 1939, Canada Gazette.
27 Dominion of Canada, *Report of the Royal Canadian Mounted Police for the Year Ending March 31, 1940* (Ottawa: 1940), p. 67.
28 Dominion of Canada, *RCMP Report, 1940, ibid.,* p. 67.
29 Dominion of Canada, *Report of the Royal Canadian Mounted Police for the Year Ending March 31, 1941,* p. 57.

sympathies for the National Socialist cause were interned.[30] By 1943, 194 German Nationals remained in internment camps. Most of these internees were German citizens apprehended on the high seas. About 9,000 Germans remained on parole; the majority of Austrians received Exemption Certificates. The revocation of Regulation 26B of the Defense of Canada Regulations in December 1942 lifted the requirement for German-born persons to register.[31] The Canadian government recognized that World War II was a war of ideologies rather than of national loyalties. The refugees mentioned in the previous chapter were fervently anti-Nazi and desired nothing more than to work for the Allied cause. One of the first to recognize the shift from ethnicity to ideological commitment was John J. Deutsch[32] who advised the Prime Minister to leave most German-born residents of Canada to pursue their normal careers unless they were identified as Nazi supporters.[33]

In 1944, 7,431 Germans were on parole and 4,682 were exempted. Austrians held 1,050 parole and 1,337 Exemption Certificates.[34] About 152 Germans remained interned. In addition to these internees were the refugees to Britain who were released by 1943 receiving parole and Exemption Certificates.

On November 20, 1944, 134 German internees were sent to Germany under a programme for the exchange of interned civilians between the United Kingdom, Canada and the German Reich. After this exchange, less than 100 persons remained interned.[35]

During the war, the investigations of the Royal Canadian Mounted Police did not discover a single case of sabotage by Germans in Canada,[36] or by Canadians of German background. A few German intelligence agents had attempted to infiltrate Canada but were soon discovered or gave themselves up. In the internment camp at Lethbridge, Alberta, an anti-Nazi German was murdered by four prisoners-of-war. They were executed in turn after the War. It is one of the ironies of history that now victim and persecutors are buried together at the Kitchener, Ontario, cemetery and their graves are maintained by the German War Graves Association.[37]

Generally, there were only sporadic and not widespread hostilities against German-Canadians as there had been during World War I. The population was more restrained and German-Canadians were more circumspect in their behaviour. Most

---

30 Dominion of Canada, *RCMP Report, 1941, ibid.,* p. 67.
31 Dominion of Canada, *Report of the Royal Canadian Mounted Police for the Year Ending March 31, 1943,* p. 36.
32 Interview with Dr. John Deutsch, Kingston, Ontario, June 11, 1974.
33 Discussion of Dr. John J. Deutsch with the Rt. Hon. William Mackenzie King, as reported in the above interview.
34 Dominion of Canada, *Report of the Royal Canadian Mounted Police for the Year Ending March 31, 1944,* p. 32–34.
35 Dominion of Canada, *Report of the Royal Canadian Mounted Police for the Year Ending March 31, 1945,* p. 35.
36 Dominion of Canada, *Report of the Royal Canadian Mounted Police for the Year Ending March 31, 1946,* p. 37–38.
37 Rex vs. Mueller, *Dominion Law Reports,* 1947, 1, p. 705. The Kitchener Cemetery Burials were arranged in 1971.

German Clubs ceased their operations. There was no general prohibition of German language newspapers, although they were censored.

A new German language newspaper, *Volksstimme*,[38] was published in 1944–45. With a strong communist orientation, it supported the goals of the Red Armies in Eastern Europe. It dealt harshly with Nazi sympathizers and attacked the Canadian government for releasing some internees whom the paper accused of being pro-Nazi.[39]

After the collapse of the Third Reich, the RCMP conducted a survey of the reactions of Germans in Canada to the defeat. They disclosed that:

> The majority of the German population of this country was relieved that the conflict was over, although their concern appeared to be for their fellowmen in the homeland, rather than in appreciation of the fact that Canada was no longer involved in an internecine war.[40]

World War II reduced the amount of language maintenance even more than the normal intragenerational attrition. The hostilities of World War I were hardly overcome when the Depression and World War II came about. Most of the pressures against the use of German were of an informal nature. Children did not want to be identified with the enemy, and therefore they did not want to speak German. Any person with a German accent was identified as a potential enemy of Captain Canuck, the hero of a comic strip. The Hun of World War I became the Jerry of World War II.

When the atrocities of World War II became known, a strong and sustained campaign against Germans began. There was little differentiation between those who were completely uninvolved and the perpetrators of these enormous crimes. The German-Canadians were not involved in these; on the contrary, a large number served in the Armed Forces of Canada. The campaign was primarily conducted by the newsmedia and by individuals who had suffered because of the war or had relatives who had suffered. This time, however, official Canada did not join the xenophobia. The senior governments acted cautiously but correctly.

World War II signalled the changing structure of the Canadian economy. Whereas formerly agriculture and the extraction of raw material were the basis of the economy with corresponding manpower requirements, now the emphasis was on the availability of workers in secondary industries. The large-scale expansion of these industries created new demands for an industrial work force. At the same time, the mechanization of the farms freed many farmers for industrial employment. There was a change from subsistence farming to the market economy. Most German farmers had remained subsistence farmers throughout the Depression. With the avail-

---

38 *Volksstimme*, published 1944/45, Horst Doehler, editor, Business Manager Frank Gattschaff.
39 Dominion of Canada, *RCMP Reports of 1946, ibid.*, p. 30. Also, Rex vs. Mueller, Dominion Law Reports, 1947, 1, p. 705.
40 Dominion of Canada, *RCMP Report, ibid.*, p. 37–8. The report singles out the internment camp in Lethbridge, Alberta, as being unduly influenced by the Gestapo.

ability of industrial employment, many farmers left for the towns and cities. The exceptions were Mennonites, Amish (in Ontario) and especially Hutterites. They continued with the traditional mixed pattern, being as self-sufficient as possible. Cash crop farming, mostly labour intensive, became prevalent in Ontario and in the irrigated lands of the Prairies.

The war period also initiated a shift in the German-Canadian population. Until then, the majority had lived in the Prairie Provinces. Now the number and percentage of German-Canadians began to increase in Ontario and British Columbia. The post-war period accelerated these shifts in population which became even more pronounced when immigration to Canada commenced again.

POST WORLD WAR II DEVELOPMENTS

After World War II, German-Canadians began to re-organize slowly with a changing emphasis, relief and support. There were approximately twelve million refugees who were living under deplorable conditions in Germany and Austria. Among these were a considerable number of Mennonites who had fled from Russia with the retreating German armies.[41] In 1945, C. F. Klassen made the first contacts with refugees in the camps and in February 1946, the Mennonite Central Committee became a member of the Council for Relief Agencies licensed for operation in Germany.[42] Non-Mennonite German-speaking Canadians followed suit. In the fall of 1946, a small group met in Kitchener to start the Canadian Society for German Relief.[43] At a later time, the Relief Society worked on behalf of refugees and lobbied the Canadian government for the admission of refugees to Canada. On January 30, 1947, an additional Order-in-Council broadened the admission criteria of the Order-in-Council of May 28, 1946 and was known as the Close Relatives and Special Projects Scheme.[44]

While the number of 1947 arrivals was relatively small, refugees who were not German citizens came in larger numbers: in 1948 about 3,000 and in 1949 over 6,000. Besides Mennonites there were refugees from the Baltic Countries and ethnic-Germans from Roumania and Czechoslovakia, Yugoslavia, Hungary, Poland and Russia. Among the ethnic-Germans from Roumania and Yugoslavia were some who were finally able to join relatives who had come to Canada between 1926 and 1930.

In 1951, the Relief Society changed its goal and became the *Deutsch-Kanadischer Zentralverband*, Canadian-German Alliance, which in turn became the Trans-Canada Alliance of German-Canadians on September 25, 1952.[45] This organi-

---

41 Frank H. Epp, *Mennonite Exodus* (Altona: 1962), p. 357–364.
42 *Ibid.*, p. 365.
43 Dr. Gottlieb Leibbrandt, *Canadian German Society, 1947–1972* (Waterloo: 1972), p. 11.
44 Frank H. Epp, *Mennonite Exodus, op. cit.*, p. 392–393.
45 Dr. G. Leibbrandt, ibid., p. 33–37.

zation tried to co-ordinate the activities of German associations in Canada. Until 1976, the Trans-Canada Alliance was an exclusively Canadian organization — all executive officers had to be Canadian citizens — but since then, the Alliance has considered itself the representative of Germans in Canada.[46]

In 1950, German citizens who had relatives in Canada were again admitted to this country. In 1951, restrictions on the immigration of German citizens were finally lifted. The post-war immigration wave began. Between 1951 and 1957, almost 220,000 German immigrants were admitted to Canada. Most of these settled in Ontario, a few in the West.

In 1958, the Canadian government placed considerable restrictions on the number of potential immigrants. German immigration figures dropped from a peak of 15,000 in 1958 to about 5,000 in 1963. In 1963, new immigration regulations became effective, selecting immigrants according to skill and education criteria rather than national origin. More German immigrants came to Canada, until about 1968, when the number dropped off sharply.

During the 1960s and 1970s, Germany underwent a prolonged period of financial prosperity which made the Federal Republic a country of net immigration. The prosperity of Germans increased considerably and the standard of living could hardly be matched in Canada. In recent years, there were annually fewer than 9,000 immigrants to Canada.

Since the second part of the 1960s, there has been a considerable return migration of Germans and German-Canadians from Canada to the Federal Republic. It is estimated that only about one-half of the landed immigrants to Canada remain here permanently. At one time, Germans, like Canadians, had virtually unlimited access to the United States; this also changed in 1968. With the political turmoils of the United States in the late 1960s, and the low amenity factors in the urban centres of the United States, that country was not the country of final destination.

If the returned were German citizens, readjustment difficulties were still evident. One German citizen who had returned from a prolonged period in Canada wrote:

> All in all, I selected upon returning to Germany; a lousy job and can only hope to change it soon. Although I do not belong to that category, who, as soon as they return to their beloved homeland, complain about the miseries of circumstances in Germany and mourn for their (although not perfect) paradise in Canada; nevertheless, I am annoyed at the narrow-mindedness and pettiness of the German circumstances. I really underestimated the effect of the rigid social hierarchies.[47]

If return migrants were Canadian citizens, the difficulties of going back to Germany were increased. From 1975 onward, all professional occupations were virtually closed to non-Germans. German authorities do not welcome former German citizens who are accused of having deserted the homeland in poor times and now wish to take part in prosperity. While this attitude does not reflect formal policies,

---

46 Trans-Alliance of German Canadians, Statutes 1976.
47 Letter of D. H., in the possession of the author.

re-migrants frequently experience hostile attitudes. For persons of German background, Canadian citizenship means an irrevocable commitment to Canada, not a temporary expedient.

The characteristics of post World War II migrants differed considerably from the pre-Depression settlers. Until 1930, most immigrants came as farmers. Only when they did not succeed in farming did they drift into the cities as unskilled and semi-skilled workers. Postwar immigrants were skilled craftsmen, technicians or professionals. Their integration into the Canadian labour force differed considerably from the earlier patterns. The new migrants were well trained, quite articulate and familiar with urban lifestyles.

In 1976, there are slightly fewer than one and a half million German-Canadians. Close to 600,000 live in Ontario, 250,000 in Alberta and 150,000 in each of British Columbia and Saskatchewan. Most are urban, with the exception of Amish, Mennonites and Hutterites, who cling to their rural lifestyles. Mennonites have begun to move to urban centres in Ontario and Winnipeg.

German-Canadians display a high degree of adjustment to urban life. They do not, with the exception of ethno-religious subgroups, form homogeneous settlements within urban areas, except during periods of mass migration. Toronto, for example, has had German settlement areas in the High Park District and in Scarborough during the 1950s and early 1960s, but now there are no longer distinctive German residential areas. Only in Winnipeg, Manitoba and Edmonton, Alberta, are distinct German settlement areas. With the upward social mobility displayed by German-Canadians, areas of ethnic concentrations give way to random distribution and socio-economic stratification. Socio-economic status, rather than ethnicity, determines the place of residence.

Chapter 7

EDUCATION AND THE PREPARATION SYSTEM

The attitudes of German-Canadians towards education comprise the entire spectrum from acceptance of minimal education to desire to obtain the best possible education. The Hutterites consider any formal education beyond Grade 8 to be sinful and inappropriate. Instead, they rely on children learning through experience from an early age the various tasks which the communal farming system requires. Some groups of Mennonites, such as Old Colony Mennonites, also maintain that formal education should be for the basic skills and that the majority should obtain their knowledge as farmers within the immediate family unit. However, most Mennonites have accepted the basic North American premise that formal education is the only legitimate pathway towards adulthood.

German-Canadians represent a variety of educational experiences. The majority of the immigrants received a Grade 8 education in primary schools, followed by an apprenticeship of three to four years. During the time of the apprenticeship, they were obliged to attend trade schools for at least one to two days per week. The apprenticeship was terminated with a journeyman's examination. Some craftsmen continued their education on a part-time basis and obtained their master craftsmen certificates after five to six years. In Europe, only master craftsmen had the right to train apprentices. They were considered to be the backbone of the skilled labour force system.

A second group of immigrants attended primary and secondary schools until Grade 10. After this, they became trainees in business or technical occupations, leading to paraprofessional status. After the completion of their training, these paraprofessionals attended colleges of applied arts and technology and obtained certification in their chosen disciplines. These graduates, although having a fair amount of practical experience, did not enjoy full professional status in Europe. The occupational integration of the paraprofessionals into equivalent positions in Canada was initially a source of continuous conflict and disenchantment. They had more formal training than the traditional craftsman, but did not reach the level of a university-trained professional person. The development of colleges of applied arts and technology in Ontario and other provinces aided in establishing parallel educational approaches leading to positions as technicians and middle management executives.

The university-trained immigrant experienced the greatest problems in adjusting to the new environment. Certain occupational skills, such as law, could not easily be transferred to Canada. Only after the graduate in law attended a faculty of law in Canada and articled under the auspices of a Provincial Bar Association, was there a possibility of his practising law again. The majority of law graduates of European universities were unable to do so and drifted into other occupations.

Canadian professional associations as self-governing bodies set the criteria for admission to the professions. Provincial Colleges of Dentistry usually admit only graduates of North American universities and a few selected British colleges. In medicine, admission to the profession is subject to a formal validation of previous training and experience. The Colleges of Physicians and Surgeons maintain lists of acceptable medical schools. Graduates of these schools are permitted to write the examination for foreign graduates in medicine. After a specified period of internship in accredited hospitals, the graduates are permitted to practise their profession in a Canadian province.

In general, graduates of German, Austrian and Swiss universities experienced few difficulties, since the majority of the universities in their homelands are on the list of accredited medical schools. German-speaking graduates from southeastern or eastern European universities have some difficulty in getting their degrees recognized and obtaining equivalent standing.

Among medical doctors, the principal obstacles toward exercising their profession are the mastery of the English or French language and the passing of the basic examinations required of foreign graduates. Contrary to popular belief, the medical associations in general have established a fair measurement system, which safeguards the interests of the Canadian public, as well as the occupational aspirations of medical practitioners. Discriminatory patterns are primarily found in the granting of hospital privileges. Hospital boards are free to grant or deny residence or internship privileges with few external controls. These discretionary powers have sometimes been used to exclude graduates of German-language universities. As a rule, graduates of foreign universities are more likely to find employment in the isolated areas of the country than in the big cities and southwestern Ontario, unless they serve their own ethno-cultural communities. Doctors trained in German, Austrian and Swiss universities have contributed significantly to the advancement of medicine in Canada and to medical research in general.

The societies for professional engineers have also created clear-cut criteria for acceptance of graduates of foreign universities. Since professional engineers do not need to be university graduates, it has been possible for technicians trained under the European system to acquire the status of professional engineer. Graduates of technological colleges and universities in German-speaking areas now find little difficulty in being accepted, although difficulties existed during the 1950s.

Admission to the teaching profession is governed by provincial standards. In general, full admission requires graduation from an accredited university and the passing of basic educational courses leading to certification. During the postwar immigration boom, 1951–1958, graduates of German-language universities found little acceptance in the teaching field; however, with the shortage of teachers in the 1960s, graduates of foreign universities were accepted for teacher training and certification. The Atlantic Provinces and Quebec showed themselves most generous in receiving graduates of foreign universities, and the Western Provinces were more willing than Ontario to accept American graduates.

The acceptance of academic qualifications by Canadian universities has been somewhat more difficult and controversial than among the licensed professionals such as medicine and engineering, which had worked out relatively clear-cut and acceptable standards of recognition. Each university is free to accept or reject the academic preparation and graduation certificates of other institutions. Initially, many universities used this freedom to the detriment of German potential students or graduates. In recent years, the Association of Universities and Colleges of Canada has assisted in developing guidelines for equivalent academic statuses of university graduates outside of North America. Although these guidelines are in the form of recommendations, they have contributed significantly towards a more uniform acceptance of academic credits earned abroad. During the period of expansion of Canadian universities from 1960 to 1970, Canada invited a large number of foreign graduates to staff the universities of the country. The majority of these graduates came from the United States and the United Kingdom, but there was also a significant number of graduates from universities of German-speaking countries. These graduates sometimes found that their academic preparation and degrees were not fully accepted, since the continental European pattern of education does not completely coincide with the patterns of Anglo-Saxon countries. After some negotiation however, about recognition of academic degrees, graduates of German-speaking universities encountered few difficulties in being accepted on a basis of their academic background.

The fairly generous treatment of German academic and professional degrees and certifications is in contrast to the treatment of Canadian academic and professional experience in the Federal Republic of Germany. The German authorities have a low opinion of Canadian academic standards, and make it difficult for Canadian professionals to work in Germany.

German-educated professors can be found in almost all Canadian universities, whether in English or French language institutions. They are not confined to departments of German but are found in almost all departments and faculties, except faculties of law. It is not necessary for professors of law to be members of their provincial bar associations, but few teachers are conversant with both the Anglo-Saxon and European continental legal traditions. While there is no restriction in the acceptance of German-trained graduates, the long period of apprenticeship and the system of examinations discourage the entrance to this profession.

THE GERMAN LANGUAGE SCHOOLS*

In contrast to the United States, where German religious groups have established colleges and universities under their own jurisdiction, there are hardly any colleges which reflect the German academic orientation. Until recently, Waterloo-Lutheran University, now known as Wilfred Laurier University, had some degree of orienta-

---

* Karl Heeb, Diplom-Volkswirt, Hamilton, Ontario

tion to the German intellectual and religious traditions. However, the change from a denominational to a provincially supported university diminished this influence. At one time, St. Jerome's College in Kitchener reflected the German Catholic educational tradition; it is now affiliated with the University of Waterloo and little remains of its German tradition. St. Peter's Abby in Muenster, Saskatchewan, is the centre of German settlement in the Prairie Provinces and for a while maintained a junior college. The German tradition of the College has diminished and now plays an insignificant role.

The main burden of language maintenance among the children of German-speaking Canadians and immigrants rests with the German language schools, which are maintained by the Trans-Canada Alliance of German-Canadians. There are no institutions in Canada in which German is the principal language of instruction. In public and separate schools there is hardly any German language instruction at the primary level; at the secondary school level, instruction in German is an option available in some schools. Public secondary schools are more likely to offer German instruction than separate schools.

The basis for education is Article 92 of the British North America Act of 1867, whereby education was reserved as a provincial responsibility. All provinces require attendance in schools which follow provincially approved curricula. In general, the language of instruction is either French or English. The first concern of many provinces is the acquisition of the second official language by the students.

Students in secondary schools have more language options than those in elementary schools and beginning with Grade 9 can learn other languages than the official ones. Whereas there is compulsory language instruction in the second language in many schools, parents may be able to demand that third language instruction also be provided. In contrast to the European practice of instruction of Saturdays, Canadian provinces do not require Saturday as a school day.

German language schools utilize the free Saturdays to provide instruction in the German language. There have been some exceptions, such as Windsor, Ontario, where schools teach during the evening hours. Most students in the German language schools are between the ages of six and fourteen; some schools offer instruction to students up to eighteen years of age.

Throughout Canada, there are private schools chiefly maintained by Mennonites at Gretna, Rosthern, Clearbrook, Yarrow, Coaldale, Winnipeg, Leamington and Niagara-on-the-Lake,[1] which offer intensive training in the German language. Due to the increasing cost of maintaining private schools, there has been a steady decline in the number of these schools.

Most Canadian universities offer at least undergraduate instruction in German language and literature. The larger institutions also offer advanced degrees. In recent years, there has been a changed emphasis in departments of German language. At one time, instruction in German was primarily seen as one of the available options

---

[1] Frank H. Epp, *Mennonite Exodus, op. cit.*, p. 446.

for liberal arts courses, or as preparation for passing the second-language examination required for advanced degrees. Now many universities have eliminated the language requirements for graduate degrees. On the other hand, there has been a renewed interest, not only among those of German parentage or background, in studying German as another academic subject. There has been a gradual increase in the number of students taking courses in German language or literature, although it appears that the demand has now levelled off without, however, losing any ground.

Although Canadians of German origin constitute the third largest group in Canada, after those of British and French background, Germans have a low rate of language retention. Of the approximately 1.5 million Canadians of German descent, there are fewer than 500,000 whose mother tongue is German.

During the last fifteen years, that is, since 1958, the last year of the large post World War II immigration wave, there have been tremendous efforts among Germans and German-Canadians, and in recent years by Canadian officials, to preserve the German heritage and to contribute to the growth in Canada of the folklore, art and culture of German-Canadians. Prior to this time, there were German language schools throughout Canadian history, but there were periods of war during which instruction ceased. Only the Mennonites have continued to teach and preach in the German language since their arrival in Canada, although English is equally used. They consider German as the language of worship, especially among Old Colony groups and make great efforts to preserve their religious heritage.

Number of Schools, Students, and Teachers in German Language Schools, Canada 1958–1972, by Province

Year	Alberta			British Columbia			Manitoba		
	Schools	Students	Teachers	Schools	Students	Teachers	Schools	Students	Teac
1958/59									
1959/60									
1960/61									
1961/62									
1961/63									
1963/64									
1964/65	29	1.450	87	11	500	33	24	1.100	72
1965/66	29	1.650	90	10	600	36	26	1.200	74
1966/67	33	1.740	92	8	1.383	69	26	1.300	75
1967/68				20	1.650	86			
1968/69				23	1.847	112			
1969/70				23	1.921	109			
1970/71				20	2.004	96			
1971/72	20	1.200	60	18	1.750	82	13	950	50

Education and the Preparation System 91

The following statistics have been for the school year 1971–1972 and are incomplete, with the exception of Ontario. The reports on British Columbia are accurate since 1964. Other provinces have not reported on all school activities. The trends in the development of German language schools can be best seen in Ontario and British Columbia, German language instruction in Quebec began in earnest only in 1970.

German language schools in Alberta, British Columbia, Manitoba and Saskatchewan are maintained primarily by various religious denominations. In Quebec, the Trans-Canada Alliance of German-Canadians maintains seven language schools directly. Another is supported by an unaffiliated German club. In Ontario, over fifty percent of the German language schools are maintained by German clubs, school associations and private individuals. The other fifty percent are affiliated with churches.

About fifty percent of all German language schools in Canada are in Ontario and the structure of these schools serves as a model in all the other provinces. Until 1965 and 1966, there was a constant increase in the number of schools. Since then, there has been a continuous reduction in the number of schools, but an increase in the number of students and teachers. This change can be attributed to the fact that some of the larger universities are integrating a number of the language schools into their systems. Since 1965 and 1966, rationalization has been affected, leading to the 1972 guidelines of the Trans-Canada Alliance which established minimal criteria for all German language schools. The peaking of the German language schools in 1965 also depended on immigration of German-speaking persons to Canada. There

	Ontario		Quebec			Saskatchewan			Total		
ls	Students	Teachers	Schools	Students	Teachers	Schools	Students	Teachers	Schools	Students	Teachers
	920	43									
	1.445	77									
	2.085	101									
	3.095	169									
	3.338	194									
	3.500	198									
	4.000	221	4	250	15	4	200	13	128	7 500	441
	4.440	218	4	250	16	4	220	14	129	8.360	448
	4.342	217	4	260	16	4	220	14	127	9.245	483
	4.770	238									
	5.069	238									
	5.720	316									
	5.800	315									
	5.460	302	8	800	45	1	80	4	106	10 240	543

has been a continuous decrease of German-speaking migrants with a present total of under five thousand per year. As a consequence, German language schools are no longer maintained by first-generation immigrants, but rather serve the needs of the second and later generations of Germans.

Until 1960, there were few problems in obtaining teachers for German language schools. Most of the teachers were new arrivals who gladly seized the opportunity to teach. Since 1965, the majority of the teachers have been young Canadian graduates of universities and teachers' colleges, whose mother tongue was German. Although these young teachers were familiar with the Canadian environment, it became necessary to have special courses for instructors in German language schools. The training was primarily in the form of internships with established schools.

The changeover from German-trained to Canadian-trained teachers increased the financial liabilities of the schools considerably. There were demands for professional remuneration which was not given previously to the German-trained teachers. Although the remuneration was small – between $5.00 and $9.00 per hour, and later between $10.00 and $15.00 per hour – salaries constituted a major item in the budget. The two most important training schools in Ontario were the German language schools of the Club Harmonie in Toronto and the German language school of London. Starting in 1964, there were special courses for new teachers, first at the Goethe House in Toronto and in 1971 and 1972, in Gummersbach, Germany. Each course was held for about twenty teachers and lasted two weeks. In 1973, all new teachers were invited to participate in this course. It was the hope of the organization that this course contributed significantly to improved standards.

Since 1956, there has been an increased professionalism in German language schools. Only a few schools do not use professionally-trained teachers, primarily because they are unable to pay the salaries. So far, there has been no support of German language schools by either the provincial or federal governments. However, Kitchener and London Public School Boards have taken over the language schools in their respective cities.

The quality of instruction in German language schools is primarily dependent upon the proficiency of teachers and the availability of adequate text books. New teaching methods had to be devised to attract and hold children in the schools, because the traditional approaches proved inadequate. Until the mid 1960s, most of the children spoke German as their mother tongue. Now the primary emphasis is on teaching German as a second language. As a consequence, the model used by German language schools abroad, which is based on the assumption that German is the primary language, cannot be maintained. The shift in emphasis was supported by the instructors who conducted the course for the teachers, most of whom had been teachers in classes in which German was taught as a second language.

There is a steady demand for books for the German language schools. These books are donated by the Federal Republic of Germany. Whereas at first the books were geared to the German school syllabus, they are now geared to teaching German as a second language. An increasing number of students in German language schools are not of German background, but use the opportunity to learn another language.[2] New books have to be found which take cognizance of the changing background of the students.

There is continuous concern about the facilities of the German language schools. Initially, the clubs and associations provided their own rooms. However, the growth of the schools prevented the further use of these facilities. Instead, the language schools tried to rent facilities from local school boards. Some school boards donated their facilities, while others, such as Metropolitan Toronto, charged up to $10,000 per year. The Fourth Volume of the *Report of the Royal Commission on Bilingualism and Biculturalism* recommended that facilities be provided for teaching of other languages beside English. However, since these recommendations are not binding upon local school boards, the implementation depends on the decision of each board.

The Trans-Canada Alliance of German-Canadians co-ordinates the activities of the German language schools in Canada. The various committees (school committee, professional committee, cultural affairs committee, German language instruction committee) work closely with provincial authorities and representatives of the Federal Republic of Germany to obtain the necessary means. At the federal level, the Trans-Canada Alliance of German-Canadians is recognized as the co-ordinating agency of German cultural activities.

Adult education in the German language is also conducted by the three Goethe Houses, which are directly supported by the Federal Republic of Germany and are staffed by German nationals. These houses are located in Toronto, Ottawa and Montreal. It is their intention to bring German cultural groups to Canada and present artists and performers to the Canadian public. The Goethe Houses also offer language instruction at nominal fees. The language instruction frequently competes with the extension courses offered by local universities and has led to intense rivalry between universities and the German institutes. In general, the Goethe Houses serve two groups: German ex-patriates who consider the Centre as their house for cultural activities and the members of the elite, whether German-Canadians or Canadians, who are attracted by specific artistic performances and exhibitions. There is a minimal effect on the broad base of the German-Canadian population.

With the recognition of two German states by Canada, there may be a development of new trends. There is fear among German-Canadians that the new political orientation of the Federal Republic of Germany will be detrimental to the support of German language schools. Indeed, the support has been diminished throughout the 1970s. Present cultural policies of the Federal Republic give low priority to German language education at the primary level. Instead, they emphasize the significance of German as a second or third language.

---

2 An article by Ruth Berndt, "Sonnabendschulen auf dem Abstellgleis?", *Courier-Nordwesten*, 26. Mai 1977, p. 9 discusses similar problems. According to her report, about 1,200 children attend the German language Saturday Schools in British Columbia. The Federal Republic of Germany supports these schools financially and with school material. However, there are concerns that this support will not continue in the near future.

Chapter 8

INSTITUTIONS AND SOCIAL STRUCTURE

The maintenance of alternate lifestyles rests upon the network of institutions which develop among ethnocultural groups. Some groups strive for institutional completeness, encompassing the members with a structure and normative rules. Others are satisfied with supplemental group structures and still other groups try to participate as much as possible in the general structure of the communities in which they reside. Canadians of German background participate in all the alternatives mentioned above, ranging from institutional separation to almost complete integration into society at large.

On the separation side of the spectrum are the Hutterites, Amish, Old Colony Mennonites and Old Order Mennonites. The Hutterites[1] form their own communal settlements throughout the West. They prefer the communal life with almost complete institutional segregation. A person is born a Hutterite, socialized for life in the community, learns his or her occupational roles within the colony and completes the life cycle in the colony as a retiree. The Amish,[2] while not living a communal life, practise a co-operative pattern with a high degree of segregation from the rest of the world. Old Order Amish continue their German-language tradition to the present time. Old Colony Mennonites, while not wearing the distinctive garb of the other Anabaptist groups, maintain their own way of life apart from the world outside, trading but not having personal ties outside the community. Old Order Mennonites[3] have their own institutions, but participate in the outside economy.

Among other Protestant groups, the unity between religion and ethnicity is equally evident. Whereas Anabaptist groups have maintained to a great degree the use of German as the language of the churches, other Protestants have displayed wider variations. While some immigrant congregations and General Conference Mennonites continue to use German as the language of worship, other groups have worked out compromises, such as using German in some services but also having worship services in English.

Among Roman Catholics, German language only parishes are rare. St. Michael's Parish in Windsor, Ontario serves only German background parishioners. Other Roman Catholic churches have services in the German language but also serve other

---

1 John W. Bennett, *Hutterian Brethren, The Agricultural Economy and Social Organization of a Communal People* (Stanford: 1967), Ch. 4. (Ref. also to John Hofstetler's recent book).
2 Orland Gingerich, *The Amish of Canada* (Waterloo: 1972), p. 59–70.
3 Frank H. Epp, *Mennonites in Canada, op. cit.*, pp. 259–279.

parishioners. These churches are in Vancouver (Holy Family), Calgary (St. Boniface), Edmonton (St. Boniface), Winnipeg (St. Joseph), Hamilton (St. Boniface), Kitchener (St. Mary), Ottawa (St. Albert), Sudbury (St. Boniface), Toronto (St. Patrick's), Montreal (St. Boniface). There are numerous parishes in Alberta and Saskatchewan which started as German language parishes but now use English instead.[4] Only occasionally will there be services in German.

The basis for the maintenance of German communities is the traditional unity between families, religion and ethnic associations. When all factors are present, German traits are maintained for several generations. With the absence of one or more factors, acculturation to the general English-speaking North American patterns has taken place.

One of the important factors in group maintenance is endogamy, marriage within a specified group. The Anabaptist groups practise the most rigid endogamy rules. Each of the three major groups of Hutterites, the Darius, Schmieden, and Lehrer Leute, is endogamous.[5] While marriage between members of the different Leute is not completely prohibited, such unions are frowned upon. It is also theoretically possible that Hutterites receive converts; in practice, however, the converts are not fully accepted by the members of the colony. A similar injunction against marriage outside the faith exists among the Amish,[6] who state that there should be no marriage between a believer and unbeliever, nor between members of different denominations. Old Colony Mennonites also frown severely upon marriage outside the group. Other Mennonite groups, however, allow marriage outside the denomination but encourage the members to stay within the group. Fundamentalist Protestant groups, such as the predominantly German background Apostolic Christian Church, prefer ingroup marriage, but do not excommunicate those who select their spouses outside the faith. In general, there is greater emphasis on religious than on ethnic endogamy, except that among fundamentalist groups, ethnicity and religion coincide. Among mainstream Protestants, as well as among Roman Catholics, the ethnic preference is less pronounced.

With the above exceptions, German-Canadians in general do not place great emphasis on marrying within the group. The amount of ethnic segregation is limited; most German-Canadians in urban areas live in mixed environments. Since the majority of marriages occur among those who grow up together, there is a high incidence of exogamous marriages. In 1951, among the ethnocultural groups, Germans ranked eighth in terms of inter-ethnic marriages. Only the Dutch and Scandinavians had

---

4 Richard O. W. Goertz and Alexander Malyaky, "German-Canadian Church History, Part II, Individual Congregations, A Preliminary Bibliography" in *Canadian Ethnic Studies*, University of Calgary, April 1976, Vol. V, 1–2, pp. 95–123, see also
K. Schindler C.S.S.K., "Die deutschsprachigen katholischen Kirchengemeinden in Kanada, Teil 2" in Hartmut Froeschle et al., *German Canadian Yearbook*, Vol. II, Toronto, 1975, pp. 276–284.

5 John W. Bennett, *op. cit.*, p. 123.

6 Rules and Disciplines of the Ontario Amish Mennonite Conference, Rule IX, quoted in Gingerich, *ibid.*, p. 221.

higher rates of out-marriage. In 1961, Germans ranked ninth of twelve ethnocultural groups, Poles, Russians and Scandinavians having higher rates of exogamy. The out-marriage rates of Poles and Russians are higher since both countries had relatively few migrants to Canada since the 1920s. The members of the Polish Army in Britain who migrated to Canada, also had high incidences of out-marriage. Scandinavians place little value on in-group marriage. Moreover, few Scandinavians migrated during the last few decades.[7] This pattern would be even more pronounced if the Anabaptist groups who frown upon out-marriage were not included in the comparison.

Frequently attempts are made to predict the socialization of children and their subsequent behaviour from the way in which the initial stages of infant socialization are handled.[8] The first variable involves planning of children or leaving fertility uncontrolled. Hutterites abhor birth control in any form and have the highest birth rates in Canada. Conception and child-bearing are considered pleasant events during which the mother receives a great deal of attention and relief from ordinarily assigned chores. Most Hutterite women, therefore, look forward to having as many children as possible. A similar attitude prevails among Old Colony Mennonites. Most other rural German-Canadian groups practise child spacing or birth control. The majority of urban German-Canadians also practise family planning and restrict the number of children. There are practically no differences between Protestants and Roman Catholics. In Europe, most urban families restricted the number of children, whereas families of rural background were larger; since migration, the majority of the population has accepted family planning.

The socialization of children occurs either in an urban, secular society or in a rural, more religiously oriented *Gemeinschaft* (people bound together in a group or society because of close kinship or friendship). Those who were brought up in an urban environment usually do not differ from other Canadians in their family patterns. The model family is composed of parents and two to three children. One difference, however, is the close proximity of other relatives, especially older parents and sometimes grandparents. If the parental family is intact, usually a daughter lives within walking distance. If one parent is deceased, the surviving spouse will reside with the children rather than live alone. There is somewhat greater emphasis on family continuity than is common in North America. While for a young couple to reside with the parents was quite usual among the extended farm families of Europe, in Canada such an arrangement would be a temporary situation; while, for example, one spouse was attending school, or in an emergency situation, while the breadwinner was unemployed. While living with parents is not seen as desirable, German-Canadians are frequently generous in providing their children with

---

7 Report of the Royal Commission on Bilingualism and Biculturalism, Book IV, *op. cit.*, p. 291.

8 Alex Inkeles and Daniel J. Levinson, "National Characters: The Study of Model Personalities and Socio-cultural Systems" in Gardner Lindzey, et al., *The Handbook of Social Psychology* (Cambridge: 1954), Vol. 11, p. 1010–1011.

financial assistance. There are numerous instances of parents buying their children a house as a wedding present, providing for the down-payment or at least endorsing the loan applications. This pattern might be a partial survival of the European dowry system. As a rule, German-Canadians do not give dowries now. Instead, they provide for a well endowed trousseau, *Aussteuer*. German-Canadians from southeastern Europe also provide for their children generously at weddings. While the financial outlay is considerable, the numerous invited guests are expected to be equally generous. It is not unusual for a young couple to receive from their friends and relatives between $3,000 and $5,000, even though the majority are of working-class background.

German-Canadians in rural areas are more likely to preserve some of their traditional European lifestyles than city dwellers. German farmers did not regard themselves as absolute owners of their property. It was given to them by their own parents in trust to be handed over to their children in due course. While the family unit worked together, there were clearly understood rights and obligations. If one of the partners broke these commitments, disapproval would be voiced and the offended party would be free to make his or her own arrangements. When the parents turned the farms over, the children had to provide housing and the necessities for old age. In turn, they received increasing responsibility and ultimately title to the land. These patterns were most pronounced among Amish and Mennonites, but did not originate among these groups. Other farmers of German background would act in a similar manner.

In rural families, the traditional division of labour between a man's and a woman's work remains. Outsiders frequently assume that German families are organized along patriarchal lines and rest on supreme male dominance. Among the Hutterites, this dominance is loudly proclaimed[9] but it is also known that the women get what they want. The power of the wives is even more remarkable since Hutterite women could never use the practice of sexual bargaining to obtain their ends. Other German-Canadian groups, while acknowledging male dominance in public, are also aware of the private spheres where women rule.

In urban families, power rests with the principal wage-earner. When both husband and wife are working, there is a sharing of responsibilities. On the other hand, German-Canadian wives are less likely to be employed than other Canadians. Work during marriage is seen as a necessity rather than as personal fulfillment. Working patterns are also influenced by social class differences, except that domestic employment does not carry the stigma which Canadian society attaches to it.

Another difference between German-Canadians and other Canadians lies in the handling of domestic conflicts. Marital disagreements are less likely to be brought up into the open. Couples are prone to hide their disagreements from outsiders and are reluctant to discuss them with marriage counsellors or clergymen. When a formal breakdown of marriage occurs, it usually happens through desertion or sudden eruption of otherwise suppressed feelings.

---

9 John W. Bennett, *op. cit.*, p. 111–114.

Many German immigrants or members of religious minority groups attempt to raise their children along traditional lines, but do not always succeed. There is less permissiveness among parents, and a greater feeling of responsibility towards their children. In ethnically homogenous areas, usually in Western Canada, there are attempts to maintain these controls. For example, if a girl becomes pregnant before marriage, the young man is usually pressed into marriage. In urban areas, these pressures are more difficult to enforce; peer group counterpressures often conflicted with the discipline which parents could impose. As a consequence, instances of inter-generational conflicts have been evident among German-Canadians. Indices of these conflicts are the relative absence of adolescents of German background in German-Canadian social activities.

Only ethnic conformists – those who speak German at home – more frequently girls than boys, are eager to participate in German events. Most Germans think that the rejection of German values is due to war hostilities and the denigration of everything German by the mass media. While this might have been so for a period after the two World Wars, the propaganda in the mass media has begun to have the reverse effect. After many years of rejection of German values, in recent years there has been a renewed pride in German achievements and an increase of visits and travel to the Old Country. This could lead to a slow healing of the generational breakdown and to greater acceptance of parental values.

German-Canadian value systems do not differ greatly from those of other Canadians. They range from other worldliness seeking the heavenly Jerusalem in the Western World, to secular orientation towards the Idols of the Market Place. Some groups, such as the Hutterites, have renounced worldly goods, others, such as the Amish, frown upon conspicuous consumption and display, still others have rediscovered the Protestant ethic in the secular context. Second-generation immigrants reject the acquisitive society for the youth culture and countercultures. One German immigrant has tried to be the town jester of Vancouver; he, however, has been looking for economic security. Without the support of the Canada Council, he would or could not operate. There are small groups, such as the Baltic Germans, who attempt to re-live the past; a minutely elaborated code of conduct regulates their behaviour. There is strong emphasis on in-group marriage or at least equality of status marriage. Personal disputes are settled by a "Court of Honour" – *Ehrengericht* – an arbitration committee which judges infringement of the traditional behaviour code.

Baltics are supposed to participate in annual social events which are conducted with punctilious protocol.

Some believe in the value of an extended family, others are lone adventurers, such as Frederick P. Grove,[10] who seek in Canada a new beginning. Those who live a rural life follow the cycle of the seasons, highlighted by the events of the farm year and the lifestyles of the small communities. The majority of German Cana-

---

10 Frederic P. Grove, *In Search of Myself* (Toronto: 1974).

dians, as other Canadians, live in urban clusters within the areas of emergent Canadian megalopolis.

In a rural society, identities changed slowly; patterns, once established, continued throughout the generations. In an urban context, there were continuous shifts, sometimes dictated by changes in the economic structure, sometimes created by the circumstances of the moment. In the nineteenth century, German-Canadians felt themselves welcomed as pioneers. Most came from rural backgrounds and moved again into a rural society. Adaptation to the new world was gradual. Many of the folkways continued, modified only slowly by the impact of social change.

In this century, Germans have undergone the traumatic experiences of two World Wars and also the shift in attitudes towards Germans from friendliness to hostility, from tolerance to rejection and again from grudging acceptance to welcome as an addition to Canadian pluralism. These shifts in attitudes were seldom caused by the value systems displayed by German-Canadians or by their behaviour within Canada; they were consequences of the political and economic forces in motion at a given moment.

The various attitudes in the dominant society are mirrowed within the minority. Pre-World War II immigrants wanted to keep their distance from post-war migrants whom they considered tainted by the events of the intervening years. This subtle differentiation within the group made no difference to the outside.

Germans in Canada easily learned to communicate in English, and sometimes in French. Even the groups with extensive language maintenance patterns, such as the Anabaptists, are usually bilingual. Language maintenance seems to be based, among other variables, on status considerations.

Through the adaptation to the anglophone society, and in some instances to francophone cultures, Germans were unable to develop institutional completeness except for otherworldly groups. The fate of German-language newspapers demonstrated this point. If there were a distinctive and separate system of German-Canadian values and identities, the impact of news media as a means of language and cultural group maintenance would be strong. In general, the newspapers eked out a precarious existence. Rather than developing a separate society, German-Canadians lived in transitional groups which borrowed their values heavily from the old and new countries. Most groups tried to mediate between conflicting values and loyalties, the European heritage versus the Canadian experience. In times of economic prosperity, German clubs and associations were hardly able to maintain themselves. In times of economic adversity, such groups flourished because of the need for mutual aid and togetherness.

German-Canadians in the West depended primarily upon their churches to provide them with the values and guidelines for everyday living. A few were little attuned to life in the cities. When forced to live in this alien environment, they formed their own little communities, such as Mennonites in Winnipeg.

Pre-World War II immigrants continued to suffer from the Depression mentality. Post-war migrants had lost their belongings, sometimes twice, and came to Canada in penury. Both groups were willing to sacrifice immediate gratification for economic security in the future. Acquisition of lands and goods became ends in themselves.

The children of the migrants did not share the experience of deprivation and seldom cared to go through similar hardships to gain economically. In this attitude, they were joined by recent newcomers from Germany who were the products of the period of prosperity.

Many German-Canadians consider education as a value in itself. Knowledge is held in high regard. There is, in contrast to Germany, little regard for knowledge in an abstract sense. Rather, there is strong emphasis on knowledge for specific purposes, such as for professions and occupations. There is respect for economic status and security.

Many Germans strive to follow middle-class lifestyles, aspiring to this status and absorbing the generally held middle-class values. Germans tend to be more conservative rather than socially innovative. Due to instant communication throughout the developed countries, a remarkable degree of convergence of value systems has emerged. The big differences and contrasts are not between one developed country and another, but between these and the "Third World countries."

The majority of the descendants of the German pioneer settlers have almost completely acculturated to their Canadian environment. Unique traits, such as names, manners of speech or self-identification can still be found, but carry little significance. Other groups try to control and slow down the acculturation process, not necessarily because of a sense of German identity but rather because of religious conviction. Most noticeable are the controlled acculturation patterns of Hutterites, Amish and Old Colony Mennonites. The Hutterites isolate themselves from the greater society and have retained their distinctive social, linguistic and religious traditions. The Amish retained the German language in Church services until the 1950s. Old Colony Mennonites use German but General Conference Mennonites use English as their language of worship.

Among twentieth century immigrants, an interesting status reversal took place. The majority of Germans who settled in Canada came from areas outside of Germany where the status of the language was high in comparison to the local tongue. The groups lived in ethnically homogeneous settlements, sometimes small enclaves in isolated areas, but they maintained their language throughout the centuries. For example, in the Baltic States, German was the language of the elite and as such was assiduously maintained. It was thought that these groups with a long tradition of minority language preservation would continue the tradition in Canada. However, this did not happen. Immigrants to Canada have, unless they belong to religious minority groups, low ancestral language retention. The first generation used German and was moderately fluent in English, the second generation used English with moderate mother tongue retention. The third generation had lost their knowledge of German altogether. Sometimes, the third generation children of native-born parents have sentimental attachment to Germany. To a limited degree, this phenomenon occurred in Lunenburg County, Nova Scotia and in Kitchener-Waterloo, Ontario.

The descendants of the early German settlers showed a great deal of interest in the architecture and handicrafts of their ancestors. Lunenburg houses and Tamcook Island dolls are Nova Scotian examples of this. The Kitchener-Waterloo *Oktoberfest* serves a similar function, going beyond the mere celebration of a beer festival. Yet these manifestations are superficial leisure time phenomena rather than deep attachments to the values of forefathers. Post-World War II migrants, seared by the personal tragedies of that time, have wholeheartedly embraced the new world society. Even those who came as adults rather than children and are recognizable by their accents prefer Canadian ways to the European ones and use English more often than German.

In the acculturation process, several stages of adjustment can be observed among newcomers. The first generation, those who came after the age of sixteen, retain most of their old world socialization patterns and usually speak English with a distinctive accent. For them, the old world is seen through the eyes of observers, whose sense of time has been frozen at the period of arrival in North America. They will seldom experience complete integration into Canadian life. Only an open society, such as is attempted by the policies of multiculturalism, or a society which is primarily composed of immigrants, can offer a new sense of identity. If the immigrants have rejected the "old world society", there is a feeling for strong emotional identity with Canada. Some leading Canadian nationalists are immigrants of German background who left Europe behind in anger and found Canada their home and passion.[13]

The countries of origin also underwent changes. Most of the migrants consider these to be unreal and understand little of them. In many cases, immigrants who came to Canada after the age of thirty-five were unable to learn the basic language skills that were necessary to function effectively in this country. Unless they found a niche in their own ethnocultural group, such as supplying the physical or spiritual needs of the community, they experienced loss of status, alienation and isolation. Many gave up and returned to the Federal Republic of Germany.

Most German immigrants arrived before the present training program in English as a Second Language. They had to find employment in order to survive. Occupational adjustment was a painful process which helped or hindered in other phases of acculturation.

After obtaining a foothold in a new career and environment, immigrants attempted to consolidate their economic position. Usually, they saved to make a down payment on a house and started acquiring North American gadgets and con-

---

11 Orland Gingerich, *op. cit.*, p. 185.
12 William L. Warner and Leo Srole, *The Social System of American Ethnic Groups* (New Haven: 1954).
13 This applies especially to pre-World War II refugees who as symbols of their identity changes, changed their names. For example, Franke to Franklin, Neumann to Newman, and Pick to Prentice.

veniences. One difference remained: German immigrants distrust credit operations and usually relied on credit purchasing only for major items, such as automobiles and housing. There was less reliance upon the disposable society but greater emphasis on conspicuous display of wealth. Symbols of affluence were cherished; ridicule was reserved for those who acquired these on borrowed money. After several years of hard work, the German immigrant felt more secure and started to identify himself with his own subculture, mostly regional rather than national, or with special interest groups. While special interest groups, such as sports groups or folk-dance groups frequently have an ethnic orientation, expertise in the special interest area is more important. A soccer player of Italian or Yugoslavian background is easily accepted in a nominally German team. Otherwise, he is a Russian-German, a *Schwabe* or a *Reichsdeutsche Landsmannschaften* take precedence over all ethnic identification. There is a certain degree of nostalgia towards the homeland, especially after an improvement in status. Sometimes this nostalgia is so strong that he longs for the German *Gemütlichkeit* and returns home. While the return visitor is treated in a friendly manner, the returnee soon gets the full impact of the competition in the labour market. Even if work is available, social stratification is more pronounced and many returnees are unhappy. It is difficult to obtain adequate housing and the level of prices in relation to income is higher in Germany. To their dismay, returnees are not welcomed with open arms and they discover that Canada was not such a bad place at all. Anthony Richmond[14] in a study of British migrants calls the process of returning home for the purpose of resettlement "the thousand dollar cure." Germans' experience is similar. Upon returning to Canada, these immigrants consider themselves as Canadians rather than as Germans.

In the period after World War II, Germans were eager to become Canadian citizens as soon as the law permitted them to do so. Many refugees were stateless and welcomed the protection of Canadian citizenship. Even immigrants with West German passports were quick to apply for Canadian citizenship. Since the economic recovery of the 1960s, Germans are reluctant to exchange their German passport for a Canadian one. For some, a German passport is a safety blanket to be used to return to the Federal Republik in case of economic failure in Canada. This phenomenon has gained greater importance in the 1970s. Canadian citizens of German background found that the Federal Republic is correct but restrictive in the treatment of former citizens. There is no right to return permanently to Germany, work permits are difficult to obtain and non-German citizens are the first ones to be laid off. German authorities show little generosity towards citizens of countries outside the European Economic Community. German pension laws discriminate against non-German citizens. Those who can expect German pensions suffer greatly when they take out Canadian citizenship.

Of course, there are those who retain their German passports because of strong

---

14 Anthony Richmond used this term "tongue in cheek" in an unpublished paper at the meeting of the Canadian Learned Societies in Sherbrooke, Quebec, in 1966. Also Anthony H. Richmond, *Post War Immigrants in Canada* (Toronto: 1967), p. 176.

personal attachments to the homeland. Some of the most ardent German citizens residing abroad are those who have suffered discrimination because of their German nationality. In this case, they cling more stubbornly to their Old Country background and identification. Germans do not possess dual citizenship. There is no right for former Germans to return and there is no automatic regaining of German citizenship except for victims of National Socialist persecution between 1933–45.[15]

One deterrant towards applying for Canadian citizenship is the attitude of many Canadians and even officials towards naturalized citizens. Full equality between naturalized and natural-born citizens is still a goal rather than a reality. In times of stress, citizenship status becomes subordinated to real and imagined threats by minority group members.

German-Canadians who were born abroad and came to Canada as children or juveniles quickly adjusted to the new environment. In lifestyles and behaviour patterns, they are indistinguishable from second-generation immigrants who were born in Canada of foreign-born parents. Second-generation German-Canadians are in a marginal position. On the one hand, they see themselves as Canadians; on the other hand, they carry their own heritage and background along. Those who have experienced rejection and discrimination because of their German ancestry turn to strong emotional identification with things German and with Germany or Austria or Switzerland. Most try to compromise between old world and Canadian patterns. While participating in some cultural activities of their group, they have adapted themselves to Canadian ways. In some instances, the adaptation has negative consequences. Whereas German immigrants are economically quite successful, their children do not subscribe to the same degree of deferred gratification as their parents. Other difficulties arise in cases of attempted upward social mobility. Canadian social mobility is frequently based on sponsorship by high status persons or peers, rather than on competition. Since immigrant families are seldom knowledgeable about the intricacies of the Canadian social structure, their children are unaware of the extent of the covert selection processes. Instead, they rely upon formal education, often selecting the proper course of study but seldom the appropriate institution with the in-group network. As a consequence, children of immigrants seldom reach positions of influence and power, but remain at best in middle-class status positions. The exceptions are those parents or children who soon recognize the successive steps required for further advancement.

In the classical study of the Polish immigrant in Europe and America, W. I. Thomas and Florian Znaniecki[16] discussed how immigrants from rural areas who had been firmly integrated into the folkways of the old country lost their orientation in the new world until other control patterns emerged which served as guidelines. Migration to Canada in earlier times was group migration, mostly under deno-

---

15 *Grundgesetz für die Bundesrepublik Deutschland* (München: 1956), Article 116, p. 43, 44.
16 W. I. Thomas and Florian Znaniecki, *The Polish Peasant in Europe and America* (New York: 1927), 2 Vol.

minational auspices. Leaders were able to retain a great deal of control over the members of their group even to the detriment of individual migrants. The Old Colony Mennonites were able to retain control over their members in Europe and North America. They followed for a long time the patterns of government which were evolved in Imperial Russia. When civil government was established in Manitoba, some adjustment difficulties occurred, but in general traditional controls remained effective. The strength of the control patterns were demonstrated in the 1920s, when Old Colony leaders were able to induce about 6,000 followers to migrate to Chihuahua, Mexico. This exodus created deprivations for the members but increased power for the leaders.

The same high degree of informal control exists among the Hutterites, who maintain their social order without resorting to government support or allowing more than minimal government interference. There is controlled adjustment to the worldly patterns of a secular society. The Amish also resort to informal control and avoid the legal forms of government. Similar reliance upon primary group control by small rural denominations, usually of the fundamentalist type had little success in maintaining the accepted old country patterns.

Lutherans and Roman Catholics although they had sponsored group migrations into rural settlements could not hope to exercise this degree of control over their members. In general, Lutheran communities were more conservative and have continued to maintain the traditional authority of the Church leaders.

Control patterns among German Roman Catholics broke down in less than one generation in urban areas, and less than two in rural areas. At first, immigrants were subjected in English Canada to strong assimilative pressures to the Irish form of Roman Catholicism. At a later time, the general breakdown of traditional ecclesiastic authority after Vatican II accelerated this pace. Social control is now exercised in an informal manner by neighbours and peers.

Roman Catholics of German background were in a difficult position. In Ontario, territorial and national parishes lived side by side. In many cases, however, the bishops wanted to end the establishment of national parishes. Until 1975, in Toronto, national parishes were seen as institutions with limited significance. In that year, a dramatic reversal occurred. Toronto was recognized as primarily a city of immigrants with native Canadians living in the suburbs. The services to Roman Catholic immigrants, including the Churches, were placed under the jurisdiction of an auxiliary bishop, an immigrant himself.

The Diocese of Hamilton gives scant consideration to services other than in English. Hamilton and Kitchener have German-language services, but in Kitchener, for example, German Catholics cannot even lay claim to churches built and financed by German Catholics and are restricted to the partial use of one church. The German-speaking priest is considered to be the associate pastor rather than the senior curate. The other dioceses in Ontario offer German-language services, some on an occasional basis, some in a more permanent way.

In Western Canada, almost all parishes are organized along territorial lines, although some parishes, such as St. Joseph, Winnipeg, serve primarily German

Catholics. St. Peter's Abbey, in Muenster, Saskatchewan, was formerly the centre of German Catholic activities. Little of this tradition remains in 1976. While services in the German language are available throughout the West, little organizational support is offered. One bishop in British Columbia is of German background and speaks the language fluently.

The Church hierarchy in the Federal Republic of Germany is concerned with the availability of German-language services and parishes and has endeavoured to support the churches by supplying liturgical books and material. Without the active support of the German Episcopate, German-speaking Roman Catholics would move rapidly towards assimilation. The German Episcopate has been unable to supply an adequate number of German-speaking priests. The papal constitution, *Exsul Familia*,[17] which was designed to regulate the rights of migrants to receive religious services and comfort in the mother tongue, has been more or less ignored by local Canadian bishops. Vatican II resulted in a shift of focus of power from Rome to local bishops and the Canadian Catholic Conference. While beneficial in many other areas, this shift has been detrimental to linguistic minorities within the Roman Catholic Church. No longer does their appeal to Rome carry any significant weight.

Roman Catholics are approximately one-third of the population of German-Canadians. All others, when professing membership in a religious denomination, are Protestants and Anabaptists. In the West, the number and percentage of Protestants and Anabaptists increases. Roman Catholics are less than twenty-five percent.

In Alberta, small Protestant sects exercised a great deal of influence, larger than their numerical strength indicated. Most Protestants belonged to the Lutheran and United Churches with Baptists third in numbers. In British Columbia, where Catholics among German-Canadians are a small minority, Lutherans and United Church members are predominant.

The Lutheran churches form the largest denominations of German origin in Canada. Slightly fewer than one-half of the Lutherans in Canada are of German background. German Lutherans came to Nova Scotia with the first settlement of "foreign Protestants" in Halifax and Lunenburg. There are 15 German Lutheran congregations alone in British Columbia, 35 in Alberta, 62 in Saskatchewan, 25 in Manitoba, about 10 in Ontario, one in Quebec and one in Nova Scotia.

The Lutheran churches in Western Canada had a two-fold orientation towards Germany and the United States. At first they were the churches of the German immigrants,[18] which stressed the unity between religion and language. The Lutheran churches and their colonization societies contributed significantly to the settlement of the West. In the early days of colonization, until World War I, they gave the main direction to the settlers and provided the principal link with the world-at-large. After World War I this pattern continued but slowly gave way to a more

---

17 Apostolic Constitution, Exsul Familia of August 1, 1952. See *Exsul Familia, The Church's Magna Charta for Migrants,* Edited by Rev. G. Tessaralo (New York: 1962).
18 Heinz Kloos, "Das Luthertum in Kanada", Stuttgart: Institut für Auslandsbeziehungen, *Mitteilungen,* Juli-September 1957, 7 Jahrgang, Nummer 3, p. 210–11.

secular approach and lay leadership because more decisive in the affairs of German background colonies. Most of these colonies did not receive new migration waves. Congregations changed from the churches of immigrants to those of the native-born. The language of worship also changed to English. German-speaking pastors were the main leaders in language maintenance but they, too, gave way to predominantly English-speaking clergymen. One reason for the change was the close affiliation between Lutheran churches in the United States and Canada which had a greater impact than co-operation with Germany. The two wars accelerated the process of affiliation. The Lutheran churches at first became an extension of their American parent bodies. Only in recent years are the three Canadian Lutheran churches moving towards greater independence from their parent organizations. Canadian Lutherans are trying to unite into the Lutheran Council in Canada as a co-ordinating group rather than stressing the uniqueness of each branch as in the United States. However, as late as 1959, the impact of American sectarianism became evident when Waterloo Lutheran College was scheduled to become the core of the newly founded University of Waterloo. All was set when the parent church, the Lutheran Church in America, vetoed the merger. For fourteen years, Waterloo Lutheran University remained the only denominational university in Ontario. In 1973,[19] the university gave up church affiliation and became Wilfred Laurier University.

In the 1970s, Canadian Lutheranism has limited contact with the Lutheran Churches in Germany. There is less support either in manpower supply or subsidies than given by the Roman Catholic Church. The Lutheran Church in Germany has no formal program under which ministers are sent abroad to German-speaking congregations.

Lutherans of German background are pietistic rather than oriented towards social activities. As a group, they are somewhat reserved and inward-looking. In Canada, there are few attempts at social action, apart from immigrant aid during the major immigration waves. While not opposed to co-operation with other churches, there is little emphasis on ecumenical activities. Individual Lutheran congregations are relatively active in language maintenance and are among supporters of German language schools. This again is in marked contrast to the assimilative tendencies of the Roman Catholic Church towards German Roman Catholics.

The United Church of Canada also has a small German background component, the Evangelical and United Brethren, who joined the Church in 1968. Most congregations were located in southwestern Ontario. Besides these, there are a few immigrant congregations which have after a few years changed from German to English as the language of worship.

Among German-Canadians, Baptists were a small minority. From the nineteenth century onward, German Baptist churches existed in Canada, primarily in Grey and Bruce counties in Ontario. When Baptists started to migrate to Canada in larger

---

19 Other presently existing denominational colleges and universities are federated or affiliated with publicly supported universities.

numbers, the older settlers insisted on retaining their own congregational identity and did not unite with the newcomers. The new migrants came primarily from East and West Prussia, Poland, and Russia, few *Reichsdeutsche* belong to the Baptist Faith. In 1976, there were about fifty immigrant Baptist churches with services in the German language.[20] The once important Moravian Brethren Church has become the smallest Protestant group in Canada. About 200 members strong, they are primarily in Alberta. A small but rapidly growing group are German background Pentecostals. There are churches in almost all metropolitan cities of Ontario and Western Canada.

In contrast, Anabaptist groups, those who believe in adult baptism, have been a numerous and important component of German-speaking North Americans from the early colonial days. The principal Anabaptist groups are Mennonites, Amish and Hutterites. South German Mennonites came to Pennsylvania after 1683 and to Canada after 1803, when they established themselves in the Grand River Valley.[21] The Amish[22] came between 1815 and 1818 and after World War II when American Amish came from Ohio. The Hutterites migrated after World War I. North German Mennonites migrated since 1874, in the 1920s, and after World War II. The impact of the Anabaptist groups is by far greater than their mere number. They have served as the main preservers of German culture and language in Canada.

Jack Thiessen sees Mennonites as having an unerring sense of direction and purpose. Their decisions where and when to migrate have been prudent and turned out to be right, if not providential as they claimed. Other students of Mennonite history do not necessarily share this opinion, especially in the analysis of the exodus of Old Colony believers to Mexico. Thiessen sees urbanization as the principal threat towards Mennonite identity. In the transition from rural to urban communities, he also sees change from a unique group to one form of fundamentalist pietistic Protestantism. Only the conservative groups appear to him as the guardians of the unique sense of identity which maintained the faith throughout the centuries. Frank Epp, Mennonite historian, sees the future in the emergence of a new identity, based not on language and *privilegium,* but on being a witness and committed to a lifestyle different from the secular society. For Epp, this unique sense of being one strand with somber colours in a multicultural society also explains the alternative ways in which the Kingdom of God can be perceived.

The division of German-Canadians along religious lines was strong in the nineteenth century and remained so, albeit diminishing, in the first part of the twentieth century. Throughout the settlement periods, first in Eastern Canada, later in the West, religion formed the mainstay of social cohesion. Most associations were organized along denominational lines, stressing the particularism of the members. Only church members in good standing were admitted to the religious organizations.

With the increasing secularization of Canadian society and the adaptation to im-

---

20 Wm. Sturhahn, DD., *They Came from East and West* (Winnipeg: 1976).
21 G. E. Reaman, *The Trail of the Black Walnut, op. cit.*
22 Orland Gingerich, *op. cit.,* p. 29.

migrant communities, the impact of religious associations, except among the fundamentalist groups, has diminished from generation to generation. At first, especially in group settlements, the religious organizations tried to provide a total lifestyle and a comprehensive service structure. With the changing characteristics of Canadian society, especially in the health and welfare field, many of these services had to adapt themselves to the new realities. Others simply closed down because of lack of funds and clientele. Now the religious groups primarily serve the spiritual needs of their members and have withdrawn from the areas of social services. They are also increasingly withdrawing from the support of educational institutions, except those directed solely towards the maintenance of religion. Religious associations show some strength in the Prairie Provinces, but seldom exceed the confines of a region. National associations of religious groups among German-Canadians are weak.

Group patterns based on the region of origin, the *Landsmannschaften,* elicit a high degree of loyalty among their first-generation members, but lose their impact in the second generation. Somewhat more successful are the associations based on social class. Among these are German-Canadian business and professional associations, associations for the preservation of music and German culture, and art societies. Most of these groups represent the aspirations of an emerging middle class or of a re-established middle class. Corresponding working class groups are soccer teams, hobby groups, and recreational clubs, such as Mardi Gras Societies. In these groups, the main emphasis is on the activity as a focal point and conviviality as the desired by-product.

Slightly apart, yet intimately interwoven with the above groups, are the singing societies, musical groups and folkdance associations. These groups maintain the musical or dancing heritage of the region from which they came, but also adapt to Canadian requirements. For example, all German dancers do not follow the Bavarian style, yet the majority of German dances performed in Canada are Bavarian.

Many outside observers consider the folk-art activities as the core of the maintenance of culture and enjoy the intricacies of music and dance. The maintenance of tradition and culture, however, is more than the occasional appearance of performing groups. While these groups add a great deal of colour and express symbolically their origin and heritage, their activities symbolize all other activities designed to maintain a separate identity in the new land.

In the metropolitan areas of Canada, multi-purpose clubs which originated in the 1930s or shortly after World War II are usually centred around large physical facilities. In many ways, these multi-purpose clubs are federations of special sub-groups. Throughout the year, the clubs provide a wide range of activities, from hobbies, sports and recreational patterns to organizing travel groups and performing social services. In recent years, the multi-purpose clubs have undergone considerable change. At one time, especially during the early periods of adjustment to the new environment, the clubs served all the needs of the new arrivals and helped them to become accustomed to the new land. At that time, the members built large facilities which could only be sustained if all members used them on a regular basis. With the growing adjustment to the new world, and the virtual standstill of immigration to

Canada by German-speaking persons, the patronage of the clubs has decreased while the expenses of maintaining the facilities have risen considerably. Some clubs have tried to compensate by widening the basis for membership, allowing all interested persons, whether German or non-German, to take part. Others have expanded into commercial catering and rental of halls for special events.

Many of the clubs are in financial difficulties, which have created a crisis among the members.[23] Some members wish to retrench to an exclusively German organization. This would mean the sale of all facilities and the establishment of the clubs on a more modest scale. Others hope to increase the activities in order to generate the revenues necessary for the continuation of the clubs. Increased activities, especially when they are designed to attract the general public, frequently create friction with the policies of provincial liquor licencing boards or commissions. They frequently compete with other licensed premises and are frowned upon by the regulatory agencies which impose numerous conditions upon the struggling clubs. When these conditions are ignored, cancellation of licences and other sanctions follow. Provincial governments in turn have to walk a tight rope mediating between the interests of conflicting groups and activities.

It may well be that the time for large all-purpose clubs for German-Canadians is coming to an end. Instead of unity of language as the basis for organization, there seems to be an increasing differentiation along specific rather than general lines. There is increasing social class differentiation among German-Canadians. At one time, almost all newcomers lived in limited circumstances. Now there is a broad spectrum, ranging from wealthy to poor. Cultural interests during times of relative prosperity become more significant than class interests. This phenomenon reverses in times of economic stress when class issues become paramount.

In the early settlements, leadership was provided by religious functionaries since religion played an important part in the life of German-Canadians. The traditional leaders of the German community were the clergy and the teachers. Guidance by the clergy provided the first point of reference to the new arrivals, who saw in them the continuation of old world patterns. However, the role of the clergy in Canada, as compared to the homeland, had changed. Their main roles in the homeland centred primarily around liturgical services. In Canada, however, their roles were those of counsellor, pastor and comforter. Another important function was the maintenance of the religious and ethnic group. Membership was no longer enforced by tradition or law; instead it depended upon persuasion and appeals to loyalty. A few clergymen saw their role primarily as preservers of the group, fearing contact with other members of this pluralistic society. They hoped that if its members were kept in isolation, the group would be maintained without contamination. Some leaders went so far as to encourage emigration to another land to preserve the purity of the faith; for example, some of the Old Colony Mennonites in 1923. Hutterites living a communal life also try to control contact with outsiders. Their

---

23 Rudy Herbst "Die Rede des Praesidenten am Versammlungsabend zur Kenntnis für alle Mitglieder, die nicht anwesend waren", in *Harmonie Nachrichten* (Toronto: 1973), p. 3–4.

policies seem to be one of minimal acculturation, only giving way under extreme pressure.

With the increasing adjustment by immigrants to Canada, the leadership of the clergy diminished considerably, especially in areas peripheral to divine service. Instead, the leadership of the groups shifted to other persons. Like the clergy who saw their role as ethnic preservers, there were leaders who tried to preserve as much as possible the patterns of the old world. These leaders, frequently of high status according to homeland criteria, tried to interest German-Canadians in the maintenance of their heritage, especially in literature and the performing arts. Quite frequently, these leaders came to Canada as middle-aged adults and were unable to learn fluent English. Some were political refugees who had left their homeland because of persecution and exile. Their point of reference was the homeland of their ideals rather than the reality of the present. For German-Canadians, the largest pre-War refugee organization was composed of Sudeten-Germans.

At local levels, the second category of leaders emerged from the various activities. Through the leadership of local groups, they grew more and more into the activities of German-Canadian associations until they became recognized not only at the local level but in national organizations. In this group are those whose primary experience lies with German-Canadian organizations with limited contact with other ethnocultural groups. These leaders represent primarily the group interests and the maintenance of their specific activities.

The leadership of the Trans-Canada Alliance of German-Canadians at one time represented a mix between successful local officers of German clubs and persons accorded high status because of academic accomplishments. These leaders in turn were replaced by business executives who attempted to shape the Trans-Canada-Alliance into an economic political pressure group. As a consequence, there was a great deal of controversy among the constituent groups. Many German-Canadian organizations preferred to work outside the umbrella group.

A third category of leaders originated from the world of work and commerce. They were union leaders, successful businessmen or recognized professionals. By virtue of their accomplishments in their chosen fields, they were recognized by those outside their sphere of immediate influence. During the period of their upward mobility, these leaders had little contact with German-Canadian clubs or activities. However, because of their success in the outside world, they were again approached by the German groups to represent their interests to the public and the governments. These leaders can be found in multicultural activities and in mediating roles between the wishes and demands of the group and the structures of the larger society. Their services are in special demand for the solution of crises and conflicts. These leaders also co-operate actively with similar leaders of other ethnocultural communities. They are recognized as mediators as long as they are able to respond to at least some of the demands of the sponsoring group or can avert disaster. Should they be unsuccessful, the sponsoring group will readily disclaim them. In contrast to the group's executive, who have spent long hours in the service of the cause, the mediator was slowly impelled into his present status. Quite often a mediator was elected into the general power structure of the community and recognized as a spokesman for ethnic groups before the group itself was willing to grant the same recognition.

Somewhat apart from these leadership patterns are those performed by the executives of German-owned multi-national organizations.[24] German societies frequently ask for help from these organizations to sponsor special events or to salvage precarious financial situations. In most instances, the contributions of the Canadian branches of German-owned enterprises to German-Canadian life have been minimal. With the possible exception of one or two multi-national companies, these organizations have contributed little to Canada, except their business activities. There are no foundations developed by these companies to support charitable or cultural activities in Canada. Not even their parent companies' foundations have supported German-Canadian or Canadian activities and endeavours to any significant degree.

Two principal factors seem to influence the patterns of intergroup relations: the relative status of a group within the Canadian social order, and the degree of group cohesion.

The status within the Canadian social order is determined by the status of the country of origin of the immigrants as well as by the behaviour of members within Canada. In general, Canada follows the preferential system ennunciated by Emory Bogardus[25] and W. L. Warner.[26] High group status is accorded to northwestern European Protestants, Catholics, non-Christians, natives of Central Europe, the Mediterranean Countries and the other non-industrialized areas of the world. An immigrant can modify this attitude somewhat; more often however, group ascription permeates the treatment the person receives.

The degree of group cohesion allows an ethnocultural group to improve its standing somewhat. By control of the members and assiduous cultivation of the values of Canadians in general, a group is able to change its relative status gradually. Of course, group statuses no longer enjoy the legal standing which were once accorded to them in immigration law and regulations. However, they still find popular acceptance.

German-speaking Canadians underwent significant changes in intergroup relations, especially during the twentieth century. In the nineteenth century, the general attitudes of the majority of Canadians as well as the behaviour of the minority were in accord. German-speaking groups were able to obtain concessions from the government, such as the Mennonite privileges. At the same time, German-Canadians participated in political decision-making. Only fragmentation along regional and religious lines prevented concerted group action. In most cases, alliances were formed on ad

---

24 The annual membership roster of the Canadian German Chamber of Industry and Commerce contains the names and officers of these multinational corporations.
25 E. S. Bogardus, *Immigration and Race Attitudes* (Boston: 1928).
26 W. Lloyd Warner and Leo Srole, *The Social System of American Ethnic Groups, op. cit.,* p. 283–96.

hoc bases and broke up once a specific goal was obtained. Up to World War I, there was primary concern about the privileges of a specific group and little emphasis was placed on universal rights and freedoms.

World War I changed this situation in a traumatic way. German-Canadians reacted to the changed circumstances with panic or naivete. The *Deutsch-Kanadischer Provinzialverband von Saskatchewan*[27] displayed this naivete when they appeared as lobbyist before the Federal Government and in 1916/17, when they solicited $5,000 to $10,000 for a propaganda and defence fund. The reaction of the authorities was predictably negative. Old Colony Mennonites were helpless when they were equivocated with other German-speaking groups and subject to great suspicion because of their opposition to conscription. Throughout the 1920s, German-speaking Canadians were subject to virulent attacks with little organized resistance or awareness of the importance of civil rights and general equality.

In the 1930s, The German Reich practiced her own theories of intergroup relations which most Canadians found abhorrent. In spite of strong opposition to these practices, however, little was done to help the refugees. At first Canadians considered National Socialism to be harmless and the propaganda had some impact in Canada, especially Quebec. Most Canadians were appaled by the crudeness of the approach and the blatant propaganda moves.

German Canadians reacted to the period of the 1930s with a mixture of acceptance of National Socialism and extreme scepticism borne out of the lesson from the past. In a period of depression, the seeming success of National Socialism to reduce unemployment, was admired. Another appeal based on the unity of all German speaking people regardless of boundaries or citizenship also found willing acceptance. Some German Canadians even returned to Germany to live in a country which could solve the unemployment problems, only to be swallowed up by mobilizations of World War II. Others, however, learned about the treatment of dissidents and minorities and severed all ties with Germany. In some ways, German associations benefitted from the increased ethnic awareness created by the propaganda network. Partially due to the depression and partially due to alienation, they huddled together in their clubs. Many of these clubs served as social centres but others helped the new immigrants of the late 1920s to survive the economic hardships of the 1930s.

World War II did not see a repetition of the mass hysteria. German-Canadians had openly dissociated themselves from the Nazi cause. But after the War, virtually all German-speaking Canadians were seen as Nazi and experienced prejudice and discrimination on a wide scale. Whereas World War II created a renaissance of the concept of civil liberties and was the beginning of the codification of principles of human rights and the treatment of minorities, but seldom was extended to German-Canadians.

---

27 Werner Entz, "Der Einfluss der deutschsprachigen Presse Westkanadas auf die Organizationsbestrebungen des dortigen Deutschtums 1889–1893", in Hartmut Froeschle, *Deutschkanadisches Jahrbuch*, Vol. II, 1975, p. 113.

German-Canadians reacted to this experience in many ways. Some denied their heritage altogether, claiming Dutch origin; some changed their names; others ceased speaking German in public. Others turned inwards, trying to rediscover the sources of the German humanism which had been buried under the debris of the war.

With the arrival of many refugees after the war from all parts of Europe, traditional dislikes and group animosities received new impetus. Victims of the Nazi persecutions still remember their sufferings, some in sorrow, some in anger and with a feeling of revenge. German-Canadians also remember their share of sorrow and grief which was not of their own making. Coming from countries outside of Germany, they usually suffered multiple persecutions and deprivations. Discrimination against German-Canadians and Germans in general occurred almost daily in the news media, especially between 1950 and 1960, up to a point when the incessant propaganda became counter-productive. Attitudes and stereotypes became muted, more engrained ones remained and became part of the folklore. Most German-Canadians were unable to counter the most blatant statements although they themselves were seldom involved in World War II activities.

With the coming of age of the post-War generation, group hatreds and dislikes lessened, became more convert or shifted to other groups and persons. Active programs advocating universal human rights, combined with greater emphasis on individual rather than collective responsibilities, lessened open discrimination.

The most important factor in the improvement of the status of German-Canadians was the economic recovery and strength of the Federal Republic of Germany. With the increasing prosperity, the Federal Republic engaged in an active public relations campaign among the opinion makers. Slowly, attitudes changed between 1960 and 1970, when the impact of World War II receded.

German-Canadians are left with a sense of ambivalence and bewilderment. They are frequently reminded of the heritage of hatred, wounds and death. On the other hand, they take vicarious pride in the cultural, scientific and economic achievements of post-war Germany. Some have overcompensated for the past and have espoused with great fervour the various peace movements. Others try to forget the past and work with iron determination to build a future, mostly perceived in economic terms, for themselves and their children. Some ignore the past but complain loudly about their own misfortunes and blame others for them. In this country, few German-Canadians were involved with the past, but many suffer the consequences. The most significant problems occurred in the political area. Until a few years ago, it was most difficult for a post-war German immigrant to be elected to public office. This changed, at least in Alberta, where an immigrant, Horst Schmidt, was elected to the provincial legislature and became a member of the province's cabinet.[28]

The mass media of communication still present the image of either the buffoon outwitted by ingenious allies or of the sinister conspirator who plans to take over

---

28 Sigismund Schlinger, "Vom bayerischen Jugendverbands-Sekretaer zum Kultusminister in Kanada", *Kulturpolitische Korrespondenz*, Vol. 151, 25, January 1973, p. 15–16.

the world. The Canadian Broadcasting Corporation has consistently disseminated anti-German stereotypes. For example, in one report about student unrest in Mexico, the arrival of the police was signalled with German military music. The CTV network in a multicultural program on Germans in Canada also referred to the World War II heritage of West Germans and the life of German-Canadians. It seemed that the producer was unaware that West Germans contribute less than one-eighth of the German-Canadian population.

German-Canadians have actively participated in multicultural activities and co-operated with other ethnocultural groups at local, provincial and federal levels. At local levels, German-Canadian groups usually have their own associational patterns and frequently do not need the services of multicultural centres, which are more often the domain of the smaller and less established ethnocultural groups. Yet in most communities, German-Canadians contribute to local activities.

At both provincial and federal levels German-Canadians in relation to their share of the population are underrepresented in multicultural activity. Most provincial councils have one or two representatives of German background, frequently fewer than other ethnocultural groups which are numerically smaller. The first Canadian Conference on Multiculturalism had approximately fifteen out of two hundred and forty participants of German background.[29] A similar disproportion was evident in the Second Canadian Conference,[30] and in the composition of the Canadian Consultative Council on Multiculturalism. While these boards and conferences do not necessarily require proportionate representation, nevertheless the scant numbers of German-Canadians reflect their low public profile.

Until recently, German-Canadians had avoided one of the pitfalls of present day intergroup relations — pitting French against other ethnocultural groups. But with the deterioration of the relations between the two official languages, German-Canadians have lined up against Francophones, as they did in the Essex County, Ontario, school crisis,[31] or in their opposition to the Quebec Official Languages Act of 1975/76. At the personal level, interaction between French and German-Canadians is amicable. Many South German origin Canadians speak French and value the language.

Many French-Canadians are opposed to multiculturalism as government policy and fear that it will weaken the case for bilingualism in Canada. Most German-Canadians, in contrast, hope that multiculturalism will enable them to preserve their heritage and lifestyles. This concern is strong in Western Canada where German-Canadians exceed French-Canadians numerically. Here it is hoped that the claims

---

29 The First Canadian Conference on Multiculturalism, October 14, 15, 16, 1973, list of participants.
30 *Multiculturalism as State Policy,* Second Canadian Conference on Multiculturalism (Ottawa: 1976) February 13–15, 1976.
31 This school crisis erupted because of the general opposition of the Essex County School Board to establish a francophone Secondary School. The leader of the opposition was the mayor of Kingsville, Ontario, who is of German background.

for the maintenance of the German language and cultural institutions will be respected.

A small group of francophone Germans in Quebec City has found acceptance among the emerging professional elite. These persons are especially active in international, cultural and commercial affairs. In orientation and policies they are opposed to the larger group of German executives in Montreal who have identified themselves with the anglophone business community.

Chapter 9

THE WORLD OF WORK

The early German settlers in the eighteenth and nineteenth centuries came as soldiers, craftsmen and farmers. Those who settled in the Maritimes added fishing as their livelihood. Their children did not remain on the land; they moved to the cities of the United States and Canada. Some of the descendants have reached wealth and power, for example, the late Hon. Robert H. Winters. The majority have remained in blue-collar occupations or joined the emerging middle class.

In Ontario, the minority position of the early German settlers was less pronounced than in the East. In the Grand River Valley, they formed an enclave within an otherwise Anglophone pioneer society. Once self-sufficient farmers, some became merchants or expanded their shops into small factories. Their descendants were later known as "Old Germans" to differentiate themselves from the twentieth century immigrants and their children. "Old Germans" entered the professions and politics; they held offices in their region. They also have their own socio-economic elite, centered in Waterloo, Bruce and Grey counties. This elite is composed of entrepreneurs in consumer products, professional and political dynasties such as the Wintermeyers and Eulers. The local farmers, although moderately prosperous, have not reached the status of large scale agribusinessmen.

In Western Canada, the descendants of nineteenth century settlers, with the exception of Old Colony Mennonites, have become successful farmers. Whereas the number of farm families has steadily decreased, the land farmed by each family has increased. Many farmers of German background work between five and ten sections of land. In general, the thrift and the knowledge of Prairie farming of Mennonites and members of Protestant sects have enabled them to prosper. In regions where success in farming is a race against the weather, such as the Peace River District, German farmers have remained on the land.

"New Germans" are the immigrants of the post World War I and World War II periods. Their occupational adjustment followed different patterns from the older generation. Post World War I migrants were primarily from "non-preferred countries." The immigration trains brought them to Winnipeg for further distribution on the land in the West. At first they were required to work as farm labourers and farmers. Some remained in this occupation but the majority drifted into the towns and cities after their prevailing stay on the land. The Depression of the 1930s limited their chances considerably, and there was concern about survival in any job rather than about occupational mobility. Only the post-war years gave these people the opportunities to develop.

At first, post-war refugees were also required to come to Canada as farm labourers. Farm work, however, had undergone considerable mechanization. Stoop labour available for newcomers, such as sugar beets, vegetable work and tobacco, became increasingly more seasonal. At the beginning of the winter the workers drifted into the urban centres. Fewer and fewer came back to the fields in springtime.

With the general post-war migration of the 1950s, immigrants drifted to the cities, primarily to Ontario, rather than Western Canada. Migrants to the cities experienced various phases of adjustment. At the time of their arrival, there was the immediate need to find inexpensive shelter. In the big cities, throughout the 1950s, were numerous boarding houses run by earlier German immigrants. The settlement officers of the former Department of Citizenship and Immigration and the denominational immigrant aid societies also provided temporary shelters.

Newcomers usually came with minimal language skills throughout the 1940s and 1950s. Many tried to obtain employment with German-speaking employers or jobs without language requirements. There were few opportunities to transfer directly into equivalent occupations commensurate with experience and training. Earlier migrants who were mainly farmers and craftsmen had few difficulties in transferring their skills from the old world to the new. After World War II, in contrast, immigrants experienced obstacles in being accepted by employers, unions, professional organizations and educational institutions.

In general, employers in the post-war period were willing to hire German immigrants according to the immigrants' background and experience. There were a few cases in which employers who had suffered from the effects of World War II in Europe refused to hire Germans. Some of these cases led to complaints before provincial human rights commissions.

During the main post-war migration period between 1950 and 1960, employees of German background often encountered difficulties in being accepted by their fellow workers. Several craft unions were reluctant to grant journeymen status to German immigrants. Immigrants had to submit all papers and have them translated for evaluation. If the training and experience did not fully coincide with the Canadian apprenticeship equivalent, the unions refused admittance. Under the closed-shop conditions which existed in many industries, this amounted to exclusion from jobs. Some unions also charged high fees for admittance of outsiders. Industrial unions demanded full documentation for acceptance as skilled journeymen, although in contrast to craft unions, they did not demand excessive membership fees.

As previously indicated, professional associations have practised similar exclusion policies. For a long time, the federal and provincial governments did not interfere in the practices of self-governing occupational groups. In 1967, the Trans-Canada Alliance of German Canadians submitted a Brief to the Special Joint Committee on Immigration in the Senate and House of Commons. It stated that there should be an adequate assessment of the educational equivalents between Canada and the countries of emigration.[1]

---

1 Trans-Canada Alliance of German-Canadians, *Brief to the Special Joint Commission on Immigration in the Senate and House of Commons,* February 1967, p. 3.

The problems of mutual recognition of professional and occupational levels have become less pressing for Germans. However, there were also immigrants who claimed greater occupational competence than they really had. Whenever people are desperate in the struggle for survival, they may resort to almost any means in securing their occupations. But when their deceptions were detected, they often complained bitterly about alleged discrimination.

After 1960, when immigrants were looking for employment at their level of education and background, they had given up the initial job and were somewhat familiar with their new environment. Some immigrants, especially those who came to Canada over the age of forty, were unable to find suitable employment and usually left Canada after a few years of hardship and frustration. Others had found jobs with equivalent status or had worked out alternate careers which satisfied them. They became adjusted to the new country and wanted to remain permanently.

The prosperity of the 1960s in the Federal Republic of Germany reflected itself in the development of German-owned companies in Canada. At the present time (1977), there are almost two hundred German-owned industrial companies in Canada, ranging from several thousand employees to service and import companies employing only a few workers. German investment in Canada amounts to approximately 2.5 billion dollars and represents the third largest foreign group after the Americans and British. Many German background workers found employment in German-owned multinational companies, primarily at the technical and skilled levels. German background managers can also be found among companies which have extensive business dealings with Europe. In these companies the managers act frequently as mediators between the Canadian and European point of view. Large companies, whether German or Canadian owned, are often members of the Canadian-German Chamber of Industry and Commerce. This organization is primarily financed by the German Chambers of Commerce (*Deutscher Industrie- und Handelstag*). It serves purposes similar to Canadian provincial and federal trade representatives in Europe. Canadian financial institutions exercise a great deal of influence in the activities of the Canadian-German Chamber of Industry and Commerce. The small businessmen and entrepreneurs who have developed their companies in response to local and regional challenges, are represented in the German-Canadian business and professional organizations that exist in many of the larger cities of Canada from Ontario to British Columbia.

In Canadian or American-owned industrial companies, German-Canadians find ready employment at the skilled and technical levels, less so in the clerical and managerial occupations. While they can be found in specialist positions, they are seldom among the ranks of generalists and upper echelon managers. In financial institutions, they can be found in international divisions or in services to ethnic clients. The Metropolitan Trust Company in Ontario is probably the most German oriented financial company in Canada. For some time, this company has extensive dealings with German clients and serves also as one of the main companies for European investors in Canada.

With the exception of the armed forces which accepted a sizable number of post-war migrants during the 1950s, Canadians of German background are underrepresented in the public services of the federal and provincial governments. In these occupations, German-Canadians are seldom found at the assistant deputy or deputy minister levels. Only two German background civil servants have reached this level in the federal public service in the present generation.[2] In the armed forces, Germans are underrepresented among the officers, but not among other military personnel.[3]

Among the German upper class in Canada, mainly in Ontario and the western provinces, there are three components:

1. members of the former German upper class, frequently members of the former nobility,
2. old German industrial families,
3. the *Wirtschaftswunder* elite, the Canadian executives of German multinational corporations.

Members of the former German upper class now in Canada are frequently refugees of the pre-war and early post-war period. They came primarily from eastern Europe, such as the Baltic nobility, who came from Estonia, Latvia and parts of Russia. There is a sprinkling of other members of the nobility who came directly from Germany or from places in Africa and South-America. The Baltic nobility ruled the countries for several centuries, first under the sovereignty of the Kings of Sweden, but since Peter the Great under the domination of the Russian Emperors. A strongly cohesive group with an elaborate code of personal and social behaviour, they owned the land and were government officials and officers. After the Russian Revolution, the Baltic States became independent until 1939. During that time, the nobility lost a great deal of their land and most of the political power. With the second coming of the Russians at the beginning of World War II, they were transferred to German held territory in Poland. At the end of the war, many escaped to the west, others were deported to Siberia and remained there for some time. Those who were able to flee to West Germany, having lost their property and their social status, negotiated for migration overseas. Through the intercession of the late General, Lord Alexander of Tunis, who had personal contact with members of the group[4], they were able to come to Canada in 1949–50.

Most of these were farmers and small entrepreneurs. Gradually the Baltic nobility succeeded in coming to terms with the life in the new country. Among the first generation, their social cohesion allowed them to continue their traditional pat-

---

2 John J. Deutsch and Andrew Kniewasser.
3 Report of the Royal Commission on Bilingualism and Biculturalism, Book IV, *The Cultural Contributions of the Other Ethnic Groups* (Ottawa: 1969), Table A33, p. 275.
4 Viscount Alexander of Tunis served in the Baltic States until 1920 and was asked for intercession after World War II. Robert Wendelin Keyserlingk, *Unfinished History* (London: 1948).

terns. The second generation, however, is losing the distinctive identity and adapting to general Canadian middle class patterns. In terms of income and occupational status, the members of the Baltic nobility are in middle class positions. A few, especially in Alberta, have succeeded in regaining upper class status. Others see themselves as upper class in terms of behaviour and self-identification. Due to lack of recognition by members of the Canadian upper class, this status aspiration is seldom acknowledged. Members of the Baltic nobility are active in horse breeding and horsemanship in general, occupations with frequent access to the Canadian upper class.[5]

Other members of the former German upper class are owners of medium sized companies or large scale farmers. For example, the former Maytag Ranch in the Cariboo Region of British Columbia, the largest ranch in Canada, is owned by such a family.

The Old German industrial families are the descendants of the nineteenth century settlers in Upper Canada. They form a distinctive local elite centered around Kitchener, Waterloo and Grey and Bruce Counties. The members of this elite have participated for some time in the economic and political life of their region and at the federal level. They are recognized by other Canadian elites and interact easily with the others. Usually, their ancestors were craftsmen who developed consumer goods industries such as furniture, electronics and textiles. Some descendants of these manufacturers still maintain the pietistic protestant tradition of avoiding conspicuous display of wealth and power.

The *Wirtschaftswunder* elite is composed of the executives of German multinational corporations who have come to Canada to manage the branch plants. These expatriates have the lifestyles of international executives, extensive travels overseas and display of affluence while in office. Because of their economic power, especially in the field of investments, they are easily accepted by their Canadian counterparts. While business relations are relatively easy, informal interaction is less open than among members of similar Canadian strata. For example, few German executives are admitted to clubs of high prestige in the metropolitan areas. Most interactions are confined to meetings of a semi-official nature, such as in receptions and during the infrequent visits of the company's chief executives. During one of these occasions, the executive officer and his Canadian representative entertained lavishly in the penthouse apartment belonging to the company. Most visitors came out of a sense of social and business obligation rather than enjoying a visit with old acquaintances.

There is also a small number of pre-war upper class migrants to Canada who were able to reestablish themselves in their former position. Karl Landegger in New Brunswick is an example. Others live in British Columbia and have generously supported the fine arts and education. Even now, these families have extensive contacts in Austria and Germany.

---

5 McKenzie Porter, "The Bush League Complex", *McLean's Magazine*, April 1972, p. 31.

The German Canadian upper class is not a cohesive group with a great deal of self-awareness. There is little feeling for the former European aristrocratic trait of responsibility for the overall well-being of German Canadians. It is a rare occasion when the members of the upper class will speak on behalf of concerns of German Canadians. One reason for this might be the limited identification of German Canadians with the Canadian political structure. No German Canadian occupies a symbolic leadership position in this country.

The German Canadian middle class is composed of two subgroups, upper middle class and lower middle class. The former is made up of professional, managerial and white collar workers, the latter of small businessmen and craftsmen. Some of the self-employed businessmen have become rather well-to-do. Yet in their lifestyles and in their ways of doing business, they differ sharply from those of the managerial elite. As businessmen, they operate family controlled firms based on personal experience rather than systematic management techniques. Often they have become successful by filling a need. As a consequence of the growth, new forms of management are initiated which exceed the capacities of the founders. As a result, many of these small companies were sold out during the 1970s or ceased to be successful. A few small businessmen recognize this problem and have preferred to limit the size of their company rather than instituting corporate management procedures. In their lifestyles, they have maintained a low profile.

Among professionals there are those who serve a predominantly German speaking clientele, such as medical practitioners and ministers of religion. Unless they practice a specialty for which there is a constant demand, these people find it difficult to maintain themselves outside the ethnic enclave. They seldom obtain high esteem in their professions, sit on policy making or regulatory boards or serve on public commissions. Exceptions are persons with outstanding reputations as researchers or innovators who have transcended the ethnic boundaries.

Many persons of German background can be found as professors in Canadian universities and colleges. Some have been trained in Europe, the majority received their education in North America. Outside the departments of German language, German background professors can be more often found in the newer universities and in the affiliated colleges of large universities rather than in the traditional institutions of higher learning. There are scientists with international reputation, such as the only living Nobel prize winner in Canada, Gerhard Herzberg, and there are average practitioners of their disciplines. Other post-secondary school teachers have been able to obtain their status because they have skills which are rare in Canada and for which there are no progressive levels of certified competence. This happened among teachers in colleges of applied arts and technology where European master craftsmen and technologists have found acceptance as teachers of their specialties. At the levels of primary and secondary school teachers, there have been initial difficulties in being accepted but these have been overcome. European trained teachers are receiving letters of standing for studies in other countries. Now, most teachers of German background have received their training in North American schools and universities.

In the teaching profession, Germans are frequent as teachers, but seldom reach administrative positions. Middle-range administration seems to be the ceiling which few are able to penetrate. Among the approximately sixty university presidents in Canada, only two have been of German background and these are natives of Canada. Two or three are university vice-presidents. A similar scarcity exists among German background academic deans. There has been only one president of a college of applied arts and technology who is of German origin.

Germans can be found in disproportionate numbers among skilled craftsmen and operators. Traditionally, Canada has not supplied all trades with training. A few trades could not obtain their training in Canada, others were numerically restricted. Foreign trained craftsmen have filled these voids and succeeded in Canada. In recent times, the Canadian provinces have restructured their apprenticeship systems, moving away from training by the craft unions and towards formal programs by community colleges or colleges of applied arts and technology. There is less reliance on immigration to fill potential needs. The future of skilled craftsmen is uncertain due to the potential impact of automation. Although the frequently expressed fears that automation would replace numerous skills are overstated, there is little growth in the demands for skilled personnel. An exception is the service industry which still has a growth potential in Canada. An increasing number of German craftsmen uses the opportunities open in the service field.

Many German-Canadians still live on farms. These farmers frequently belong to the small Protestant groups who consider farming as one of the preferred occupations. To these people, farming represents a calling rather than an occupation. Most farmers work for the market economy, only Hutterites strive to be as self-sufficient as possible.

There are few poor German-Canadians. Recent German immigrants who were unable to succeed in Canada returned to Germany and were absorbed in the expanded labour market of that country. Poverty can be primarily found among the elderly. Their pension has been eroded by continuous inflation and their German pension rights have frequently been ignored in spite of an agreement between Canada and the Federal Republic of Germany on Social Security.[6] Many individual requests to obtain pension credits for contributions in Europe were ignored by German authorities or interpreted narrowly. Similar experiences can be found among the Jewish victims of National Socialist persecution, now living in Canada. Many incurred permanent damage to their health. However, slow recognition of claims and bureaucratic red tape have created delays and hardships for those involved.

Another group of poor Canadians of German background are the returnees from the Old Colony Mennonite settlements in Latin America and Belize. Most of these returnees are migratory farm workers who sometimes live under conditions of great deprivation. Their parents had prosperous farms in Manitoba and Saskatchewan,

---

6 Convention on Social Security between Canada and the Federal Republic of Germany, signed Ottawa, March 30, 1971.

but the children have returned as poor and frequently illiterate peasants. Since 1970, sizable colonies of returnees have been formed in southwestern Ontario, around Waterloo County, in the tobacco region around Delhi, Ontario and in the Wheatley-Leamington areas of Essex and Kent Counties.

Chapter 10

POLITICAL IDENTITY AND EXPERIENCE

Immigrants who come to Canada from another country quite frequently use a country of reference for comparison purposes. This country of reference does not need to be the homeland of their ancestors; it can also be a country of identification. In the course of generational succession, memories about the country of origin dim and Canada is finally seen as the country of orientation and reference.

Among German-Canadians especially, the actual countries of origin are less significant than the countries of reference. The earliest settlers in New France or in the Maritimes did not see themselves as Germans, but rather as subjects of a ruler to whom they owed allegiance. Lines of demarcation were based on allegiance and religion. Only in the nineteenth century did the shift toward national identity occur. It was a gradual process, since Germans came from many lands and had little in common except a common language.

To German United Empire Loyalists, the countries of reference were Britain and the United States. Many came to North America to build a new society. Similarly, the religious refugees in the Maritimes found freedom in the new land and an opportunity to establish themselves. Germany ceased to be anything but a nostalgic reminiscence of the forefathers.

The Pennsylvania Dutch had a sense of allegiance not to Germany, but to the British Crown which offered them the chance to live their particular lifestyles. While they displayed a strong loyalty to the German language, they were not loyal to Germany in the political sphere.

The nineteenth century settlers in Ontario and parts of Quebec saw the awakening of national identity, but did not foresee the conflicts which might arise out of this situation. Laws were limited in scope and wars were fought for dynastic objectives rather than involving the passions of entire nations. The impact of wars was limited only to those who took up arms in defense of a cause.

Significant changes occurred in these attitudes as a consequence of the Franco-German War of 1870–71. That war raised great passions and created a feeling of identity among Germans. In many ways, the unsuccessful revolution of 1848 had already initiated this feeling of national identity, but fewer refugees from this revolution came to Canada. The impact of this group on Germans in the United States was considerable and was conducive to the extensive development of ethnic organizations among Germans there.

Subsequent German-speaking immigrants, such as Russian Mennonites, had a deep loyalty to the cultural patterns of their forefathers and a high rate of linguistic retention, but little identification with and interest in the fate of Germany. They considered themselves a unique group. When it suited their convenience, they did not see themselves as Germans but as Dutch, since the revered founder, Menno Simons, came from the Netherlands and some of his early followers came from the Low Countries and Friesland. A similar situation existed with the Alsatians who spoke German but identified politically with France and French political patterns. In their marginality, they followed the prevailing moods of the time: Germans during the time of German glory and Frenchmen whenever France was in ascendancy.

The period between 1870 and World War I allowed a significant degree of dualism. German-Canadians, especially Protestants, saw no conflict between their origin and the land of their choice. On the contrary, in public events the common heritage of all Germanic groups was stressed and emphasized.

When the political alignments in Europe changed and there was a confrontation between Great Britain and Germany, German-Canadians were at first confused and bewildered and withdrew from political involvement. They still felt that their loyalty to the Crown was a sufficient safeguard to protect them from harm.

The wars of the twentieth century differed significantly from previous wars. They involved the total population and required stridently proclaimed loyalty to the country. The new nationalism took ethnic origin as a simple index of allegiance. As a consequence, Canadians of German origin were seen as potential traitors and were deprived of freedoms they had taken for granted and treated as citizens without rights.

The period between the two World Wars brought to Canada new groups of Germans who came from the remnants of the Austrian Empire and from German settlements outside of Germany. Many of them had suffered the effects of rampant nationalism or of violent class struggle, as in the Soviet Union and the Baltic States. They were already geared to survival as minorities, but also saw themselves as Germans rather than as citizens of the countries whose passports they happened to possess. In Weimar Germany, concern also emerged for all persons of German-speaking background. Their persecutions in any country led to attempts at German intervention and aid. As a consequence, even groups which prior to World War I had no feeling of identity with Germany, such as the Mennonites who came in the 1920s, became strongly pro-German.

National Socialism, while claiming to speak on behalf of all persons of German language background, actually started the disintegration of loyalty based on ethnic origin. National Socialism did not recognize as Germans those who for religious or pacifist or political reasons did not accept the ideology of the Greater Germany. These were people obviously of German background who nevertheless wished fervently the defeat of that political system. Instead of loyalty based on nationality, loyalties based on political orientation, religious background and minority status became significant. World War II became a war of ideologies and the post-War periods have intensified antagonism based on ideologies or social class positions.

With the exception of Transylvania and a few isolated areas of the Soviet Union, World War II destroyed German minority settlements in Europe. Only in border regions did German linguistic groups slightly exceed the national boundaries of the two Germanies, Austria and Switzerland. Again, many refugees were unable to adjust themselves to life in Germany or Austria and were little welcomed in some areas. Those Germans, frequently stateless, saw themselves as Germans but with no home. Canada was one of the countries offering the refugees a new beginning. The countries from which Germans were expelled ceased to be the countries of reference. While refugees still speak about the life in the ancestral home regions, there is no desire to return. At best, there is a desire to get relatives to come to Canada. These refugees are Canadians with no split loyalties. The same situation prevails with the victims of National Socialist persecution. They experienced much horror themselves or had relatives who did not survive the holocaust. For these also, Germany has ceased to be the country of reference, except in a negative sense that there are demands for restitution or for the punishment of criminals.

The situation is somewhat different for those who come from the two Germanies, Austria and Switzerland. Until the recent East-West reconciliations, the Federal Republic of Germany laid claim to exclusive representation of all German nationals regardless of their region of origin. Most German-Canadians accepted this position and acted accordingly. As non-citizens, they asked for West German passports and in all official relations utilized the services of the German consulates and the embassy. In official events, representatives of the Federal Republic were honoured guests. Canadian citizens of German background saw the Bonn government as the only legitimate government of Germany. Even those of Swiss or Austrian background depended primarily on the cultural services provided by Bonn.

Because of the multicultural division of Switzerland, the country engages little in cultural relations with other nations. German-speaking Swiss Canadians depend on German or Austrian cultural assistance. Austria's external relations are on a very limited basis. Whereas Austria has career ambassadors and external trade officers, consular activities are confined to honorary consuls. As a consequence, there are few Austrian government sponsored activities in Canada. More significant are the external trade activities of Austria. The country serves frequently as a meeting and exchange post between western trading partners and COMECON (the East Block) States.

Until the last few years, the German Democratic Republic (East Germany) and Canada had most tenuous relations. Canada did not recognize German Democratic Republic passports and its citizens had to travel to Canada on a certificate of identity issued by the Allied Travel Bureau in West Berlin. Canadians travelling throughout Eastern Germany were subjected to petty restrictions and rigid controls. The situation was especially difficult for former residents of East Germany, who were subjected to arbitrary measures without recourse to diplomatic channels.

Whereas there was little dejure recognition, defacto trade and commerce were maintained. Canada traded with Eastern Germany, whose ships entered Canadian ports, especially in Newfoundland. At the same time, the German Democratic Republic tried to impress German-Canadians with their presence in Canada. One newspaper in Montreal was heavily influenced by East Berlin until it was disowned by its former sponsors. There were also bookstores which distributed East German propaganda.

The German Democratic Republic seems to be well informed about life in Canada. German-Canadians visiting that country are frequently astonished at the high degree of knowledge of even confidential material pertaining to Canada. Canada was also used to legitimate agents of the German Democratic Republic who were subsequently infiltrated into the Federal Republic.

At the cultural level, the German Democratic Republic has invited leaders of German-Canadian groups to visit the country. While there, visitors are repelled by the heavy hand of the GDR's security forces even in petty matters. It seems that the prolonged international isolation of the German Democratic Republic has created a mentality which is unknown elsewhere, even in East Block countries. Many outstanding differences remain to be settled before normal diplomatic relations are feasible.

Most German-Canadians have little love for the political and socio-economic aims of the GDR. They abhor their totalitarian approach and clumsy interventions in Canadian affairs, especially the cynicism with which their collaborators are used or discarded, whenever their usefulness has ceased. They suffer the petty regulations when travelling in the East for the sake of their families, who might be subjected to reprisals.

In their relationship to West Germany, German-Canadians who were natives of Eastern Europe shifted their attitudes towards the Federal Republic of Germany. The FRG definitely has remained the country of reference; however, the country is seen from a point in the past when they left it in search of Canada. Recent changes and re-alignments are seen with a certain degree of ambivalence.

On the one hand, there is great admiration for the economic recovery and the prosperity of the Federal Republic. There is also recognition that the increasing presence of German controlled businesses has improved the economic status of German-Canadians. There are continuous exchanges between Canada and the FRG in economic and cultural affairs. On the other hand, German-Canadians see the developments in Europe from the point of view of Canada. They recognize the increasing isolation of Canada with the disintegration of the Western Alliance into economic super-blocks, which have little room for a Canadian position except as buffers and peacekeepers.

The special concern for German-Canadians is the *detente* between the COMECON countries and Western Europe. They feel that many of their legitimate interests, especially those having to do with problems of families and property, are sacrificed for the sake of political expediency. There is further concern that the Federal Republic of Germany which has given up the claim to represent all Germans will use this as an excuse to curtail her financial commitments to Canadians. Two areas of concern seem to emerge: compensation towards victims of National Socialist persecution and payments under the Canadian-West German Treaty of Social Security.

German-Canadians are also concerned about the low degree of priority which the German Foreign Office assigns to German-Canadian relations. One of the consistent concerns is that Canada is seen as an annex to the United States and German-Canadians are seen as meltables in the Great Melting Pot, rather than as a unique group in the Canadian multicultural experience.

In general, German-Canadians would like to be recognized as a component group of Canada. They have contributed from the colonial period onward to the growth of Canada and wish to be respected for this achievement. While maintaining friendly relations with their country of reference, the Federal Republic of Germany, they see themselves as Canadians first. They are aware of the opportunities which this country offers to conscientious immigrants and to its citizens. Second and third generation German-Canadians cease to consider the Federal Republic of Germany as their country of reference. There is little which reminds them of the country of their forefathers except some feelings of nostalgia when visiting Europe. Otherwise, Europe is seen from a Canadian perspective. When Mennonites, for example, re-established *Die Mennonitische Post* in 1976–77, a German language publication appealing to Old Colony readers, their mandate to the publisher was the emphasis on Mennonite traditions rather than on German culture maintenance.

PARTICIPATION IN CANADIAN POLITICS

Beginning with their arrival in colonial Canada, German-Canadians have discharged their civic duties first as settlers, later as British subjects and Canadian citizens. During the pioneer period, service in the militia was an important aspect of civic responsibility. Germans served in the militia of New France and after 1763 defended British North America against the new republic.

Throughout the nineteenth century, the right to vote and to hold public office was expanded and responsible government introduced. Newcomers, before they became British subjects, did not participate in the political process; even after naturalization they were hesitant to take an active part. Mennonites and some other Anabaptist groups had only recently emerged from noninvolvement in political activities. The more traditional groups, such as Amish and Hutterites continued their policies of separation from the world outside.

In the nineteenth century, German-Canadians saw a harmony between their background and their loyalty to the British Crown. In the Maritimes, the settlers were well established and their children participated fully in local, provincial and federal politics. The Tupper and the Steeves families in Nova Scotia and New Brunswick were proud of their German heritage. Similarly, German-Canadians were active in Quebec; they were provincial administrators, like Baron von Rottenburg,[1] and political leaders and judges. With the political organization of Western Canada, German-Canadians were found in prominent positions in Manitoba and British Columbia.

This situation changed with World War I. Citizens whose virtues had been extolled

---

1 Herbert W. Debor, *op. cit.*, pp. 27–31.

for their contributions to Canada became the hated enemy. The reversal of attitudes had a dramatic impact on the political behaviour of German-Canadians. Prior to the war; they proudly stressed their heritage; as of 1914, they tried to conceal it or played it down. Throughout the 1920s, Germans were attacked as "unassimilated foreigners."[2] Political candidates expressed their families' contribution to Allied causes, even when these causes were re-constructed from the past.[3] The negative perception by outsiders extended to native-born Canadians of German background, such as John Diefenbaker, who considered his name a liability in politics; he always emphasized his maternal Scottish heritage.[4]

The sustained hostility, sometimes open but more frequently covert, extended until the 1960s. While German-Canadians did not cease to vote, as they did during World War I, it was difficult to be elected to public office. In the 1970s, there was an upsurge in political participation at the federal, provincial and municipal levels.

In post-Confederation nineteenth century, Germans were likely to vote Conservative, especially in Manitoba, where William Hespeler was prominent. Germans did not form a distinctive ethnic block for voting purposes; they manoeuvered between various alliances. The War Times Election Act of 1917 alienated German-Canadians from conservative politics and brought about a lasting alliance between the Liberal Party and German-Canadians. The growth of Diefenbaker populism in the 1950s brought Westerners back to vote Conservative. The Roman Catholic German enclave in Saskatchewan, Humboldt, remained Liberal. In Eastern Canada, mainly Ontario, the alliance between German-Canadians and Liberals has survived the death of MacKenzie King.

In provincial politics, German-Canadian voting patterns followed regional issues. Lunenburg voted primarily Conservatives into the Nova Scotia legislature. In Ontario, Waterloo County was Liberal, the Bruce and Grey ridings were more frequently Conservative. In Manitoba and Saskatchewan, Germans tend to vote for the New Democratic Party.[5] In Alberta, Social Credit was formerly preferred, and now the Progressive Conservative Party.[6] In British Columbia, Social Credit seemed the preferred party.

The Twenty-ninth Parliament (1973–1974) had ten members of German background out of 264, or 3.8 percent. Of ten, eight were Progressive Conservatives, two were Liberals. The Thirtieth Parliament, since 1974, also has ten members of German background, again eight Progressive Conservatives and two Liberals.[7] One

---

2 The Rt. Rev. Exton Lloyd.
3 Dr. Uhrich, the Saskatchewan Minister of Health in the 1920s, elected from Rosthern, Saskatchewan, stressed in the 1929 *Who's Who in Canada* that his father fought on the French side in the Franco-Prussian War of 1870/71, although in that war, British sympathies were for the emergent Germany.
4 Pierre G. Normandin, *The Canadian Parliamentary Guide, 1976* (Ottawa: 1976), p. 224.
5 Norman Ward and Duff Spafford, *Politics in Saskatchewan* (Don Mills: 1968).
6 Horst Schmidt, a post-War immigrant from Germany, is a member of the Alberta Cabinet.
7 Pierre G. Normandin, *ibid.*

Progressive Conservative, Frank Oberle, Prince George – Peace River, is a native of Germany and a post-War immigrant.

Since Confederation two former Prime Ministers were of German background, Sir Charles Tupper (1896) and John Diefenbaker (1957–63). The Tupper family originated in Hessen-Kassel and migrated via Guernsey to North America. The Diefenbaker family settled in Neustadt, Grey County, but later moved to Saskatchewan. There were also eight federal ministers of German origin.

Among the living members of the Canadian Privy Council, besides John Diefenbaker, there are two other members of German descent, namely Otto Lang and Eric Kierans. Otto Lang comes from the predominantly German Humboldt settlement. Eric Kierans' mother is German.

At the provincial level, three premiers, Sir Charles Tupper of Nova Scotia, William Aberhart of Alberta and Ernest Schreyer of Manitoba are of German background. About sixteen provincial ministers have either been natives of Germany or of German descent, so are three speakers of provincial legislative assemblies and four Lieutenant Governors.

Ten German-Canadians are members of the provincial legislature of Saskatchewan, mostly New Democrats. They readily describe their German background in the Canadian Parliamentary Guide. German-Canadians of other parties are reluctant to do so; for example, a Liberal member of the Saskatchewan Legislature, elected in a predominantly German provincial riding, preferred to be identified as being of Dutch origin. Arthur R. Lower described the shift from German to Dutch ancestry – also known as *Hollaenderei* – in times of political tensions as an escape device against discrimination.[8]

Alberta has four provincial legislators who are of German background. Other provinces who have provincial legislators of German background are Manitoba (five), Ontario (four), British Columbia (three), Newfoundland (one), and Nova Scotia (one).[9] In many cases, except for representatives of well known German enclaves, legislators prefer not to be identified as German, but call themselves Canadian.

Besides the elected politicians, there exists in Canada a substantial number of political appointees at the federal and provincial levels. The members of regulatory agencies, judicial and quasi-judicial agencies and other commissions and councils are mainly selected on the basis of patronage. Appointees of German background in these bodies are relatively rare. For example, the Province of Ontario has over 350 boards, commissions and agencies. Fewer than six percent of these members are of German origin. Relatively few German-Canadians can be found in the appointed boards and commissions at the federal level.

German-Canadians are also relatively under-represented in the federal public

---

8 Arthur R. M. Lower, *Canadians in the Making: The Social History of Canada* (Toronto: 1958).
9 Pierre G. Normandin, *ibid*.

service and in the various provincial public services. No region or province even approaches proportional representation.[10]

It would be unwise to attribute all forms of under-representation to discrimination. German-Canadians could often have preferred business or professional careers to civil service ones. Members of small religious groups are less likely to be represented in civil service occupations than in self-employment. On the other hand, it can hardly be assumed that minority under-representation is accidental.

---

10 *Report of the Royal Commission on Bilingualism and Biculturalism,* Book IV, Table A 36, p. 277.

Chapter 11

RECREATION, CULTURE AND COMMUNICATION

Among the urban population, recreation and the use of leisure time are to a great degree influenced by social class patterns, rather than by ethnicity. However, among rural groups, especially if they belong to religious minority groups, distinctive patterns can be identified.

Among urban upper classes and the upper-middle class, patterns of employment and leisure are closely interwoven, forming a distinctive lifestyle, rather than being clearly defined periods of work and recreation. Work and business associates also form the main reference group for the pursuit of leisure. Clubs and community activities, the latter primarily among the wives, form the basis for leisure-time interaction. The activities are to some degree directed by the annual cycle of events, as well as those for special occasions. This cycle usually commences in the early autumn when the various groups gear up their annual activities. The importance of outdoor activities diminishes in favour of indoor sports and the interwoven demands of occupational commitments and entertainment begin.

The activities of German-Canadian businessmen differ somewhat from those of Anglo-Saxon Canadian business and professional persons.[1] German-Canadian businessmen and professionals usually interact with their peers in noon-time or formal club activities, but are less likely to have an extensive schedule of home entertainment across cultural lines. Anglo-Saxon and German-Canadians will meet for business luncheons and participate in sport activities, but have different evening and weekend patterns.

German-Canadians see their weekend as a distinctive break from formal participation and reserve it for family contacts, meeting with friends or exploring nature. Those who are active in sports find the weekends full of events in which they participate either as performers or spectators. Upper and upper-middler class German-Canadians are less likely to be seen on the golf courses than Anglo-Saxon Canadians; they prefer tennis or horsemanship.

The upper classes are somewhat more formal in their lifestyles than their Canadian equivalents. Participation in formal cultural events is seen as a requirement for status validation and acceptance. German-Canadians are more likely to arrange formal balls and receptions to celebrate specific events in honour of their traditions. During these events, they re-create the glory which was theirs or to which they aspired. Some of these events have an aura of unreality because they refer to the distant past.

---

1 German-Canadian businessmen are more formal in their approach and utilize social events for prestige purposes.

The lower-middle and working classes, in their recreational patterns, depend primarily on ethnic clubs and associations. In sports, soccer is the principal participant and spectator sport. In Canada soccer is primarily played among the groups of European immigrants. Most soccer leagues follow ethnic lines, although recently these lines have been broken. For example, a German might play for Italian soccer or an Italian may be a star on a soccer team with a German name. Soccer has adopted the star system which transcends ethnic demarcation lines.

German-Canadians are also fond of hunting and fishing. To them, the freedom to do so is seen as one of the great freedoms which this country offers. Whereas in Europe hunting and fishing are strictly regulated and a preserve for the rich and elite, in Canada even the common man can engage in these activities. Throughout the hunting season, teams of hunters go across the fields and through the woods in search of prey. Several times, throughout this time, hunters will organize banquets in which the bounty of the fields and forests is served as stew or *Hasenpfeffer.*

In the cycle of annual festivities, three seasons are especially celebrated by German-Canadians: the Christmas season, the Mardi Gras season and the summer festival events culminating in the Octoberfest.

Since the first Christmas tree was lit in Canada by the Baroness von Riedesel in the eighteenth century, German-Canadians have continued to use Christmas trees, a custom which was taken over by other European groups. Most German-Canadian groups prepare extensively for the Christmas show which seems to be obligatory for every organization. The show depicts the traditional Christmas scene and songs and performances from the old world. St. Nicholaus, the Bishop, and his servant, Rupprecht, come to reward the good children and punish those who misbehave. There are fruits and nuts as well as toys and trinkets. Each group tries to re-create the spirit of a Christmas in Germany in the past century and the old songs are rehearsed and presented.

The Mardi Gras season is a time for bacchanalian revelry, during which traditional restraints are relaxed. Fancy-dress parties and elaborate rituals which caricaturize existing fashions and modes are devised. This season ends abruptly with Ash Wednesday. Originally, the Mardi Gras revelry was a cultural trait of the Rhineland of Germany. However, in Canada an intracultural exchange of traits has occurred and all persons of German-speaking background have accepted what have been regional festivities. The summer season is a period of outdoor festivals, during which German Days are held in various parts of Canada. Regional associations also use this period to reinforce the traditional bonds of common origin. Picnics and excursions are the principal ways in which old friends meet again.

The summer season is also the period of group travel. In the travel field, it used to be profitable for groups and organizations to arrange charter flights to Europe and especially to Germany. These charter flights offered round trip transportation at substantially reduced rates but still produced revenues for the sponsoring groups.

The *Oktoberfest* signified the end of the summer and the beginning of the winter season. Originating in Munich, it started on a small scale in Canada in the 1960s, under the sponsorship of German clubs. Soon there were many such events throughout Canada, with that at Kitchener, Ontario developed as a tourist attraction. Although many *Octoberfests*[2] have become purely commercial ventures, Kitchener tries to promote the event as a cultural heritage celebration. In 1976, the Rt. Hon. John Diefenbaker, a teetotaller, acted as the Grand Marshall of the event. As commercial enterprises, the sponsoring clubs use these celebrations in order to reduce the substantial deficits which most of the clubs incur throughout the year. Frequently, festivals, balls, and banquets are necessary to support other German cultural events. Public support, in the form of multicultural grants by the federal and provincial governments, are usually token contributions to the real costs. Without subsidies by commercial activities, other worthwhile cultural events would not take place.

In Ontario, cultural activities are frequently supported by the provincial lottery, Wintario. All grants need matching contributions, usually two-thirds, from other sources. Commercial activities or private contributions become necessary to obtain the desired support. It is not unusual that activities are arranged in such a way that they qualify for public grants.

Other attempts to create a broader basis for specific activities are based on cooperation between different ethnocultural groups. Recent trends seem to indicate that the large ethnocultural communities, such as the German or Italian, have increased their co-operation in recreational activities and special events. There is a slow breakdown of ethnic boundaries. In arts, literature and music especially, appeals are made to all interested persons rather than to one group.

In fine arts, Germans have contributed their perceptions of Canada or Canadian events from the earliest colonial period. William von Moll-Berczy[3] was a portrait painter and early city planner, his son William Bent Berczy,[4] a landscaper, painter and political figure. Probably the best known painter of rural scenes and folk-life was Cornelius Krieghoff (1815–1872) whose father came from Thuringia and who himself was born in Düsseldorf. Later his family moved to the Netherlands and Krieghoff subsequently came to Canada. Krieghoff's paintings now belong to the priceless artistic heritage of Canada.

In the nineteenth century, German painters were active in the Royal Canadian Academy of Arts. O. R. Jacobs[5] was president from 1890–1893. The involvement with Canadian background and artistic experience continued into this century. At present, a sizable group of German-Canadian painters lives in southern Ontario and British Columbia. At irregular intervals, German cultural institutes, *Goethe Häuser*,

---

2 The Oktoberfest syndrome has been studied by Elliot Avedon, University of Waterloo. See James E. Curtis et al., *Directory of Sociologists and Anthropologists in Canada, and their Current Research* (Montreal: 1973), p. 4.
3 John Andre, *Infant Toronto as Simcoe's Folly* (Toronto: 1971).
4 John Andre, "William Bent Berczy (1791–1873)", in Hartmut Froeschle, *Deutschkanadisches Jahrbuch* (Toronto: 1975), Vol. II, p. 167–80.
5 Herbert W. Debor, *Die Deutschen in der Provinz Quebec, 1664–1964* (Quebec: 1964), p. 41.

display exhibitions of German-Canadian painters. In 1973, Karl May[6] had a one-man exhibition at the National Art Centre. Moreover, there are from time to time exhibitions by local and regional galleries.

Sculptors of German background have also left their creations in Canada. Emmanuel Otto Hahn (1881–1957)[7] is generally considered as the outstanding artist of his period. Generally, about ten artists produce primarily in the multidimensional art.

Handicraft, the more utilitarian cousin of the arts, received a great impetus after World War II from artists coming from Europe. Weavers and potters, metal workers and other artisans have found an environment in Canada conducive to their creativity. Of note are Jan and Helga Grove of Victoria, British Columbia, who have exhibited their ceramics throughout Canada. Others have elevated their occupational skills as craftsmen into the work of artisans. Rather than using pre-patterned designs, they have created new expressions and interpretations of functional or ornamental pieces.

Helmut Kallmann, the musicologist,[8] in a recently republished study examined the German contributions to the world of music in Canada. He makes a distinction between the work of local significance and the contributions to music in a universal sense. In the latter category are the works of composers and performers who have transcended their own heritage and have become universally acclaimed. They are part of the global rather than regional tradition.

Of regional significance was the work of British bandmasters of German background. From the conquest of Quebec (1759) to Confederation in 1867, the bandmasters tried to instill musical appreciation not only into their audiences but also to their students and the general public. Bandmasters were jacks of all trades who worked with military bands and civilian orchestras alike and predicted music scores to the general public.

Frederic Henri Glackemeyer, the most versatile of them all, wrote many musical scores which are still preserved at Laval University and composed the regimental march of the British Royal Fuseliers, the Normandy. In 1820, he founded the Quebec Harmonic Society, one of the oldest musical societies of the country. The others became music teachers and organists after demobilization and writers of musical manuals.

During the nineteenth century, sacred music became differentiated along denominational lines. French Canada produced its own organists with distinctive traditions and musical patterns. English Canada turned towards English and Scottish organists. German-Canadians henceforth worked primarily in English-speaking Canada. Their special talent was in instrumental music. Performing in all towns and cities, their stay was limited in duration. Among these travelling musicians and teachers, the most outstanding ones were L. S. Pfeiffer (1831–1878), violinist,

---

6 *Deutsche Woche,* 27th September to 3rd October, Program (Ottawa: 1973).
7 Herbert W. Debor, *ibid.,* p. 42.
8 Helmut Kallmann, "The German Contributions to Music in Canada", in H. Froeschle, *ibid.,* p. 152–166.

organist and music teacher, and the Bohrer family who lived for some time in Montreal.

German musicians were active in Toronto and Winnipeg. August Stephen Vogt (1861–1926) founded the Mendelsohn Choir in Toronto which has been, since 1894, one of the outstanding choirs of the City. Besides directing the choir, Vogt taught at the University and the conservatory. Joseph Hecker founded the Philharmonic Society of Winnipeg in 1880.

The twentieth century saw fewer German artists coming to Canada than during the pioneer period. This was partially due to growing opportunities in Europe and to the growth of musical life in the United States which offered more attractive remuneration than Canada. In the twentieth century, Canada preferred sacred music to other forms, giving limited scope to musical talents.

As a consequence of political persecution and World War II, musicians and conductors of German background came again to Canada. Many of the well known German musical personalities were refugees or came shortly after the war. Helmut Kallmann himself is an example of this trend. Forced to flee via Shanghai, he came to Montreal as a post-war settler. Other musicologists, conductors and performers also found a home in Canada. The post-war period also witnessed the growing awareness and appreciation for classical music in Canada and corresponding support for the performing arts. Artists of German background play an important role in this revival.

Immigrants also preserved their heritage of folk music and of church hymns in the German language.

There has not been a systematic study of German folk music in Canada or of the Mennonite and Hutterite songs which have been retained in Canada, but are no longer known in Germany. Hutterite songs recall the sufferings and persecutions of the members, whereas Mennonite songs follow the German pietistic tradition.

Lunenburg, Nova Scotia, had the first German singing society in Canada (1828). Kitchener had singing groups and brass bands since the nineteenth century. There was hardly a picnic without a brass band. The Berlin Musical Society was founded about 1865, and in 1878, there was a band of twenty-two players and a quadrille group with six players. In 1882, the Waterloo Music Society was founded. Even today, Kitchener and Waterloo have remained the centres for brass bands.

Singing societies started in Kitchener in 1841, in Victoria, B. C. in 1861, and in Hamilton, Ontario in 1864. These singing groups developed an active life with music and social events. Usually they were under the direction of professional musicians, who continuously strived for musical perfection.

Most German-Canadian music societies suffered from the restrictions of World War I and the subsequent attitudes towards Germans. After World War II, a limited renaissance of singing societies became evident. Many societies followed the tradition of the groups which were founded in the nineteenth century: Harmony-Toronto, Concordia-Kitchener, and Germania-Hamilton. In 1955, there was an important singing festival in Kitchener. From that time on, singing festivals have become annual events, changing from city to city. There are also exchange visits between choirs in the Federal Republic of Germany and Canada.

Since the 1950s, German professional opera groups and orchestras have visited Canada. During German Week in Ottawa, 1973, German performers presented their dramas to the Canadian public.

While folk and choir music is closely associated with a given ethnocultural group, the performing arts transcend the narrow confines of a given group. The attitudes towards German music in Canada demonstrate this point. During World War I and, to a lesser degree, during World War II, German music was frowned upon or even prohibited. However, there was a growing awareness that musical traditions are universal, shared and appreciated by all. Post-war patterns of instant communication have enlarged the scope of activities and have made the world an appreciative audience, transcending cultural boundaries.

LITERATURE*

There appears no general agreement regarding the qualities which a literary work in German ought to possess in order to deserve the classification of "German-Canadian literature." At either extreme of the argument stand two fundamentally opposed schools of critics, the "purists" and the "imperialists." The "purists" would restrict the term "German-Canadian literature" to those German-language works which were written in Canada by citizens or residents of Canada primarily for Canadian readers; while the "imperialists," among whose number many *Reich* Germans may be found, tend to inflate the corpus of German-Canadian literature by including all German-language works which in one way or another refer, however obliquely, to Canada.

Hence, convenience suggests a discussion of the subject of German-Canadian literature under several headings:
1. Literature in German about Canada, i. e., those marginally Canadian works recruited by the "imperialist" school;
2. Canadian literature in German, written primarily for a Canadian audience, and
3. as a modern variant to 2., Canadian literature in German, written for no specific audience.

1. Literature in German about Canada dates back to the eighteenth century and continues to the present day. Much of it was, and is, travel literature authored by occasional German visitors to North America. One of these early visitors was Johann Gottfried Seume (1762—1810), a Hessian soldier, sold to the British and transported to America to defeat the American rebels. Seume spent some time in Nova Scotia and wrote, after his return to Germany, a poem entitled "Der Wilde" ("The Savage"), extolling in the trite fashion of his times the supposed natural virtues of the North American Indian. Yet the opening lines of this mediocre poem,

---

* Fritz Wieden, University of Windsor

> Ein Kanadier, der noch Europens,
> Übertünchte Höflichkeit nicht kannte...
>
> (A Canadian, who still was ignorant
> of Europe's whitewashed courtesy...)

became a staple selection in German school readers; the whole poem started an equally false picture of Canada in German literature which persists to the present day.

Seume was, of course, not writing for a Canadian audience, and neither was the Austrian poet Nikolaus Lenau, who had visited Niagara Falls in 1832. Their literary reports from Canada as well as the numerous contributions to travel literature in German concerning Canada, make up a good part of the bibliographies of "German-Canadian" literature. But these works, which were not written in Canada and were not destined for Canadian readers, do not really constitute a form of Canadian literature. Only the "imperialists" would affirm this without hesitation. For the majority, German travel literature about Canada is no more Canadian than Shakespeare's *Hamlet* is Danish literature.

2. The beginnings of an undeniably Canadian literature in German took place about the middle of the nineteenth century, i. e., at a time when large numbers of German immigrants settled in Canada. Amongst the pioneers of a Canadian literature in German were such clergymen as Father Eugen Funcken (1831–1888) and the Rev. Heinrich Rembe (1858–1927), who spun out folksy tales and popular playlets with an eye on moral instruction. Throughout the second half of the nineteenth and the first half of the twentieth centuries, Canadian literature in German appeared in increasing quantity, as the number of German-speaking Canadians multiplied. That type of literature was mostly destined for the German-language newspapers, periodicals and almanacs; it was written for local interest and did not aim at high intellectual content.

Not much else could be expected. Canada then attracted pioneers, and not professionals, and government authorities invited hewers of wood rather than men of letters until World War II. German-Canadian immigrants fared no better than their fellow newcomers in experiencing an initial penury from which they could only rise by exceptionally hard work. Competitive survival and the harsh imperatives of cultural adjustment left little or no time and energy for literary production.

But once the German-Canadian had emancipated himself from daily drudgery, he faced a fatal cultural choice. He had to decide either to retain his cultural heritage, or to abandon it for the culture of the majority. The newcomer could expect more rapid social advancement by shedding his ancestral ways. In terms of literary appreciation, the German-Canadian could always look to literature in English as a source of aesthetic gratification. Editions of Shelley or Shakespeare were more readily available to him than copies of Schiller's works.

Hence "native" Canadian literature in German seldom rose beyond the level of rural and regional interest until the 1940s. The literary career of Frederick Philip Grove is a case in point. His real name was Felix Paul Greve, and he left behind him a promising record as a literary figure when a criminal conviction in Germany drove him to the anonymity of faraway Canada around 1912. Though anti-German hostility during World War I may also have played a part in his decision, Greve chose to become Grove, a major figure in English-Canadian literature during the twentieth century. Greve would clearly have remained a local figure if he had maintained the use of the German-language as his literary vehicle.

As a result of World War I, a 1918 Order-in-Council prohibited all publications in German. This dealt a lethal blow to German-Canadian literature except in those areas where German remained not only the language of farmers, tradesmen and small businessmen, but also the language of worship. This situation prevailed amongst the Mennonites of Canada. Hence a considerable portion of German-Canadian literature produced since 1918 is Mennonite literature in both High and Low German, and it is thoroughly Canadian in all respects. Its leading representative is generally acknowledged to be Arnold B. Dyck (1889–1970). There are, however, some signs that this Mennonite literary tradition in German is now ebbing away, just as the whole Canadian literary scene has undergone profound changes since the 1950s.

3. In the wake of the Allied victory in 1945, masses of immigrants entered Canada who, although for the most part as penurious as their predecessors, included an unprecedented quantity of well-educated and sophisticated people. Their cultivated tastes would eventually demand, and begin to supply, cultural and intellectual fare which so far had scarcely existed in this country.

In terms of Canadian literature in German, a marked shift from amateur regional writers to educated professional writers took place. The literary production of the latter, more recent group, is appreciated beyond Canada's borders, though its spirit is sometimes less distinctively Canadian than German-Canadian literature of the late nineteenth and early twentieth century was. Some of the most notable contributors to contemporary Canadian literature in German teach, or taught, at Canadian universities. As German-Canadian literature migrated from ethnic clubs and regional periodicals to the campuses, the role of the German ethnic societies as supporters of German cultural and literary traditions steadily diminished.

Amongst those writers who had established themselves in that role before coming to Canada, the names of Ottfried Graf Finckenstein (born 1901), Walter Bauer (1904–1976), Carl Weiselberger (1900–1970), and Petra von Morstein (born 1941) deserve special mention. It is unfortunate that Finckenstein, a novelist of some note, has not published anything of consequence since his arrival to Canada. But Walter Bauer wrote a number of short stories and fine verse. In obtaining an academic appointment to the University of Toronto, he became the successor to Ernst Stadler. Carl Weiselberger's Canadian reputation was first established by his English-language contributions to Canadian periodicals before his artful tales in German achieved recognition. Petra von Morstein is a gifted lyrical poet of a younger generation; it is not yet certain whether she will make Canada her permanent home.

Else Seel (born 1902), Anton Frisch (born 1921) and Ulrich Schaffer (born 1942) have, on the other hand, begun writing since their arrival in Canada. Else

Seel has published both verse and prose in German and English, but has decidedly done better in her native German. Anton Frisch, however, has done quite well in German, English, and French, though he has lately published little. Ulrich Schaffer is a young lyrical writer of promise, whose successful amalgamation of German, American and other poetic traditions, still leaves room for a distinctly Canadian flavour in his interesting verse.

There is still no comprehensive survey of Canadian literature in German available. But when and if such a survey is compiled, three distinctive periods may well stand out: 1. The early reflections of Canada in German travel literature published since the late eighteenth century. If the Canadian credentials of this type of literature are dubious, a brief treatment of its role would please some. 2. The gradual evolution of a regional, indigenous literary tradition in both High and Low German. Its chief qualities were identical with the properties of a literature of the soil (*bodenständige Literatur*), and nearly all of that tradition's varied products were destined for German-language periodicals in Canada, and written mostly between 1850 and 1950. Its role is now diminishing. 3. Contemporary Canadian literature in German, written mostly by academics or by university graduates. It is sophisticated and frequently of high calibre. But it is published in German-speaking Europe for a world-wide German-speaking readership and has little connection with the remaining German-Canadian communities and organizations. These trends are very likely to determine the course of Canadian literature in German for some time to come.

THE GERMAN CANADIAN PRESS

The new arrivals of the 1750s in Nova Scotia were re-enforced by the German auxiliary troops during the period of the American Revolution. Therefore, the German speaking population printed their own newspaper, *Halifax Zeitung* in the 1780s. Little is known or preserved about the early endeavours, except an extract of June 4, 1782, which reports Rodney's victory over the French fleet.[9]

In 1833, Benjamin Eby, a bishop of the Waterloo District of the Mennonite Church, persuaded the citizens of Ebytown (Berlin) to grant him an interest-free loan for the acquisition of a printing press which was hauled from Pennsylvania to the Grand River Valley. On August 27, 1835, *Das Kanadische Museum und Allgemeine Zeitung* (Canadian Museum and General Newspaper) came into existence.[10] H. W. Peterson was the first editor. By 1840, Benjamin Eby transferred the ownership to his son, Henry, who replaced the Museum with *Der Deutsche Kanadier* (The German Canadian). One year earlier, Benjamin Burkholder published *Der Morgenstern* (The Morning Star) in 1839. The Eby family continued publishing German

---

9 An extract of the Halifax Zeitung of June 4, 1782 is deposited in the William L. Clement Library at the University of Michigan, Ann Arbor.
10 Frank H. Epp, *Mennonites in Canada, op. cit.*, p. 127.

language newspapers in addition to German spelling and reading books and reading primers. In 1857, the printing plant was sold to an English speaking family.

Between 1850 and 1914, German language newspapers flourished in southwestern Ontario, especially in villages and towns along the Niagara Escarpment. The newspapers were local and regional in content and orientation and seldom dealt with national and international issues. In many ways they reflected the attitudes and opinions of pioneer settlers who, due to isolation and limited means of communication, were at once starved for information and at the same time intensely parochial. Each newspaper had limited circulation, some appeared in split issues with different mastheads in different regions, and seldom exceeded 2,000 copies per issue. Most of these publications were short-lived, up to a period of five years after the initial printing.[11]

In 1877, the *Mennonitische Rundschau* (Mennonite Survey), was published in the West. This Winnipeg paper is the oldest continuously published German language newspaper in Canada. A non-denominational newspaper followed in 1889, *Der Nordwesten* (Northwestern). Werner Entz[12] discussed the growth and decline of these papers and their impact on German Canadian organisations as well as the participation of groups and individuals in public life. *Der Nordwesten* continued, with an interruption during the First World War and the immediate post-war period, until 1970, when it was merged with its rival, *Der Courier*. This newspaper originated in Saskatchewan in 1907 and was a partisan paper supported by the Liberal Party. It gradually developed into a regional newspaper and later into a national German language newspaper chain. *Der Courier* had as its aim not only the dissemination of news and information, it also intended to unify the German communities in the Prairie Provinces and develop a consciousness of kind beyond the denominational and parochial divisions. Prior to World War I, Conrad Eyman, the editor, tried to organize the German Canadian communities into an effective block. Even during World War I, he attempted to overcome the open hostilities against German Canadians but with limited success.

World War I signalled the end of German language newspapers culminating in the prohibition of any publication in the German language. Some newspapers tried to continue their efforts by publishing English language editions until the lifting of the restrictions in 1920. The majority, however, folded up, never to appear again. The background of the prohibition which occurred towards the end of the war, had never been fully explored. W. Bausenhart[13] saw the prohibition as a culmination of

---

11 Herbert Karl Kalbfleisch, *The History of German Newspapers in Ontario, Canada, 1835–1918*, unpublished doctoral dissertation, The University of Michigan, Ann Arbor, 1953. It was re-edited as *The History of the Pioneer German-Language Press in Ontario, 1835–1918* (Toronto: 1968).
12 Dr. Werner Entz, "Der Einfluß der deutschsprachigen Presse Westkanadas auf die Organisationsbestrebungen des dortigen Deutschtums, 1889–1939" in H. Froeschle, *op. cit.*, p. 92–138.
13 Werner Bausenhart, "The Ontario German-Language Press and its Suppression by Order-in-Council, 1918", *op. cit.*

general sentiments, treatment of Union Government candidates during the elections of 1917 and anti-foreign feelings in the population. W. Entz[14] also saw the attempts in Saskatchewan to influence the election of candidates favourably disposed towards German Canadians as one of the contributory factors leading to the prohibition. He contrasted strong public sentiments with the more cautious approach of the censors.

After 1920, the two major newspapers appeared again. In 1923, the newspapers became active in organizing the Prairie Provinces' German background population into associations which transcended the traditional boundaries of religious affiliation, regional origin and local interests. In 1924, *Der Deutsch-canadische Provinzialverband von Saskatchewan* (German Canadian Provincial Association of Saskatchewan) was revitalized.[15] A new approach was attempted with the establishment of annual German days which were held each year from 1928 to 1939. At first quite successful in rallying German Canadians for meetings and presentations in public, they were later treated with caution and subsequently boycotted when National Socialists tried to use the events for propaganda purposes.

During the 1930s, both Communists and National Socialists tried to establish their own newspapers. The communist paper had few readers and folded up because of lack of interest. The National Socialist paper, *Deutsche Zeitung fuer Canada,* German Newspaper for Canada, which appeared between 1935 and 1939, reached about 6,000 subscribers and was heavily subsidized by the Government of the Third Reich. It was the aim of the paper to influence German Canadians and others to a favourable attitude towards Germany. Besides German language articles, there were news in English intended for wider dissemination. For example, the *Deutsche Zeitung fuer Canada* reported in great details all the speeches and events of the German days. The Consul of the German Reich, Dr. Seelheim, reported in a letter to the German Foreign Office of September 5, 1935, how the German days were to be used for promoting National Socialist causes. His wrath was especially directed towards the German Communists who in their paper, *Deutsche Arbeiterzeitung* (German Newspaper for Workers) attacked the Nazi propaganda. In general, the *Deutsche Zeitung fuer Canada* was more intemperate in the German than in the English section. The German section frequently attacked and ridiculed the refugees from the Third Reich.

The other two newspapers, *Nordwesten,* Winnipeg and *Courier,* Regina, took a more careful approach. While reporting on general events, they did not fully equivocate the cause of Germans in Canada with the aims of the National Socialists. This reluctance to join wholeheartedly the Nazi cause was one of the reasons for the establishment of the Nazi newspaper. The two traditional papers were primarily concerned with the difficult economic problems which Canada encountered during the Great Depression and with regional concerns. They also cautioned against

---

14 W. Entz, "The Suppression of the German Language Press in September 1918", *Canadian Ethnic Studies,* Vol. VIII, No. 2, 1976, pp. 56–70.
15 Werner Entz, in Froeschle, *op. cit.,* p. 119.

wholehearted commitment to specific causes which might not be in the interests of German Canadians.

German language newspapers, after the *Deutsche Zeitung fuer Canada* ceased publication in 1939, were not suppressed during World War II. While the contents were censored, there were no additional obstacles such as the prohibition of the use of the mails or similar devices. However, German Canadians feared a repetition of the events of the First World War and many ceased subscriptions. During the war, another short-lived Communist newspaper appeared in 1944/45 containing strong propaganda messages denouncing stridently any form of covert Nazi sympathies.

The post World War II migration waves, for *Volksdeutsche* (ethnic Germans) and for *Reichsdeutsche* (German Nationals), the former since 1948 and the latter since 1951, brought new readers to German language newspapers. Because of the post-war migration waves to Ontario, this province became the largest German speaking area. The 1950s and 1960s witnessed an expansion of German language publications and a shift from Western Canada to Ontario and Quebec. Since that time, subscription decreased at first gradually and in the 1970s dramatically. Among the principal reasons were the lack of sustained migration to Canada, increases in postal rates and unreliability of postal services which rendered regular delivery impossible. In the 1960s, German background residents moved in larger numbers to British Columbia which added to the readership of the *Pazifische Rundschau,* a German language publication in Vancouver.

In the 1970s, three newspaper groups were publishing in the German language, the Längin Group, the Reprich Group and the Ackermann Group. Bernard Längin, the Editor-in-Chief of the *Courier,* edited the *Montreal Courier, Toronto Courier, Manitoba Courier, Saskatchewan Courier, Alberta Courier* and *Vancouver Courier.* The main texts of the *Courier* split editions were identical, with local news varying according to the edition. Ontario had slightly over 9,000 subscribers, over 14,000 in the Prairies and several hundreds in other parts of the country. Moreover, the *Courier* distributed the Canadian Edition of *Die Zeit* (The Times), a newspaper of record aimed at German Canadian opinion leaders with over 7,000 copies.

The Reprich Group, named after Eric O. Reprich, the principal owner, published the *Hamilton Journal,* close to 6,000 copies, *Kitchener Journal,* 6,700 copies, *Montreal Zeitung,* over 11,000 copies and the main paper, *Torontoer Zeitung* with 12,600 copies.

Baldwin Ackermann's newspaper, the *Pazifische Rundschau* (Pacific Survey) had about 10,000 subscribers, mainly in British Columbia, and represented the Western Canadian point of interest.

Whereas the *Courier* generally supports the positions taken by the Canadian federal government, the *Journal* is close to the government of Ontario. At most times, the *Courier* reflects the attitudes and opinions of the readers. During the 1950s and 1960s, the *Courier* had a right wing orientation.[16] In the 1970s, there

---

16 Ottmar Kliem, *Deutsche in Canada,* doctoral dissertation, University of Erlangen-Nuernberg, November 1966, published 1969.

were some concessions towards the East Block Countries, however, in general, the attitudes were rather cautious against appeasement towards the East. In the 1970s the paper also reported nostalgic visits to the old East German homelands. On the other hand, they frequently report about the intelligence network of East Block powers and the work of their agents. An example is the June 9, 1977 edition of the *Courier* with headlines: "10 East German Agents Caught in the Web of Counter Intelligence."

In Canadian matters, the *Courier* deplores the limited participation of German-Canadians in public affairs. Both the *Courier* and the *Torontoer Zeitung* also supported strongly the Kitchener faction of the Trans-Canada Alliance of German-Canadians who took over in 1974, replacing a widely diversified group of former executives. This support was evident in the publications surrounding the criminal procedures against the former executives which ended in acquittals on October 26, 1976. As a consequence, the new executive as well as the two newspapers were sued in turn before the Supreme Court of Ontario. During this controversy which sharply divided the German-Canadian community, the *Pazifische Rundschau* was at first sceptical and later antagonistic toward the new executive of the Trans-Canada Alliance. Support of the Alliance dwindled considerably from 90 clubs in 1974 to slightly over 20 dues-paying member societies in 1977. The Alliance however maintained that "the German ethnic group is one of the strongest and best organized groups."[17]

Until the demise of the paper in 1975, Mario von Brentani, a colourful journalist and artist, published the *Montrealer Nachrichten* with about 16,000 copies during the peak time. This paper changed from an ardently free enterprise publication to an advocate of East German interests. Later, because of several failures in starting a letter campaign on behalf of the German Democratic Republic, this arrangement was disowned. Thereupon, Mario von Brentani was viciously attacked by a group of East German letter writers, especially Gerhard Moest, Leipzig, whose diatribes were faithfully reprinted by the *Courier* throughout 1975/76.

Religious organizations maintain their own periodicals. The *Mennonitische Rundschau* has at present about 6,000 subscribers. Other Mennonite papers are *Der Bote*, Saskatchewan, and *Die Mennonitische Post*, Steinbach, Manitoba. Roman Catholics have a controlled circulation paper, distributed without charge, *Der Deutsche Katholik in Kanada*. There are also periodicals, issued by associations and special interest groups, such as the *Ottawa Herald* which reports organizational activities in Ottawa, Ontario, the *Sudeten Bote*, Pouce Coupe, B. C., for the Sudeten refugees, *Der Heimatbote*, Toronto, for Danube Swabians, *Annagennesis*, Montreal, for pre-war political and religious refugees, *Vorwaerts*, a socialist monthly, Toronto, as well as *Kontakt*, Toronto, the house publication of the German Democratic Republic (East Germany).

Most German-language newspapers are financially barely able to publish. Were it

---

17 Letter of the Ontario Branch, Trans-Canada Alliance of German-Canadians of 29th May, 1977 to the Ontario Advisory Council on Multiculturalism.

not for the hidden support of the governments via public service advertisements, the newspapers would have been even more curtailed. Mr. Reprich has been trying to sell his newspaper chain because of dwindling circulation for some time and actively advertised in Germany for potential buyers. Before its demise, the *Montrealer Nachrichten* was available at bargain rates, but without any takers.

With the exception of highly motivated special interest publications, German-language newspapers try to appeal to a mass audience. Other news are frequently direct translations from the wire services or re-writes of German news.

Generally, German-Canadians are more likely to read their regional English-language newspapers than the German weeklies. Those readers who prefer European news can easily obtain airmail editions. In contrast, specialized audience periodicals have constant readers but no dramatical increases in publications.

German-Canadian papers have two target groups, new arrivals and special-interest readers. New arrivals who do not know enough English or French need the ethnic press for information and orientation. The press mediates between German background and new Canadian experience. The second group consists of those who are active in German-Canadian organizations and affairs and those who have special causes to plead. All ethnic newspapers by publishing occupational and personal advertisements in a non-official language can appeal directly to a target group rather than to the general public. German-Canadian newspapers, for example, carry "lonely hearts" columns in which people request friendship or marriage partners. This practice is more acceptable in German-language publications than in English-language media. There are also requests for employment guarantees which would allow applicants to come to Canada. Two kinds of employment offers appear regularly: 1) for German occupational specialties, such as bi-lingual German-English office help or German tile setters for tile-oven construction and 2) requests for household help or for work in German-owned farms and forests. Other advertisements are for exchange of property between West Germany and Canada.

Most German-language newspapers, but not the periodicals, are primarily for information and entertainment. In the post-war period, they did not as openly align themselves with political parties as in earlier periods, but their political bases are reflected in editorial policies. *Die Zeit* (The Times) can be considered as a newspaper of record, analyzing and interpreting current events rather than describing matters which attract readers.

Unless there is going to be the resumption of large-scale migration of German-speaking people, the impact of the newspaper is lessening each year. Subscriptions are dwindling and rates increasing. Delivery problems have not been solved and will continue to damage the ethnic press. The clientele is aging and not replaced by new audiences. Due to delivery problems many groups publish their own news bulletins for local information, a situation which further damages paid circulation. Whereas publications for special interest groups will have a relatively constant list of subscribers, the future of the weekly newspapers in the German language is clouded.

GERMAN LANGUAGE BROADCASTING*

The policy of the Canadian Broadcasting Corporation (CBC) is not to broadcast in any other languages but English and French, except in its Northern Services, where native languages are used, and in its International Service. This policy, which has remained unchanged in spite of some protests from ethnic groups, leaves the task of providing broadcast services in languages other than English and French to Canada's many private stations. The restriction applies to broadcasts in German. Private radio stations must depend on advertising revenues, and this dependence influences the kind and the quantity of programming, which this or that station may offer to the German-speaking public.

In general, German-language broadcasts in Canada are today of two types: 1. The broadcasts of regional interest, directed at socially and culturally homogeneous groups of German-Canadians, such as southern Manitoba, and 2. Broadcasts directed at a relatively substantial German-speaking element in some of Canada's major cities or industrial centres.

The first type consists mostly of broadcasts directed at such groups as the Mennonites. A typical example is provided by stations CFAM in Altona, Manitoba, and CHSM in Steinbach, Manitoba. Both stations are owned by the same company and are situated in towns with a high concentration of German-speaking Mennonites. A little more than three hours each week is devoted to programs in Low German and the same amount to programs in High German. The Low German part is directed exclusively at the Mennonite population and consists of religious, historical or cultural programs featuring various aspects of Mennonite life in the past and the present. The High German segment adds some entertainment and occasional reports from the Old World.

2. German-language broadcasting in Canada's urban centres has largely come about in the 1950s as an advertising initiative of small German businesses wishing to address themselves to German-speaking residents in the area. In the late 1960s, large German companies have also figured as sponsors of these programs. For many a German immigrant in the 1950s and 1960s, these broadcasts were the only source of information since the newcomers' English could not always keep pace with the rapid speech of English-language announcers. The decline of immigration, the assimilation of earlier immigrants and the limited scope of these ethnic programs have lately diminished their importance and their audience. Fewer and fewer residents of Canada are exclusively dependent on them, and fewer and fewer erstwhile immigrants prefer the somewhat amateurish ethnic programmes to the slick, well-financed and well-produced programs of the majority language. As a result, German-language programs that still exist have neither the financial backing nor the appropriate audience to accomplish anything ambitious. Professional shows on

---

* Fritz Wieden, University of Windsor

videotape in German are indeed more likely to appear, with English or French dubbing, on the CBC than on the "German broadcasts."

The following list of German-language programmes in Canada was compiled in 1973, and reflects the approximate state of German-language broadcasting in Canada:

GERMAN LANGUAGE BROADCASTING IN CANADA

Province	Station/Frequency	Location	Weekly Broadcast Time (Hours)
Ontario	CKQS/FM	Oshawa	13
	CHIN/FM	Toronto	6
	CFPL/FM	London	1 1/2
	CHLO/AM	St. Thomas	1 1/2
	CHYR/AM	Leamington	1 1/2
	CKOT/AM	Tillsonburg	1
	CFMO/FM	Ottawa	2
	CHYM/AM & FM	Kitchener	5
	CFCA/FM	Kitchener	2
	CKPR/AM & FM	Thunder Bay	1
	CKMP/AM	Midland	1
Alberta	CKUA/AM	Edmonton	2 1/2
	CHFA/AM	Edmonton	1 1/2
British Columbia	CKOO/AM	Osoyoos*	1/2
	CJDC/AM	Dawson Creek	1
	CKCQ/AM	Quesnel**	1/2
Saskatchewan	CJUS/FM	Saskatoon	Upon Demand
Manitoba	CKSB/AM	St. Boniface	1
	CFAM/AM	Altona	3 1/2 High German
	CHSM/AM	Steinbach	3 1/4 Low German
	CFRW/AM	Winnipeg	1
Quebec	CFMB/AM	Montreal	1/2
	CKVL/AM & FM	Verdun	4

* Okanagan Valley
** Northern British Columbia

In addition to these, a number of German-language broadcasts are received in Canadian border cities from stations in the United States.

Television programs in German are confined to weekly, fortnightly, or monthly offerings lasting one hour or less on cable television. Again, financial reasons can be cited for this. The sponsors are German firms, or small German-Canadian businesses, who are either unwilling or unable to put a great deal of money into them, and the viewers must be determined Germans indeed if they resist the temptation to flip their receiver dial to the next channel for a top-notch and top-rated Canadian or American programme. Hence German-language television has so far survived in very few centres, and only with considerable difficulty. Future financial pressures may indeed put an end to it.

Chapter 12

CONCLUSION

From the dawn of European settlements in Canada to the present, German-speaking people have contributed to the growth and development of the country. They came as soldiers and adventurers, albeit not always voluntarily. Once in Canada, they stayed, pioneered on the land and contributed to the many coloured tapestry of Canadian culture.

In the colonial periods, both French and British, they tried to escape the vicissitudes of the homeland, persecution as Catholics when they came to New France, persecution as Protestants when they entered Nova Scotia in and after 1750. During the wars of the eighteenth century, they served as soldiers, the Swiss for the King of France and Germans for the British Crown. During the American Revolution, they were lent as mercenaries and did garrison duties in Nova Scotia and Quebec.

In the last century, Germans found peace and security as well as freedom of worship in Upper Canada. Hungry for land, they made the virgin forest into fertile farms. Well known for their industry and thrift, they were welcomed and solicited for settlement.

Without the Mennonites from Eastern Europe and their successful experience in the Prairies, the other immigrants would not have come to the West and made the Prairie, that frozen wasteland, the granary of the world. Followed by other German-speaking settlers, the Prairies became the testing grounds for the Canadian experiment in which many peoples tried to live peacefully together without being deprived of their identity. Of course, in times of stress, the strident voices of self-anointed patriots were to be heard; common sense, however, prevailed in the long run and new patterns of tolerance were created.

The population realignments in Europe which began with World War I found their culminations in World War II. Millions of people were on the move and a large percentage found in Canada a new home and cherished land. Processes of adjustment were not always easy. Dominated by economic necessities, they took personal tolls. The old and the weak could not stand the pressure. They looked for a refuge in their communities; others turned back home for support, only to fail to find happiness in the land of their dreams. Canada remained indelibly in the memories even of those who left. The children in Mexico of some of those who left because their religious freedom ceased being recognized, long for the land of their parents and dread the developments in their host country.

The immigrants saw Canada as a land of opportunity, a place to raise a family in peace, to acquire property and to live a life of challenge. Their children hoped to participate in the public life of the country and be fully recognized as equals. At first, they encountered the vertical mosaic and the discrimination of the charter groups; in later times, they were given gradual recognition for their accomplishments.

German-Canadians have done well economically. Within the employment structure, they have found new niches and responded to the challenges of a growing economy. They established industries, they invested and prospered. Those who came from peasant stock frequently remained on the farms, but adapted to the changing requirements of a cash-crop economy. Others gave witness to alternate lifestyles either by conservative practices with quaint horses and buggies trotting along the side roads or by living a communal life, sharing wealth and poverty with their brethren. Only the elderly and the deprived Old Colony returnees from Mexico know grinding and debilitating poverty.

With the exception of those who cling to their way of life, German-Canadians adapted themselves well to Canada. Language maintenance was the goal of the religious minorities but it was seldom attained in an urban environment. The patterns of third-generation return did not include the re-learning of the ancestral language. It was confined to the preservation of cultural patterns, artifacts and handicrafts. Germans have married freely with people of other backgrounds, easily blending into the mainstream of Canadian life.

The contributions of German-Canadians to Canadian culture has been manifold. They were among the earliest poets of Canada, and throughout their long stay in this land they have tried to cope with the environment and the people who inhabit it. They have pioneered in the performing arts, in music, drama and folk art. Others used the various visual arts to express their interpretations of people and events. Many of their contributions have entered Canadian life not as ethnic creativity, but as universal or as Canadian as the Bluenose.

In only one area have Germans been underrepresented — in the political life of the country. Those who did not come for the earthly kingdom withdrew to serve the heavenly one; even in withdrawal they suffered discrimination. Others, however, experienced the dramatic changes dictated by outside events which made friends into foes overnight and created scapegoats. It took a long time to overcome the mistrust and guilt by association. While the younger generation was relatively free from this burden, the inhibitions created remain a long time after.

In the multicultural decade of the 1970s, German-Canadians find new opportunities to preserve and to share. The preservation should be not only to the things specifically ethnic, but also of values and cultural contributions. Experiences to be shared are those with universal appeal and the various traits which are blended in the unique Canadian way.

German-speaking Canadians have come from many countries and regions. While considering the Federal Republic, Austria or Switzerland their countries of reference, they are Canadian. At first hyphenated, later have grown to be an integral part of the diversity which is Canada's contribution to the world. This land is living witness that people of many backgrounds can share the same basic values and pursue similar goals without forsaking their own identity.

The future of German-Canadians lies in the development of their unique identity. One aspect of it is the lessening of the impact of European politics and economics on the well being of the group. Political alignments are subject to change with profound impact on German background residents of Canada. Likewise, the economic balance is subject to fluctuations. There are already indications that large-scale foreign investments are diminishing, a process which might increase in the future. German-Canadians cannot depend on German enterprises to maintain their prosperity, they need full integration into the national economy. The same applies to political alliances and processes. Participation in Canadian public life needs encouragement and organization. The maintenance and growth of German-Canadian culture depends primarily on the will of those who cherish it. Only if German-Canadians display the same determination they have shown in the economic life in the cultural sphere, are they able to present to Canada their heritage and traditions which might become a valuable component of Canadian life rather than only of a part of it.

BIBLIOGRAPHY

John Andre: *Infant Toronto as Simcoe's Folly*, Toronto 1971.
—: "William Bent Berczy (1791–1873)", in: *Deutschkanadisches Jahrbuch*, ed by Hartmut Froeschle, vol. 2, Toronto 1975.
Utz Aysslinger: Letter of the President of the Trans-Canada Alliance of German-Canadians to the Ontario Advisory Council on Multiculturalism, May 29, 1977.
Milton L. Barron: *American Minorities*, New York 1957.
Werner A. Bausenhart: "The Ontario German Language Press and its Suppression by Order-in Council in 1918", *Canadian Ethnic Studies*, vol. 4, 1972, No. 1–2.
Alexander Begg and Walter R. Nursey: *Ten Years in Winnipeg*, Winnipeg, 1879.
Winthrop P. Bell: *The Foreign Protestants and the Settlement of Nova Scotia*, Toronto 1961.
John W. Benett: *Hutterian Brethren; The Agricultural Economy and Social Organization of a Communal People*, Stanford 1967.
Ruth Bernd: "Sonnabendschulen auf dem Abstellgleis", *Courier*, May 26, 1977.
Eugene F. Bliss: *Diary of David Zeisberger; a Moravian Missionary Among the Indians of Ohio*, Cincinnati, 1885.
John Blue: *Alberta, Past and Present*, vol. 1 Chicago 1924.
Hermann Boeschenstein: "Is there a Canadian Image in German Literature?" *Seminar*, vol. 3, 1967, No. 1.
Emory S. Bogardus: *Immigration and Race Attitudes*, Boston, New York 1928.
—: "Racial Distance Changes in the United States During the Past Thirty Years", *Sociology and Social Research*, vol. 42, 1958, Nov.–Dec.
Bernhard Bott: *Confidential Memorandum to the German Foreign Office, Division VIA, of August 25, 1934*.
Joseph A. Boudreau: *The Enemy Alien Problem in Canada 1914–1921*, Los Angeles 1965 (doctoral dissertation).
Censuses of Canada, 1665 to 1871, vol. 4, Ottawa 1876.
Convention on Social Security Between Canada and the Federal Republic of Germany, Ottawa 1971.
British Columbia Historical Association: *Victoria, B.C. 1843–1943*, Victoria 1943.
George Bryce: *Mackenzie, Selkirk, Simpson*, Toronto 1906.
—: *The Romantic Settlement of Lord Selkirk's Colonists*, Toronto 1909.
Mabel Burkholder: *Out of the Storied Past*, Hamilton, no date.
James M. S. Careless: *The Union of the Canadas: The Growth of Canadian Institutions 1841–1857*, Toronto 1967.
Champlain Society: *The Town of York, 1793–1815*, Toronto 1962.
Martha B. Clark: "The Hessians". *Papers and Addresses of the Lancaster County Historical Society*, vol. 4, 1900.
Commission de Revocation: *Rapport du secretaire d'état du Canada pour l'année financière close le 31 mars 1947*.
G. I. Cooper: "The Germans in Nova Scotia; the Bi-Centenary of the Halifax Community", *American German Review*, vol. 16, 1950, February.
P. Cornell, J. Hamelin, F. Quellet, M. Trudel: *Canada, Unity in Diversity*, Toronto 1967.
Bruce Creighton: *High Bright Buggy Wheels*, Toronto 1951.
Helen Creighton: "The Folklore of Lunenburg County, Nova Scotia", National Museum of Canada Bulletin, vol. 1950, No. 117.
Alfred H. Crowfoot: *This Dreamer; Life of Isaac Hellmuth, Second Bishop of Huron*, Vancouver 1963.
James E. Curtis and Desmond M. Connor: *Directory of Sociologists and Anthropologists in Canada, and Their Current Research*, Montreal 1970.

Bibliography

L. Curtze: *Geschichte und Beschreibung des Fürstentums Waldeck*, Arolsen 1851.
Carl A. Dawson, ass. by R. W. Murchie: *The Settlement of the Peace River Country; a Study of a Pioneer Area*, Toronto 1934.
—: "The German Catholics", *Group Settlement*.
Herbert W. Debor: *Die Deutschen in der Provinz Quebec 1664–1964*, Como 1964.
—: *The Cultural Contributions of the German Ethnic Group to Canada*, Ottawa 1966.
Mather Byles DesBrisay: *History of the County of Lunenburg*, Toronto 1895.
Deutsche Gesellschaft zu Montreal in Kanada: *Statuten*, 1859.
Horst Doehler (ed.): *Volksstimme*, published 1944/45.
Dominion Law Reports, vol. 1947, No. 1
Dominion of Canada: *Reports of the Royal Canadian Mounted Police*, for the years 1940 to 1946.
Mabel B. Dunham: *Grand River*, Toronto 1945.
—: "Mills and Millers in Western Ontario", *Western Ontario History Nuggets*, vol. 1946, No. 9.
Lord Durham: *Report on the Affairs of British North America*, vol. 11 Oxford 1912.
Johann Peter Eckermann: *Conversations with Goethe*, London, New York 1935.
Robert England: *The Colonization of Western Canada; a Study of a Contemporary Land Settlement 1896–1934*, London 1936.
Werner Entz: "Wilhelm Hespeler, Britischer Parlamentarier aus Baden", *Mitteilungen des Instituts für Auslandsbeziehungen*, vol. 7, 1957, No. 3.
—: "120 Jahre deutschkanadische Presse", *Mitteilungen des Instituts für Auslandsbeziehungen*, vol. 7, 157, No. 3.
—: "Der Einfluss der deutschsprachigen Presse Westkanadas auf die Organisationsbestrebungen des dortigen Deutschtums 1889–1939", in: *Deutschkanadisches Jahrbuch*, ed. by Hartmut Froeschle, vol. 2, Toronto 1975, 92–138.
—: "The Suppression of the German Language Press in September 1918", *Canadian Ethnic Studies*, vol. 8, 1976, No. 2, 56–70.
Frank H. Epp: *Mennonite Exodus; the Rescue and Settlement of the Russian Mennonites since the Communist Revolution*, Altona, Manitoba 1962.
—: *Mennonites in Canada, 1786–1920; the History of a Separate People*, Toronto 1974.
Exsul Familia, The Church's Magna Charta for Migrants, of August 1, 1952, ed. by Giulirio Tessarolo, Staten Island, N.Y. 1962.
Albert B. Faust: *The German Element in the United States, with Special Reference to its Political, Moral, Social and Educational Influence*, New York 1927.
Emerich K. Francis: *In Search of Utopia; the Mennonites in Manitoba*, Glencoe 1955.
—: "Mennonite Institutions in Early Manitoba", *Agricultural History*, vol. 22, 1948, July.
William B. Fraser: *Calgary*, Toronto 1967.
German Consulate, Winnipeg: *Letter to the Foreign Office, Germany, of April 15, 1929*.
—: *Letter to the Foreign Office, Germany, of August 16, 1930*.
German League of Canada: *Application Form and Guidelines*.
Geschichte des Teutonia Vereins, Windsor 1965.
John M. Gibbon: **Canadian Mosaic; the Making of a Northern Nation**, New York, Toronto 1938.
Orland Gingerich: *The Amish of Canada*, Waterloo, Ont. 1972.
Glenbow Archives, Sessional Papers in various vols. 1887–1920.
Richard O. W. Goertz and Alexander Malacky: "**German** Canadian Church History, Part 2", *Canadian Ethnic Studies* vol. 5, 1976, Nos. 1–2.
Government of Canada: *Orders-in-Council of September 2, 1939, and September 3, 1939*, Canada Gazette.
Friedrich von Grafenried: "Sechs Jahre in Kanada", *Tenth Yearly Report of the Geographical Society of Berne*, Switzerland, 1890.
Greene's: *Who is who in Canada*, 1928/29.
Harry Gregson: *A History of Victoria, 1842–1970*, Victoria, B. C. 1970.

Wilfred T. Grenfell: *The Romance of Labrador*, New York 1934.
Frederick P. Grove: *In Search of Myself*, Toronto 1974.
Grundgesetz für die Bundesrepublik Deutschland, München 1956.
Ken Hand: "Remember the Sudeten Czechs?", *Canadian National Magazine*, 1952, February 9.
James Hanny: *History of New Brunswick*, St. John 1909.
James B. Hedges: *Building the Canadian West; the Land and Colonization Policies of the Canadian Pacific Railway*, New York 1939.
Carl Heiler: "Von Hanau nach Quebec", *Volk und Scholle*, vol. 9, 1931.
Rudy Herbst: "Die Rede des Praesidenten am Versammlungsabend zur Kenntnisnahme fuer alle Mitglieder, die nicht anwesend waren", *Harmonie Nachrichten*, vol. 1973, 3–4.
Karl Hern: *Wenzel Jaksch, Sucher und Künder*, München 1967.
Rudolf Hubner: "Die Sudetendeutschen in Skandinavien", *Sudeten-Jahrbuch*, vol. 1952.
House of Common Debates, April 14, 1908, Ottawa 1908.
Alex Inkeles and Daniel J. Levinson: "National Charakter: The Study of Modal Personality and Socio-Cultural Systems", in: *The Handbook of Social Psychology*, ed. by Gardner Lindsey et al., vol. 2, 1954.
Institut Drouin: *Dictionnaire National des Canadiens Français, 1608–1760*, Partie Généalogique, Tome 1 et Tome 11.
Wenzel Jaksch: *Europe's Road to Potsdam*, New York 1963.
Charles M. Johnston: *The Valley of the Six Nations; a Collection of Documents on the Indian Lands of the Grand River*, Toronto 1964.
Herbert K. Kalbfleisch: *The History of the German Newspapers of Ontario, Canada, 1835–1918*, Ann Arbor 1953 (doctoral dissertation).
–: *The History of the Pioneer German Language Press of Ontario, 1835–1918*, Toronto 1968.
Hellmut Kallmann: "Der deutsche Beitrag zum Musikleben", *Mitteilungen des Instituts für Auslandsbeziehungen*, vol. 7, 1957, No. 3.
Howard A. Kennedy: *The Book of the West*, Toronto 1925.
Robert W. Keyserlingk: *Unfinished History*, London 1948.
Ottmar Kliem: *Deutsche in Kanada; eine empirische Orientierungsstudie über den Integrationsprozess der Mitglieder des deutschen Klubs in Calgary/Alb. im Vergleich zu den Führern der deutschen Klubs in ganz Kanada*, Erlangen-Nürnberg 1969 (doctoral dissertation).
Heinz Kloos: "Das Luthertum in Kanada", *Mitteilungen des Instituts für Auslandsbeziehungen*, vol. 7, 1957, No. 3.
Emil Kutscha: "Sudeten Germans in Canada", *American German Review*, vol. 23, 1957, February-March.
Ernest J. Lajeunesse: *The Windsor Border Region*, Toronto 1960.
Heinz Lehmann: *Das Deutschtum in Westkanada*, Berlin 1939.
Gottlieb Leibbrandt: *Canadian German Society 1947–1972*, Waterloo 1972.
Life History of a German Immigrant, unpublished manuscript.
Life History of a German Background Ontario Resident, unpublished manuscript.
Arthur R. M. Lower: *Canadians in the Making, A Social History of Canada*, Toronto 1958.
Norman MacDonald: *Canada's Immigration Policy, 1840–1903*, Toronto 1957.
James G. MacGregor: *A History of Alberta*, Edmonton 1972.
E. H. Macklin: *Letter to the Consul General of Germany*, Montreal, November 28, 1972.
Manitoba Library Association: *Pioneers and Early Citizens of Manitoba, A Dictionary of Manitoba Biography from the Earliest Times to 1920*, Winnipeg.
Gotthard L. Maron: *Facts About the Germans in Canada*, Winnipeg 1920.
McArthur: "Immigration and Colonization in Western Canada, 1900–1930", in: *Pioneer Settlement*, ed. by Robert England and C. A. Dawson.
Jean N. McIlwraith: *Sir Frederick Haldimand*, Toronto 1910.

Mennonite Mirror, Winnipeg, Manitoba, 1972.
Friedrich Michael: "Verschollene der frühen 'Insel' ". *Börsenblatt für den deutschen Buchhandel*, vol. 1972, No. 17.
Henry Milton (ed.): *The Speeches and Addresses of the Rt. Hon. Frederick Tempel, Earl of Dufferin*, London 1882.
Alan Morley: *Vancouver; from Milltown to Metropolis*, Vancouver 1961.
William F. E. Morley: *Pioneer Life on the Bay of Quinte*, Belleville, Ont. 1972.
Desmond Morton: *The Canadian General, Sir William Otter*, Toronto 1974.
William L. Morton: *Manitoba; a History*, Toronto 1957.
Multiculturalism as State Policy, Ottawa 1976.
Frederike Charlotte Louise von Mussow, Freifrau von Riedesel: *Briefe der Generalin von Riedesel auf dieser Reise und während ihres sechsjährigen Aufenthalts in America in den Jahren 1776—1783, nach Deutschland geschrieben*, Berlin 1800, Albany, New York 1867.
Pierre G. Normandie: *The Canadian Parliamentary Guide 1973*, Ottawa 1973.
John Offenbeck: *The Nazi Movement and German-Canadians 1933—1939*, London 1970 (doctoral dissertation).
Ordinances of the Northwest Saskatchewan School Act, 1901.
Ostdeutscher Kulturrat (ed.): *Deutsche Presse im Ausland*, Düsseldorf 1972.
Howard Palmer: *Land of the Second Chance; A History of Ethnic Groups in Southern Alberta*, Lethbridge 1972.
Victor Peters; "Schicksal und Leistung der Mennoniten in Kanada", *Mitteilungen des Instituts für Auslandsbeziehungen*, vol. 7, 1957, No. 3.
Carl Peterson (ed.): *Handwörterbuch des Grenz- und Auslandsdeutschtums*, Breslau 1938—40, vol. 3.
Alexander C. Pincombe: *The History of Moncton Township*, Fredericton 1969 (M. A. thesis).
Stephan Popp: Popp's Journal, 1771—1783", *Pennsylvania Magazine of History and Biography*, vol. 24, 1902.
McKenzie Porter: "The Bush League Complex", McLeans Magazine, vol. 1972, April.
Jacob F. Pringle: *Lunenburg, or the Old Eastern District, its Settlement and Early Progress*, Cornwall, Ont. 1890.
Friedrich Prinz (ed.): *Wenzel Jaksch — Edvard Benes: Briefe aus dem Londoner Exil 1939—1943*, Köln 1973.
Thomas H. Raddall: *Halifax, Warden of the North*, Toronto 1948.
Bruce Ramsay: *A History of the German-Canadians in British Columbia; the Contribution of the Vancouver Alpen Club towards British Columbia's Centennial Year*, Winnipeg 1958.
George E. Reaman: *The Trail of the Black Walnut*, Toronto 1957.
J. G. Rempel: *Die Rosenorter Gemeinde in Saskatchewan*, Rosthern 1950.
Anthony H. Richmond: *Post-war Immigrants in Canada*, Toronto 1967.
Norman Robertson: *The History of the County of Bruce and the Minor Municipalities Therein*, Toronto 1906.
Agnes E. Rothery: *The Ports of British Columbia*, Garden City, New York 1943.
Royal Commission on Bilingualism and Biculturalism: *The Cultural Contributions of Other Ethnic Groups*, Ottawa 1969.
Harry L. Sawatzky: "Viability of Ethnic Group Settlements, with Reference to Mennonites in Manitoba", *Canadian Ethnic Studies*, vol. 11, 1970, No. 2.
—: *They Sought a Country; Mennonite Colonization in Mexico, with an Appendix on Mennonite Colonization in British Honduras*, Berkeley 1971.
Sbirka zakonu a narizeni statu Ceskoslovenskeho (Collection of Laws and Decress of the (zechoslovak State), 1945.
K. J. Schindler: "Die deutschsprachigen Katholischen Kirchengemeinden in Kanada", in: *Deutschkanadisches Jahrbuch*, ed. by Hartmut Froeschle, vol. 2, Toronto 1975, 276—84.
Sigismund Schlinger: "Vom Bayerischen Jugendverbandssekretär zum Kultusminister in Kanada", *Kulturpolitische Korrespondenz*, vol. 151, 1973, January.

Walter Schmiedehaus: *Eine feste Burg ist unser Gott; der Wanderweg eines christlichen Siedlervolkes*, Cuauhtemoc, Mexico 1948.
P. Schweers; *Maria Immaculata*, Marburg 1907–08.
James Scott: *The Settlement of Huron County*, Toronto 1966.
Johann G. Seume: *Seume's Selbstbiographie (im Auszug)*, Hildburghausen 1834.
–: *Mein Leben; mit anderen biographischen Texten und dem Bericht von C. A. Clodius*, Bremen 1964.
H. J. Siemens: *Report of the Sudeten Settlement, Tupper B. C.*, Edmonton 1955.
Clifford Sifton: "The Immigrants Canada Wants", in: *Immigration and the Rise of Multiculturalism*, ed. by Howard Palmer, Toronto 1975.
Colin Simpson: *The Lusitania*, Boston 1972.
George Simpson: *An Overland Journey Round the World, During the Years 1841–1842*, Philadelphia 1847.
Friedrich W. Sintenis: "Sintenis' Chronik der Stadt Zerbst, 1758–1817, narrated by Reinholt Specht", *Zerbster Jahrbuch*, vol. 15, 1930.
Rufus D. Smith: "Immigration and Government", in: *One America*, ed. by F. J. Brown and J. S. Roncek, New York 1947.
Douglas O. Spettigue: *FPG: The European Years*, Ottawa 1973.
D. O. Spettigue and A. W. Riley: "Felix Paul Greve redivivus: Zum früheren Leben des kanadischen Schriftstellers Frederick Philip Greve", *Seminar*, vol. 9, 1973, No. 2.
Statutes of Canada, several volumes, Ottawa.
William J. H. Sturhahn: *They Came from East and West; A History of Immigration to Canada*, Winnipeg 1976.
Sudeten Jahrbuch, vol. 22, München 1973.
William I. Thomas and Florian Znaniecki: *The Polish Peasant in Europe and America*, Chicago 1918–20, 2 vols.
Trans-Canada Alliance of German Canadians: *Brief to the Special Joint Committee on Immigration in the Senate and House of Commons*, February 1967.
H. Troper: "American Immigration to Canada, 1896–1914", in: *Immigration and the Rise of Multiculturalism*, ed. by Howard Palmer, Toronto 1975.
Bernard A. Uhlendorf: *Revolution in America*, New Brunswick 1957.
William V. Uttley: *A History of Kitchener, Ontario*, Waterloo, Ont. 1937.
Vorwärts, demokratische Monatsschrift, vol. 25, 1973, No. 1/2.
Vorwärts Festschrift, Hamilton, Ont. 1971.
Wiki Wanka (ed.): *Sudeten-Bote*, vols. 1968 and 1969.
Norman Ward and Duff Spafford: *Politics in Saskatchewan*, Don Mills, Ont. 1968.
Abe Warkentin: *Reflections on our Heritage; a History of Steinbach and the R. M. of Hanover from 1874*, Steinbach, Manitoba 1971.
William L. Warner and Leo Srole: *The Social System of American Ethnic Groups*, New Haven 1945.
Henry Weisbach: "Auf der Suche nach neuem Zuhause", *Sudeten-Jahrbuch*, 1973.
Maximilian Alexander Philipp, Prinz von Wied-Neuwied: *Reise in das innere Nord-America in den Jahren 1832 bis 1834*, Coblenz 1839–41.
Peter Windschiegl: *Fifty Golden Years, 1903–1953; a Brief History of the Order of St. Benedict in the Abbacy Nullius of St. Peter, Münster, Saskatchewan*, Münster, Saskatchewan 1954.
James S. Woodsworth: *Strangers Within our Gates; or Coming Canadians*, Toronto, Ont. 1909.
Esther C. Wright: *The Loyalists of New Brunswick*, Fredericton 1955.
James F. Wright: *Saskatchewan, the History of a Province*, Toronto 1955.
"10 Agenten im Netz der Spionageabwehr", *Ontario Courier*, June 9, 1977.

VIERTELJAHRSCHRIFT FÜR SOZIAL- UND WIRTSCHAFTSGESCHICHTE
Beihefte
Herausgegeben von W. Conze, H. Kellenbenz, H. Pohl, W. Zorn

38. **Anton Ernstberger: Hans de Witte.** Finanzmann Wallensteins (vergriffen)
ISBN 3-515-03079-4
39. **Fritz Redlich: De Praeda Militari.** Looting and Booty 1500—1815. 1956. X, 79 S., kt. DM 17,—
ISBN 3-515-00299-5
40. **Hermann Kellenbenz: Sephardim an der unteren Elbe.** Ihre wirtschaftliche und politische Bedeutung vom Ende des 16. bis zum Beginn des 18. Jahrhunderts. (vergriffen)
ISBN 3-515-00300-2
41. **Alexander Bergengruen: Adel und Grundherrschaft im Merowingerreich.** Siedlungs- und standesgeschichtliche Studie zu den Anfängen des fränkischen Adels in Nordfrankreich und Belgien. 1958. X, 219 S., 2 Ktn., kt. DM 40,—
ISBN 3-515-00301-1
42. **Margareta Schindler: Buxtehude.** Studien zur mittelalterlichen Geschichte einer Gründungsstadt. (vergriffen)
ISBN 3-515-00302-9
43. **Winfried Trusen: Spätmittelalterliche Jurisprudenz und Wirtschaftsethik,** dargestellt an Wiener Gutachten des 14. Jahrhunderts. 1961. VII, 245 S., kt. DM 34,—
ISBN 3-515-00303-7
44. **Ivo N. Lambi: Free Trade and Protection in Germany 1868—79.** 1963. XII, 267 S., kt. DM 48,—
ISBN 3-515-00304-5
45. **Hans Pohl: Die Beziehungen Hamburgs zu Spanien und dem spanischen Amerika in der Zeit von 1740—1806.** 1963. XIII, 371 S., 1 Tab., 1 Taf., kt. DM 54,— ISBN 3-515-00305-3
46. **Subshi Y. Labib: Handelsgeschichte Ägyptens im Spätmittelalter (1171—1517).** 1965. XII, 586 S., kt. DM 88,—
ISBN 3-515-00306-1
47./48. **Fritz Redlich: The German Military Enterpriser and his Work Force.** A Study in European and Social History
Part I: From the Embryonic to the Full-fledged Military Enterpriser 1350—1600. Part II: The Heyday of Military Entrepreneurship 1600—1650. 1964. XV, 532 S., kt. DM 92,— (Beih. 47)
ISBN 3-515-00307-X
Part III: The Decay and Demise of Military Entrepreneurship 1650—1800. 1965. VIII, 322 S., kt. DM 66,— (Beih. 48)
ISBN 3-515-00308-8
49. **Heinrich Rubner: Untersuchungen zur Forstverfassung des mittelalterlichen Frankreichs.** 1965. XI, 232 S., 2 Taf. u. 4 Abb. i. T., kt. DM 40,—
ISBN 3-515-00309-6
50. **Erich von Lehe: Die Märkte Hamburgs von den Anfängen bis in die Neuzeit.** 1966. X, 98 S., 2 Faltktn., 9 Taf., kt. DM 26,—
ISBN 3-515-00312-6
Ln. DM 32,—
ISBN 3-515-00311-8
51. **Ulf Dirlmeier: Mittelalterliche Hoheitsträger im wirtschaftlichen Wettbewerb.** Zur Frage des Verhaltens staatlicher Gewalt gegenüber dem Bereich der Wirtschaft im Raum des Deutschen Reiches vom 12.—14. Jh. 1966. VIII, 239 S., kt. DM 50,— ISBN 3-515-00313-4
53. **Dieter Lindenlaub: Richtungskämpfe im Verein für Sozialpolitik.** Wissenschaft und Sozialpolitik im Kaiserreich, vornehmlich vom Beginn des „Neuen Kurses" bis zum Ausbruch des Ersten Weltkrieges (1890—1914). 1967. 2 Teilbde. m. zus. XII, VIII, 481 S., kt. DM 98,—
ISBN 3-515-003415-3
(Beih. 52 — ISBN 3-515-00314-2; Beih. 53 — ISBN 3-515-00315-0
54. **Karl-Heinz Allmendinger: Die Beziehungen zwischen der Kommune Pisa und Ägypten im hohen Mittelalter.** Eine rechts- und wirtschaftshistorische Untersuchung. 1967. VIII, 109 S., kt. DM 32,—
ISBN 3-515-00316-9
55.-57. **Wolfgang Frhr. Stromer von Reichenbach: Oberdeutsche Hochfinanz 1350—1450.** 1970. XXVI, 607 S. m. 18 Urkundenbeilagen, 2 Ktn., 2 Falttaf., kt. DM 106,—
ISBN 3-515-02903-6
(Beih. 55 — ISBN 3-515-00317-7; Beih. 56 — ISBN 3-515-00318-5; Beih. 57 — ISBN 3-515-00319-3)
58. **Hansheiner Eichhorn: Der Strukturwandel im Geldumlauf Frankens zwischen 1437 und 1610.** Ein Beitrag zur Methodologie der Geldgeschichte. 1973. XVI, 437 S., 2 Taf, 11 Ktn. u. 44 Abb., kt. DM 72,—
ISBN 3-515-00320-7
59. **Johann Hellwege: Zur Geschichte der spanischen Reitermilizen.** Die Caballeria de Cuantia unter Philipp II. und Philipp III. (1562—1619). 1972. VI, 183 S., kt. DM 28,—
ISBN 3-515-00321-5

60. Frauke Röhlk: **Schiffahrt und Handel zwischen Hamburg und den Niederlanden in der zweiten Hälfte des 18. und zu Beginn des 19. Jahrhunderts.** 1973. Teil I: X, 187 S., Teil II: VI, 209 S., 1 Faltkt., zus. kt. DM 54,— ISBN 3-515-01195-1
61. Martin Kutz: **Deutschlands Außenhandel von der französischen Revolution bis zur Gründung des Zollvereins.** Eine statistische Strukturuntersuchung zur vorindustriellen Zeit. 1974. XII, 395 S., kt. DM 56,— ISBN 3-515-01801-8
62. Eberhard Schmauderer: **Studien zur Geschichte der Lebensmittelwissenschaft.** Teil 1: Qualitätsbeurteilung und Versorgungsprobleme bis zur Renaissance. Teil 2: Das Lebensmittelwesen im Spiegel der frühen deutschen Literatur. 1975. X, 314 S. m. 14 Abb., kt. DM 60,— (Werk wird fortgesetzt) ISBN 3-515-01908-1
63. Hans Pohl: **Die Portugiesen in Antwerpen (1567—1648).** Zur Geschichte einer Minderheit. 1977. X, 439 S., 2 Faltktn., kt. DM 78,— ISBN 3-515-02380-1
    Ln. DM 86,— ISBN 3-515-02381-X
64. Hannah Rabe: **Das Problem Leibeigenschaft.** Eine Untersuchung über die Anfänge einer Ideologisierung und des verfassungsrechtlichen Wandels von Freiheit und Eigentum im deutschen Bauernkrieg. 1977. XII, 128 S., kt. DM 28,— ISBN 3-515-02678-9
65. Franz Irsigler: **Die wirtschaftliche Stellung der Stadt Köln im 14. und 15. Jahrhundert.** Strukturanalyse einer spätmittelalterlichen Exportgewerbe- und Fernhandelsstadt. 1979. VIII, 413 S. m. 7 Ktn. u. 15 Graphiken, kt. DM 88,— ISBN 3-515-02743-2
66. Ludolf Kuchenbuch: **Bäuerliche Gesellschaft und Klosterherrschaft im 9. Jahrhundert.** Studien zur Sozialstruktur der Familia der Abtei Prüm. 1978. XVI, 443 S., 20 Ktn., 1 Abb., 4 Tab., kt. DM 64,— ISBN 3-515-02829-3
67. Jörg Jarnut: **Bergamo 568—1098.** Verfassungs-, Sozial- und Wirtschaftsgeschichte einer lombardischen Stadt im Mittelalter. 1979. X, 330 S. m. 6 Ktn., kt. DM 72,—
    ISBN 3-515-02789-0
68. Erich Maschke: **Städte und Menschen.** Beiträge zur Geschichte der Stadt, der Wirtschaft und Gesellschaft 1959—1977. 1980. XX, 532 S., kt. DM 88,— ISBN 3-515-03329-7
69. Helmut Grieser: **Die ausgebliebene Radikalisierung.** Zur Sozialgeschichte der Kieler Flüchtlingslager im Spannungsfeld von sozialdemokratischer Landespolitik und Stadtverwaltung. 1945—1950. 1980. XII, 185 S., 1 Taf., kt. DM 38,— ISBN 3-515-03110-3
70. Reinhard Liehr: **Sozialgeschichte spanischer Adelskorporationen.** Die Maestranzas de Caballeria (1670—1808). 1981. X, 380 S. m. 4 Abb., 4 Ktn. u. 3 Schaubilder, kt. DM 74,—
    ISBN 3-515-02923-0
71. Wilfried Reininghaus: **Die Entstehung der Gesellengilden im Spätmittelalter.** 1981. X, 361 S., kt. DM 68,— ISBN 3-515-03428-5
72. Wolfgang Hartung: **Die Spielleute.** Eine Randgruppe in der Gesellschaft des Mittelalters. 1982. VIII, 112 S. m. 5 Abb., kt. DM 38,— ISBN 3-515-03690-3
73. Wolfgang Hartung: **Süddeutschland in der frühen Merowingerzeit.** (Studien zu Gesellschaft, Herrschaft, Stammesbildung bei Alamannen und Bajuwaren. 1983. X, 227 S. m. 10 Abb., kt. DM 48,— ISBN 3-515-03418-8
74. Klaus Zernack, Hrsg.: **Schichtung und Entwicklung der Gesellschaft in Polen und Deutschland (16.—17. Jahrhundert).** Nebeneinanderstellungen, Verknüpfungen und Vergleiche. Referate der zweiten Konferenz des Verbandes der Historiker Deutschlands und der Polnischen Historischen Gesellschaft in Thorn vom 16.—21. März 1981. 1983. VIII, 310 S., kt. DM 68,— ISBN 3-515-03805-1

FRANZ STEINER VERLAG WIESBADEN GMBH